DANGER SOUND KLAXON!

DANGER SOUND KLAXON!

The Horn That Changed History

MATTHEW F. JORDAN

University of Virginia Press

CHARLOTTESVILLE AND LONDON

University of Virginia Press
© 2023 by the Rector and Visitors of the University of Virginia
All rights reserved
Printed in the United States of America on acid-free paper

First published 2023

9 8 7 6 5 4 3 2 1

Library of Congress Cataloging-in-Publication Data

Names: Jordan, Matthew F., author.
Title: Danger sound klaxon! : the horn that changed history / Matthew F. Jordan.
Description: Charlottesville : University of Virginia Press, 2023. | Includes
    bibliographical references and index.
Identifiers: LCCN 2022016284 (print) | LCCN 2022016285 (ebook) |
    ISBN 9780813947952 (hardcover) | ISBN 9780813947969 (paperback) |
    ISBN 9780813947976 (ebook)
Subjects: LCSH: Automobiles—Horns
Classification: LCC TL274 .J67 2023 (print) | LCC TL274 (ebook) | DDC 629.2/6—
    dc23/eng/20221011
LC record available at https://lccn.loc.gov/2022016284
LC ebook record available at https://lccn.loc.gov/2022016285

Cover art: From *La Publicité,* April 1911 (Bibliothèque nationale de France), and
rawpixel.com

For Meri, Claire, and Ellis

Just as the entire mode of existence of human collectives changes over long historical periods, so too does their mode of perception. The way in which human perception is organized—the medium in which it occurs—is conditioned not only by nature but by history.

—WALTER BENJAMIN

CONTENTS

ILLUSTRATIONS

ACKNOWLEDGMENTS

I can only begin to thank the many people who gifted me with the time, resources, support, and ongoing conversations that go into writing a book like this. I first picked up the scent of this story while on sabbatical doing archival work in Paris looking, as often happens, for something else. Endless gratitude is owed to the Kent-Radici family, in Paris, and later to the Hogan family, in Washington, DC, for opening their homes to me while I was spending my days in the archives. Many thanks to the Donald P. Bellisario College of Communications at Penn State University, and in particular to Marie Hardin and Anthony Olorunnisola, for supporting me with the time and resources to do the work and for their faith in my ability to realize it. I am grateful to many friends, students, and colleagues in and beyond State College—especially Matt McAllister, Mary Beth Oliver, John Christman, Matt Jackson, and Greg Eghigian—who helped me immensely by listening to me talk about the story and the issues it raised as it went through its various stages.

As the manuscript took final form at the University of Virginia Press, I am grateful to the anonymous reviewers who engaged with it, asked great questions, and pushed me to clarify what I meant. I cannot imagine a better editor to work with than Nadine Zimmerli, who read through multiple revisions with a keen eye for detail and a wonderful ear for tuning the prose for audience resonance. Andrew Edwards and Marjorie Pannell helped bring the manuscript to the finish line with polish and precision.

Of course, everything worth anything that I do is made possible by the unwavering support and patience of my family. My brothers and their families, and my dad, continue to lend an arm and an ear, even when they are not quite sure what I am driving at. Most important, I would be nothing without the love and support of my wife, Meredith Doran, and our children, Claire and Ellis. Every day you let me know that I am the luckiest.

DANGER SOUND KLAXON!

Introduction
SOUNDSCAPES AND SCHEMATICS

When Count de Souaie opened the door to his favorite automobile dealer sometime late in 1910, he was looking for something new. An early convert to horseless carriage technology, he was well known in the motoring world, frequenting the salons and car races that spread the evangel of automobile culture. The Parisian dealer was known to stock the newest and most expensive accessories on the market, and the count, who considered himself a pioneer of sorts, liked to be the first to adopt the latest technological applications.

As it happened, on that very day an American salesman was also in Paris trying to sell the busy dealer on a new electrical signaling device that was all the rage in America. The conversation piqued the curiosity of the eavesdropping count and his young wife. Five years before, they had bought for their car new French squeeze bulb horns, the loudest signaling device on the market. It swelled the count's pride when their sound caused people to look as he cruised the boulevards in his Bébé Peugeot. These days, however, it seemed everyone had one; he wanted something new. Interrupting the American's sales pitch, the count said, "Let's hear it." The dealer shrugged and pulled an eight-volt battery from a shelf. The salesman quickly connected it to a shiny black metal apparatus and, with a glint in his eye, pushed a button.

"*AaOOgah!*" it shrieked. The metallic noise of the American device was unlike anything anyone in the shop had ever heard. The countess stumbled backward into a chair, unable to say a word. The half-terrified count dropped his hat. Slowly a smile crept across his face as he caught the eye of the satisfied salesman, who nodded and said, "It's a klaxon."

"I must have it—NOW!" exclaimed the count. "Quick! How much is it?"[1]

Why a French count, whose apocryphal story was told to *Harper's Weekly* readers early in 1911, would want an American klaxon, a new communication device so shockingly loud that it assaulted the sensibilities of everyone who heard it, is the question at the heart of this book. What needs did this electrical technology promise to serve in a new century rapidly being transformed by a new disruptive technology, the automobile? What does its rise and fall tell us about how emergent technologies become dominant, how they are advertised and monetized, embraced or replaced? What does it teach us about how quickly we adapt after new technologies disrupt the way we hear, see, and perceive things in our everyday lifeworld?

This book tells the story of the rise and fall of the klaxon, a mechanized signaling device that promised to help solve the safety problems that accompanied the age of the automobile. The klaxon's mechanical shriek was first heard as a brain-rattling noise, but as the conversations that helped usher it into the culture shifted, the public's perception of that sound changed over time: *aaOOgah* became associated with a commitment to public safety made possible by electricity. In less than a decade, the klaxon cornered the accessories market as the dominant communication technology for the automobile. At its height, three out of every four cars on roads the world over utilized it. Then, just as quickly, despite massive marketing campaigns to retain the association of its sound with public safety, it was rejected as an unwanted nuisance and replaced. Why? What forced the klaxon—once an exciting technology for early adopters—into a decrescendo?

Sound plays an outsized role as a driver of our ongoing negotiation of the space we share with each other, spurring us to confront how we want to live. In the late 1920s, John Dewey argued that the "connections of the ear with vital and out-going thought and emotion are immensely closer and more varied than those of the eye. Vision is spectator: hearing is a participator."[2] As anyone who has been kept awake at night by noise can attest, it is not possible to avoid unwanted sound. New sounds or unwanted noises become sites of cultural contestation, producing the conversations through which our sense of self and society emerges. I think this is what George Simmel meant when he asserted that "hearing is by its very nature supra individual; what happens in a room must be heard by all those present."[3] So when people make sense of their changing soundscape, they are negotiating changes in the world they share, working through their hopes and concerns about aspects of society they confront every day.

In what follows, when I use the word *soundscape,* I mean to signify and evoke something more than just the "general acoustic environment of a society," as R. Murray Schafer conceived it when he coined the term.[4] The sonic environment is important for understanding the changes in everyday life and the ongoing conversations by which we make sense of them. As the cultural sociologist Nick Couldry writes, aural terms have "advantages as a source of metaphors for thinking about the social world."[5] When people talk and argue about the sounds they hear and the things or people that produce them, they are making sense of cultural change.

Of course, *how* we interpret the different sounds that fill our lifeworld is culturally contingent and also changes over time. This phenomenological point, that the sounds we hear not only are related to the physical vibrations bouncing around us all the time but also are mediated by the cultural discourse that conditions our interpretation of them, is an important one. Both sides of the soundscape—the physical and the cultural frames of perception that guide our hearing—are apt to change when we adopt new technologies. The dialectical interplay between the objects that produce raw sounds and the discourses—social, political, commercial, juridical, academic, medical, scientific—that guide how we hear them is an extremely revealing resource for scholars of culture who study changes in how we perceive things over time.

Plainly stated, our sense of hearing is conditioned by the things we hear every day. The French sociologist Henri Lefebvre, who turned the examination of everyday life into a field of study, once argued that our modes of perception, through our senses, are historically conditioned and contingent. "Our activities," he wrote, "are born from seeds contained in everyday practice." We learn, quite simply, from doing things every day. Our "reason is formed in social practice. As day follows trivial day, the eye learns how to see, the ear learns how to hear. . . . Feelings, ideas, lifestyles and pleasures are confirmed in the everyday."[6] How we listen to, interpret, and evaluate everyday sounds is the product of this dialectical relationship between the things that produce physical sounds in our lifeworld and our cultural frames for understanding them.[7] In short, how we make sense of sound is historically contingent on the ongoing conversation about sound that is always happening around us.

The word *soundscape,* then, is meant to connote this complex interplay between sounds produced and how our culture conditions us to hear them. Here I echo Emily Thompson's emphasis in *The Soundscape of Modernity,* where she argues that "the soundscape is simultaneously a physical environment and a way of perceiving that environment; it is both a world and culture constructed to make sense of that world."[8] What we hear is contingent on the ways of understanding sound that are established by culture as people negotiate the complex relationship between new sounds and our conditioned expectations of what the world around us should sound like. In this book, I trace how a sound created by a new technology, the klaxon automobile horn, underwent a metamorphosis of perceived value, molded by the ongoing conversation about its presence in the changing human soundscape. Like Thompson, I turn to history and archival material to understand the klaxon's presence in the soundscape, situating its revolutionary sound in a rapidly changing modernity during a period when the automobile was disrupting every nook and cranny of everyday life. As a case study, the story of the rise and fall of the klaxon, the first great electrical communication device of the automobile age, dramatizes how the soundscape is tied to our everyday use of and faith in technology.

One could say that every age is defined by the technologies that transform how people live. In the story of modernity, few technologies have been as dynamically disruptive as the automobile. At the beginning of the twentieth century, this now dominant technology quickly became a site for the contestation of meaning, spurring an ongoing conversation about its place in society. In many ways, I see the debate surrounding the emergence and eventual dominance of automobiles and automobility as a precursor to the feverish contemporary debate we are having about smartphones.[9] Today smartphone technology is causing major disruptions, changing everything about the way we mediate and orient ourselves to our physical space, and transforming the way that we experience it. It has changed the way we think and communicate, the way our economy works, the way we govern ourselves, the way our cities are designed, and the way we work and live.

At the turn of the twentieth century, it was automobile technology that revolutionized our shared world. It shifted our frames of cultural orientation and altered our sense of perception, especially our experience of the soundscape.[10] To understand the paradigm shift in the soundscape, I searched for traces of that ongoing debate in the archives and reconstructed the conversations around them. The striking thing about this debate is that, like the technology it followed, it is at the same time remarkably transcultural or global *and* extremely local. Like the automobile, the klaxon disrupted the global soundscape simultaneously. Yet klaxon technology and the various modern modes of communicating, advertising, and doing business associated with it originated in America, which made the klaxon an early example of a kind of technological and cultural Americanization that was contested in whatever local context its herald sound was heard. That anxious tension about what the new American sound meant for cultures where its presence was heard—what they had been, what they might become—remained a constant throughout its rise and fall. To understand how it was heard, we first need to understand the radically different soundscape of the nineteenth century before the arrival of the automobile.

The soundscape of the global city street at the end of the nineteenth century had already gone through reverberating changes brought on by the Industrial Revolution. Steam engines and factory machinery, the whistles, bells, and gongs of public and private conveyances, and the rapidly growing population of major metropolitan cities, where people from the hinterlands and colonies alike crowded together—all were sources of sound disturbance and discussions about what it meant. As the world entered the new century, noise, and what to do about the aggregation of machines and people who made it, was a major topic of conversation everywhere. As they had for centuries, cultures debated and deliberated the significance of these sounds and sought to manage and ameliorate them as much as possible, often employing technology to do so.

The streets are a particularly important site for the ongoing negotiation of sound in culture. It is in the streets where we witness the agonistic dynamism of the agora, where people moving and acting in the world create sound and where anyone venturing out into public must hear the sounds that other people make. Since the time of the Greeks, there have been laws designed to limit street noises to ensure that people can enjoy some modicum of quiet.[11] There are all kinds of linguistic and extralinguistic means for communicating with other people in the streets ("Excuse me," "Pardon," "Look out!," and so on) that not only are about teaching us to accept the sounds that others make but also about how to participate in a normal way as a member of a community. Over millennia, such communicative acts, though taking a myriad of forms, remained a constant aural experience chronicled in the descriptions of multitudes of writers. These are invaluable sources for us today as we seek to evaluate the similarities and radical differences between the past and our own aural present.

Transportation technologies caused the most profound change in the sounds of our shared streets. Indeed, as new technologies and populations made their way into the soundscape of everyday life, the modern public reacted to these new sounds with new modes of listening. One of modernity's great critics, Charles Baudelaire, was keenly aware of what the new modes of transportation were doing to nineteenth-century Parisian streets. Faster transportation technologies, such as the omnibus and carriage, moving on smoother macadam streets sped up life and made it louder. For Baudelaire, they became symbols of an urban modernity leaving old ways of life behind. At the time, Georges-Eugène Haussmann was transforming Paris, leveling older neighborhoods, widening the boulevards and smoothing their surfaces, all to make way for new transportation technologies that communicated the message of modernization. In *Paris Spleen*, Baudelaire's narrator describes "crossing the boulevard in a great hurry, splashing through the mud in the midst of a seething chaos, and with death galloping at me from every side." Whereas horses, people, and carriages used to share the old cobblestone streets, the flâneur now had to worry about safety every time he entered this new space. Giving voice to the experience of pedestrians having to dodge an omnibus in increasingly dangerous streets, Baudelaire wrote, "I gave a sudden start and my halo slipped off my head and fell into the mire of the macadam. I was far too frightened to pick it up."[12] The relentless speed of these noisy new modes of transportation pushed older ways of life aside, yet that newfound speed and the separation from older forms of life were also liberating and exhilarating. The narrator, reflecting that "every cloud has a silver lining," becomes "bored" with the older, slower, quieter world. Baudelaire's anecdote gives us a doorway through which to imagine the disruptive and transformative impact of new technologies on everyday life, their ambiguous impact on society, and the ambivalent cultural response to the changes they spurred.

The modern city soundscape was indeed transformed by such technologies as the omnibus and the steam engine. Walt Whitman provided a good indication of the sounds filling New York City streets just before the automobile arrived on the scene. In *Song of Myself*, he praised a polytonal democratic soundscape experienced while riding the omnibus up and down the paved avenues, the perfect sonic symbol of an urban modernity whose public space was filled with polyphonic diversity:

> The blab of the pave, tires of carts, sluff of bootsoles, talk of the
>   promenaders,
> The heavy omnibus, the driver with his interrogating thumb, the clank
>   of the shod horses on the granite floor,
> The snow-sleighs, clinking, shouted jokes, pelts of snowballs,
> The hurrahs for popular favorites, the fury of rous'd mobs,
> The flap of the curtain'd litter, a sick man inside borne to the hospital,
> The meeting of enemies, the sudden oath, the blows and fall,
> The excited crowd, the policeman with his star quickly working his pas-
>   sage to the centre of the crowd,
> The impassive stones that receive and return so many echoes,
> What groans of over-fed or half-starv'd who fall on the flags sunstruck or
>   in fits,
> What exclamations of women taken suddenly who hurry home and give
>   birth to babes,

What living and buried speech is always vibrating here, what howls
    restrain'd by decorum,
Arrests of criminals, slights, adulterous offers made, acceptances, rejec-
    tions with convex lips,
I mind them or the resonance of them—I come again and I depart.[13]

Whitman was exhilarated by the sonic pluralism of New York's crowded
streets, where people, animals, and technologies, old and new, negotiated a
rapidly changing social space and created a wonderfully democratic din. From
the perspective of our current modes of listening in soundscapes dominated
by one form of transportation, the automobile, the sounds are strikingly different. Indeed, part of the dramatic arc of the klaxon's story is how a more
diverse sonic world became increasingly monotonic as automobiles rose to
prominence as the dominant technology.

Yet Whitman's acceptance of the multitudinous modern soundscape,
where no sound is unwanted noise, stands out in its ethical embrace of all
sounds as wanted. Historically, new sounds have often been characterized
as noise. To be fair, Whitman never anticipated the speed of technological
innovation and its disruptive power over urban space and the modern soundscape, a force that caused so many nineteenth-century writers to lament the
changing sounds associated with modernity as unwanted noise. Baudelaire
in *Paris Spleen,* for one, described the noise-fueled rage caused by hearing the
piercing, discordant cry of a glazier one morning invading his repose. He was
"seized with a hatred . . . as sudden as it was despotic"[14] against the person
or thing that produced the noise. A similar rage against the changes in the
modern soundscape was all too common at the end of the long nineteenth
century. Writers like Dickens, Mayhew, and Carlyle in England lamented the
noise, often fantasizing about strangling or throttling noisemakers who disturbed their quiet.[15] Many sought relief in sound-mitigating technologies to
keep the unwanted sounds of the street out of their private space. Calls for
silence through the law or a cultural call to action in response to perceived
changes in the physical soundscape are a recurring theme, a narrative leit-
motiv, that we will encounter repeatedly in the story of how global culture
dealt with the crescendo of klaxon technology.

Yet while cultural conservatives railed against new technological and social
objects that produced unwanted sounds, a more typical response to the problem of noisy and speedy technology was what might be called a *technocentric
response:* to mitigate the problems of modern technology, forward-looking critics called for newer technologies to solve the problems created by the older

technologies. Increasingly, technology was offered to consumers all over the world as a solution to new social problems. As we will see manifested in the reaction to the automobile and automobile culture, people's relationship to everyday life was increasingly tied to the promise of technologies with which and through which they lived. Each new technology, from the automobile to the klaxon, carried with it the self-promotion of a technocentered ideology, of the technologization of everyday life. This techno-utilitarianism, grounded in a rhetoric of progress that James Carey has called the "technological sublime," began to dominate the cultural imaginary as the new century emerged. As it did, it flattened the conversation about living and experiencing what ethicists often call the good life, reducing everyday life to a process of identifying problems and then acquiring the latest consumer technologies that promised to solve them.

As noise created by modern forms of transportation became a social problem, inventors and engineers offered technological solutions for noisy streets. Seeking to quiet unwanted sound, engineers in France, America, Germany, and Britain tried different road surfaces, tinkered with wheels, inserted gaskets, and coated springs. In this response, we see a mode of listening and reacting to technology that I have come to think of as the "engineering mode": when they heard a problem, cultures turned to engineers to diagnose and fix a social world increasingly conceptualized as a machine to tinker with.[16] With each attempt to lessen the noise and safety problems brought on by new transportation technologies, engineers all over the world listened for the results with an ear toward improvement.

The work of the London Metropolitan Sanitary Commission of 1871, seeking to solve the social problem of urban noise, provides a great example of this engineering mode of listening. The commission's engineers studied different countries' responses to the problems caused by new transportation technologies, and recommended best solutions. Adding tramways or street cars, for example, helped alleviate the congestion caused by horse traffic because it moved people through the streets en masse; fewer vehicles meant less noise. Similarly, outdated street construction that used such surface materials as cobblestones or quarried stone pavers led to "noise, the rattle and the vibration of traffic over them, to which strong people become accustomed, and do not mind, but from which weakly and ailing people suffer very much."[17] Newer paving technologies fixed this problem. German city planners, the commission noted, had experimented with tarred concrete to reduce noise and dust, while New York and Parisian engineers utilized *Val-de-Travers asphalte*, "a sort of elastic surface." The Metropolitan Sanitary Commission recommended paving London's streets with asphalt to make them quieter and more hygienic. The commission's recommendations always conveyed an underlying belief that the latest technology could solve the problems of noise caused by modern technologies in the first place. Even better, newer streets would allow the newer transportation technology, the "hot air engine, with India rubber tyres"—an early version of the automobile—to quietly share the street with horses and buggies. Smoother roads, which could be surfaced economically with the help of the new steamroller technology, would alleviate noise, reduce traffic by allowing the consolidation of transport into heavier loads of people or goods, and lead to better, more silent forms of transportation.

The ideology contained in the Metropolitan Sanitary Commission's argument for a proper technological solution is worth scrutinizing, for it went beyond the printed page. One could say, following James Carey, that each new form of transportation was a form of communication because it embodied the message of the lifeworld it promised.[18] Each self-propelled vehicle passing over these smooth streets would communicate the ideology of technological progress, of a modernity constantly improved by speedy adoption of the latest technology. The techno-utilitarian ideology, one of the recurring themes in the story of the klaxon I tell in this book, has remained uppermost in cultural discourse: if properly studied and applied, technology can and will transform life and bring urban society into a friction-free modernity. Yet the impact of new technology on everyday life is rarely linear, and the progress it affords seldom lives up to the promise accompanying its adoption: each new fix is invariably accompanied by new creaks, bumps, and groans as new technologies bring a new cascade of problems. Smooth street surfaces, in this case, led to more vehicles traveling at ever more treacherous speeds, which made collisions more frequent and more impactful. A sped-up world was hardly a safer world.

A decade later, newer and faster transportation vehicles of all varieties were indeed moving on smoother city streets across the globe, communicating with each use the message of a new form of modern life. Automobiles, omnibuses, trolleys, and trains, powered by steam, electricity, ethanol, and gasoline, shared the streets with older forms of transportation.[19] Yet it became obvious everywhere that the unregulated streets of the nineteenth century were rendered unsafe by twentieth-century forms of conveyance. More machines moving at greater speeds meant traffic problems, which required new modes of governance, engineering, and regulation to manage. The situation demanded new ways for people using these technologies to communicate and to negotiate civic space, media technologies appropriate for the speed and number of people sharing the roads. Engineers were once again tasked to innovate ways to signal to others in noisy streets shared by old and new modes of transportation.

This brief historical synopsis sets the stage for the story of the rise and fall of the klaxon automobile horn. The following chapters examine how a communication technology imagined as a solution to the problems caused by automobile transportation technology went through a profound metamorphosis in value, an aural and ideological paradigm shift that speaks to a dramatic change in the soundscape. The history of the klaxon dramatizes how, in an ever-faster world where we are always looking for the next big fix, we quickly adopt new technologies, causing older and previously dominant technologies to fade away. Playing major roles in this story are creative inventors, ambitious American tycoons, advertising revolutionaries, ruthless lawyers, politicians, novelists, poets, songwriters, and soldiers in the trenches of the Western Front, all of whom bore witness to and made their contribution to the klaxon's rise and fall.

1
SOUND COMPETITION
Make Way for the Automobile!

By the end of the nineteenth century, transportation technologies aided by the power of steam had transformed the experience of time and space, communicating a profound cultural shift in everyday life experiences. Pedestrians shared urban streets not only with horse-drawn carriages and bicycles but also with newer forms of industrial age conveyance. Yet in the 1890s, the steam-driven omnibus and tramway—each a technological marvel in its own right, heralding a new era of greater mobility in which groups of people could be conveyed swiftly over distance—began to cede the right of way to a new invention that afforded individuals a new private mode of mobility: the internal combustion engine–driven horseless carriage, or automobile.

Henri Lefebvre once proposed that the "most extraordinary things are also the most everyday."[1] Of the extraordinary inventions that transformed everyday culture in the twentieth century, few had as much impact and were tied so closely to the notion of modern technical progress as the automobile. From its emergence, the automobile was seen as an exemplar of technologized modernity, a paradigmatic machine with the power to transform people's relationship to the natural world and alter every aspect of everyday life for the better. The automobile was a transportation medium that was its own message; no invention better communicated the technological promise of a new century filled with new possibilities and challenges.[2] Yet debates arose in Europe and the United States over the role of acoustic signaling technology as the automobile emerged as an agent of change. What kinds of devices were best suited to safely communicating in noisy traffic while their operators were driving an automobile? What should the devices sound like? What kinds of affordances made some devices more effective than others? How did these communication devices, when heard by pedestrians or drivers, compare with older forms of verbal or nonverbal communication used by people to navigate shared public space? What signals were too loud to be effective? Too quiet? How did using new technology every day transform the behavior of the people who used it? These debates across different cultures reveal the ongoing work of communities trying to come to terms with a rapidly changing soundscape while managing the powerful interests invested in promoting the automobile and the new social and biopolitical norms tied to it.

Horns, Whistles, Sirens, and Bells

When the automobile entered public space, it had to navigate through traffic, just as the forms of transportation that came before it had to, by communicating its presence through sight and sound to other vehicles and pedestrians occupying the streets. Older forms of transportation, of course, had sound signaling devices: carriage bells that banged rhythmically along with shod hooves, tramway gongs and trolley bells that announced the arrival and departure of streetcars, steam whistles that preceded oncoming trains and warned pedestrians at intersections. All were necessary sounds in a shared civic space because there were almost no traffic laws to speak of. Absent governmental regulation of movement on roads, people relied on communication technology to avoid collisions.

As the automobile took its place among traffic conveyances, cultures all over the world discussed its promise and perils. The automobile signified modernity, speed, and mobility.[3] Choosing the automobile as a transportation option—a consumer technology that would transform riders' relationship to time and space—meant embracing this new relationship to the social and physical world; being an early adopter of the technology signaled faith in the promise of modern technology.

Led by advertising copy and zealous prophets of a technological future, the discourse surrounding the emergence of the automobile reveals a cluster of sites or topoi for the generation of a modern technocentered ideology. The negotiations that came in the noisy wake of the automobile reveal a great deal about the social expectations, hopes, and fears tied to it. Such normative conversations about the way people should use new technologies, communicating and relating to one another in modernity, continue to this day. Of note for the story of the klaxon horn, people all over the world discussed the aural impact of the car on the rapidly changing soundscape and sought remedies for the social problems it created.

It seems remarkable today, when people persistently complain about automobile noise, that the horseless carriage was billed as a machine that would make the social world *less* noisy when it first entered the world's soundscape. In comparison to its predecessors, the automobile was a technology that seemed to solve transcultural complaints about street noise caused by horse and steam engine traffic. As a machine that improved on existing modes of communication and transportation, it embodied the techno-utopian promise of an increasingly technologized modernity tied to whiggish notions of progress. Though the automobile became associated with noise over time, it was consistently framed as an object that could always be improved through better engineering or design.

Though people quickly came to complain about the noises early automobiles made, these critiques of the technology's unwanted sound were not antitechnology. Complaints about automobile noise often had a utilitarian function: they were a signal for engineers to respond, to solve the identified problem by creating quieter technology. In the future, according to this underlying assumption, the automobile would fulfill its cultural promise.

As early as 1895 there appeared symptoms of what Karen Bijsterveld, Eefje Cleophas, Stefan Krebs, and Gijs Mom describe as a "diagnostic mode" of listening: listening undertaken to fix the problems making the noise.[4] "We have crusaders against visible and moral ugliness," opined an editor in *Harper's Weekly* in 1895. "Why not against the ugliness that offends the ear?" Whether people should be forced to endure sound was a crucial moral question, a challenge for a technologized modernity. The issue of noise and its imprint on people sharing social space should be weighed when evaluating the utility of any new technology. For the diagnostic listener with this social ethic in mind, the aesthetic or moral dimension of unwanted sound, though present, usually indicates that a piece of technology requires better engineering. As such,

> A bare catalogue of the urban noises that are avoidable or mitigatable, yet which no one thinks it a duty to suppress or literally tone down, would fill a page . . . steam-engines, steam-whistles, engine—bells, trolley and cable car gongs, cable brakes, thunderous coal-carts, carloads of sheet or rod iron, the rattle of the omnibus. . . . No projector of "improvements," no inventor of things for daily use, thinks of noise-suppressing as part of his problem. One sure test of a well-served table is the noiselessness of the service. There luxury combines with good taste to hide the friction of the function. . . . As to the inventor, if the noise in his engine—whatever it may be—represents an avoidable loss of power, he may better matters because it saves power.[5]

Just as servants should aspire to silent service, technology designers should aspire to noiseless efficiency. Every invention, from the eggbeater to the automobile, worked better when there was less noise-causing friction. Interpreted this way, moral and utilitarian concerns aligned perfectly, serving a notion of progress that would both increase efficiency and decrease the "roar of the city." Here again, though it may seem strange to contemporary ears, many advocates of the automobile described it—especially the early electric vehicles often overlooked by historians[6]—as relatively silent.

Harry Marillier gave a sense of the giddy expectations tied to the automobile and its potential to transform life. Writing in the *New Review* in 1895, he argued that the automobile would become modernity's most significant invention, a symbol of "the scheme of general progress, and in the direct line of civilization."[7] He marveled at how the speed of the new machines "takes one's breath away at first. . . . For there is joy in going quickly and in doing no work. It is probable that in a year or two every one will be wanting to drive without horses. . . . Within a decade at most, we should see considerable changes in our present modes of travelling."[8] With such change on the way, legal and social norms needed to adapt to new conditions. Indeed, Marillier believed a society's ability to adapt its laws to technological innovation was a sign of its functionality.

Noting that the British had been early adopters of steam carriage technology—an early form of the automobile—Marillier lamented that British law, in particular the Locomotive Act, had not adapted faster to the speedy new technology. By limiting speed on roads to under 10 miles an hour, national and local bylaws made the automobile practically illegal in England. France, by contrast, was already adapting its laws to the new automobile technology. Once British laws were free from "the interference of bumpkin officialism"[9] that stood in the way of utilitarian progress, everyday life would be transformed by this faster and quieter technology. If Britain continued to resist adapting to automobile technology, citizens would be "doomed" to endure "the purgatory to the weary brain" caused by riding crowded metropolitan railways or being trapped and "swayed on an omnibus through the roar of London streets."[10] The automobile promised greater speed and relief from the noise. Fantasizing about a well-designed and well-engineered urban space of the future, a kind of thinking that Gabrielle Esperdy has characterized as "autotopian,"[11] Marillier believed an automobile would "glide noiselessly along all the main arteries of the city . . . giving melodious warning of its approach and dealing with that endless stream of human traffic which makes one, looking over London at night, feel as if the sea were sounding in one's ears. All the jar, the rattle, the patter of the hoofs would be gone from it, gone with a hundred other things that one would gladly miss."[12] By virtue of its improved technology, its "light rubber tyres," the automobile would "pass and leave no scar upon the fair-laid asphalte," replacing the unsightly sight and sound of horses being "lashed and jagged and galled into hatred of life. "[13] Better engineering would make for a quieter city. "We shall have worked wonders in our cities, which now will be clean and sweet instead of foul and muddy. . . . Heads will no longer throb with disagreeable sights and sounds." The busy prosperous man of Marillier's imagined future would breeze around town in an automobile, "able to think as he drifts along on wheels of softest motion; not agitated by thoughts of the wretched beast in front, nor distraught by noises round him. Modern life will have lost a few of its worst terrors."[14] Marillier had faith that no matter what problems the automobile might create, better-engineered technology would solve them. This modern techno-utopian fantasy—an automobile version of the rhetoric James Carey has described as the "technological sublime," a discourse that always seems to accompany "transformative" technologies—was a constant feature of conversations about the automobile, which itself quickly became the medium for this idyllic ideological message.

Across the Atlantic, T. A. de Weese echoed this techno-utopian rhetoric a year later, in 1896, as he promoted the coming of the "age of the horseless carriage." He foretold a world in which it would be possible "to dispense with the horse and attain the highest measure of comfort and speed over smoothly paved boulevards in a vehicle propelled by mechanical power."[15] He could understand why the United States, with its vast rural spaces, would nostalgically cling to the horse, but such backwardness was not the mark of "utilitarian people." Horseless carriage technology, he argued, was safer, cleaner, cheaper, faster, and quieter. Unless one had a fondness for the smell of manure or the clack of horseshoes on cobblestones, the horseless future would be less oppressive to all the senses.

The physician J. H. Girdner joined the chorus, praising the automobile as a less noisy technology that would promote better health. Citing the link between noise and health problems that was well established by turn-of-the-century science, Girdner prescribed the automobile as a technological remedy for the "plague of city noises" disturbing modern urban life. "The time has come," he wrote in 1896, "when something should be done to lessen the constant and largely unnecessary outrages committed on the sense of hearing of the residents of large cities."[16] The sensorium of modern man, he argued, was attacked by a "constant shock or concussion of unpleasant and non-musical sounds," which had an impact not only on the ears but also on

the brain and the whole nervous system: "The jarring and actual pain produced on the sensorium by the endless roar in which we live . . . [is] a bane of
modern city life."[17] He conceded that some of the noises produced by horses
and wheeled vehicles were "largely necessary noises" that people accepted as
trade-offs for everyday convenience. But if technology had produced a noise
problem, it also could provide the cure for it. "Much can be done to lessen
their annoying effect. Asphalt pavement on all streets is the one thing needed
above all others. It is practically a noiseless pavement." Beyond better road-
surfacing technology, horseless carriages—that is, automobiles—would quiet
the "clatter of horses' feet."[18]

Choosing quiet technology also had a pedagogical function, helping to
teach people to be more aware of the noises they made. From Girdner's perspective, using the latest noise-reducing technology improved social order and
showed one's sense of social obligation. Individuals in a civil society needed
to be "careful to respect the rights and comforts of others in the matter of
noise as they are in other respects." "Noise-makers," he argued, "belong to
all classes, and . . . the so-called refined and religious are often as neglectful
of the rights of others as the rude and the uneducated."[19] Since noise caused
nerve damage and weakened the individual, the work of the engineer was of
paramount importance for improving public health. Cities could improve
conditions for all by engineering smoother roads and adopting the automobile as the mode of public conveyance. This normative ethic of making less
noise would guide the engineers to develop quieter technologies suited to
the problems of modern life and guide consumers to adopt these new technologies. It lent both the production and the consumption of technology
a moral dimension.

Better signaling technology and a more judicious use of it was also needed
for a quieter future. Carriage bells "should be abolished," as the clatter of the
horses' feet "is all that is necessary to warn pedestrians of their approach."[20]
In the name of public health, Girdner called for laws that would prohibit the
trolley conductor from ringing his bell "every time he is paid a fare" since
it caused "outrage, after a passenger has paid his passage, to have his auditory apparatus irritated." All of these unnecessary noises would be reduced,
he believed, as soon as the horseless carriage was adopted. "Horseless carriages and wagons, with rubber tires, on properly constructed asphalt pave-
ments, are noiseless . . . an ideal means of locomotion in city streets." In
short, better technology would "extend the Golden Rule into a new field of
social life."[21] Engineers could, like the physician, cure the social body with
better technology.

Not everyone thought the automobile was a quiet technology. While rubber tires on asphalt streets might be quieter than hooves, engine noise and the signaling devices increasingly used by automobile drivers to communicate with one another certainly were not. In *The Horseless Age*—one of the first journals dedicated to promoting automobile culture as a social fact and everyday need—one observer weighing in on the "noise question" strongly supported using vibrating bells, which were less noisy than horns. "There are noises, and then again there are noises," he wrote. "Deliver me from living in a city with the driver of every vehicle tooting a horn."[22] As the number of cars on the roads grew, noisy anecdotal evidence piled up to counter the assertion that the automobile and its ancillary technology were quiet.

Responding to an editorial in *The Spectator* praising the quietness of the "motor-car," one British writer in 1899 provided an experiential account that asserted the opposite. He told of a woman in a horse-drawn carriage who met a motor-car, "puffing its nasty smoke, making its hideous noise, and completely upsetting the nerves of the horse. . . . The animal bolted, the reins broke, and the coachman was precipitated into the middle of the road." Such noise-triggered disturbances were becoming common: "The roads now teem with these infernal machines. . . . It is curious that in an age which calls itself aesthetic, and adores beauty, these inventions should originate and flourish." Describing the impact on the soundscape, the writer lamented that "the songs of the birds" would be replaced by "the noise of the engines. These straight, level roads will bristle with monstrous steam rollers and shrieking, throbbing motors emitting jets of steam."[23] He called for better regulation, better engineering, and better communication technology to protect those who used the older forms of travel from these speedy new machines.

Yet while most writers touted the silent design of automobiles, in so doing they had to concede that this technological advantage led to other problems, especially in relation to safety. The natural sound of locomotion that accompanied the trolley, tram, or carriage allowed pedestrians and other drivers to know what kind of vehicle was approaching, what its speed was, and the direction it was coming from. The silent stealth of faster cars, especially when driven poorly, made them a danger to pedestrians. Grisly editorial reminders of the collateral damage from automobile technology increasingly appeared in graphic form in print media of all kinds. It was common knowledge that speed, the most revolutionary part of automobile travel, made the technology less safe.

One need not have been opposed to the new technology to admit that it was dangerous. Even popular songs that celebrated the new transportation

Le " Monde Automobile ". - LES AUTOPHOBES.

Figure 1. "Autophobes standing in the way of progress." From *Le Monde Automobile,* April 27, 1907. (Bibliothèque nationale de France)

technology, like the joyful "Automobiling," a W. C. Parker tune recorded by John Ford and Mayme Gehrue, acknowledged the carnage it caused. In verse three, the song's narrator dreams of having "my own private hospital with fresh doctors every day / To patch up all of the victims that ever happen in my way." Another verse predicted that "Senators over in Washington, and our President so True / Will soon pass no laws except those that tell you just what you Au-to do."[24]

Cartoonists in the American illustrated magazine *Puck* portrayed the "speed madness" caused by automobile culture as an irresistible thrill, analogous in its results to the fate of moths drawn to a flame. Everywhere, journalists and editorialists wrote on the speed, danger, and noise of the new transportation technology, demanding commensurate regulatory responses from governments. The French journal *Le Monde Automobile* acknowledged, while gently mocking, the "autophobia"[25] of those who resisted the new technology; autophobes were old-time dotards, passive-aggressively resisting the speed and change of the modern world.

In light of the problems caused by its "quiet" speed, more effective signaling technology was absolutely necessary. One article in *The Horseless Age* acknowledged this need for signaling technology that older forms of conveyance lacked. The horse-drawn carriage, for example, did not need extra signaling devices as the "horse announces his coming with his hoofs." This was also the case with the trolley, "second only to the locomotive in the noise it makes in motion. This noise, a buzzing or whirring sound due to the rotary action of its motor, can be heard a long distance, and in spite of the complaints of the nervous and the invalid, is not an unmixed evil." Even so, because the trolley operated on busy streets, it needed a distinctive signaling device. "The trolley is built for relatively high speed in public streets and the further its danger signals can be heard the greater the speed it can with safety attain."[26] Its representative sound, the gong, allowed people to know what was coming. When sounded, the "person hearing it knows at once the kind of vehicle that is approaching. . . . If the eyes are averted, as often happens, the ear 'sees' the approaching car, and the will is enabled to act quicker than it otherwise would and carry us out of danger." Here, commentators cast sound signaling technology as a communication medium that extended and augmented the senses. If the problems of urban street traffic involved too many distractions from people and machines, then appropriate technology that extended the senses to accommodate greater speed was the solution.

Like trollies, automobiles—"carriages propelled by power within, especially when equipped with rubber tires"—needed effective signaling technology to be safe in crowded streets. In response, more and more governments legally required automobiles to sound a warning signal on approach. "The authorities complain that the new vehicle is *too* noiseless, while some of the literary critics of the new vehicle find it too noisy."[27] Perhaps it was not desirable at all that the "motor carriage be noiseless in its operation." The author of "The 'Noise' Question" argued that "public benefit will result from the peculiar sound which the machinery of the motor carriage will produce when in motion? Will it not also become familiar, and, being heard at some distance, render the use of an emergency signal less frequent?" If indeed engineers continued to make automobiles more quiet, then the automobile would surely need effective and representative signaling technology to let people know what was approaching.

Producers of signaling technology for other forms of transportation heeded this growing call for effective automotive signals and used the opportunity to adapt their existing technologies to the new automobile age. The Bevin Brothers bell foundry, for example, which had been manufacturing bells for horse carriages and bicycles in its East Hampton, Connecticut, shop since 1832, created a device based on a carriage bell that the automobile driver could sound by pushing a pedal with a foot. Yet many thought this adaptation of older communication technology to the automobile bred confusion. One observer in

The Horseless Age suggested vehicle-specific sound, "The tinkle of the bicycle bell is peculiar to that vehicle. . . . On hearing it one is immediately aware of the proximity of a bicycle and takes precautions to avoid its path." It would be confusing to put a gong on a bicycle as "the ear would not be able to distinguish the bicycle from a trolley, and the eyes would have to supplement the ear, involving a loss of time. The same confusion would result if the gong or the bell were adopted for the motor carriage."[28] Similarly, steam whistle technology was "too suggestive of the locomotive," so the only alternative "seems to be the horn, one form of which is now in use among the French manufacturers." This Paris horn, the author suggested, was not "a musical one, but a danger signal should startle rather than please."[29] Here, a discourse of safety was used to promote technologies that produced startling noise, a sound that preceded aesthetic interpretation or pleasure and worked directly on the nervous system. The same sonic properties that might startle a horse might save a pedestrian who failed to look before crossing the street in front of oncoming traffic.

As the new technology caught people's attention, it sparked an ongoing debate over its impact on the soundscape and whether sound signaling might help address the safety problems the automobile had created. If culture is created through an ongoing negotiation of contested issues, the contours of automobile culture were coming into focus. It was clear that sound would be increasingly important.

The Crescendo of the Automobile Horn

Legislative assemblies in countries being transformed by the presence of the automobile grappled with its immediate impact. They issued new statutes and ordinances attempting to regulate the automobile and institutionalize the user's relationship to it. Many expressed a desire to standardize the sound of the audible signal used by automobiles. As the City of Chicago debated the issue in 1900, one local writer described the conundrum: "What should constitute the warning sound for automobiles? In Europe the pneumatic horn is commonly used, making a noise similar to that of a steam whistle. In this country the tendency is to employ a gong for the same purpose. This, however, is open to the objection that the equipment is similar to that of the electric street car, so that accidents are liable to arise through mistaking the approach of an automobile for that of the latter, the passer therefore deeming himself out of danger when clear of the car tracks."[30]

Chicago legislators were not alone in calling for standardization and uniformity in automobile signals. Across Europe and America, automobile clubs promoting motor cars debated the appropriate representational sound and took suggestions to legislatures in the hope those bodies would arrive at consensus. In 1909, following an international conference of Recognized Automobile Clubs, the French government organized an international meeting of similar officials from across the world, hoping to reach agreement on how to control automobile traffic. Representatives from France, Germany, Austria, Hungary, Belgium, England, Italy, Russia, Holland, Spain, Portugal, Romania, Switzerland, Serbia, Montenegro, Monaco, Sweden, Bulgaria, and the United States all took part. They resolved that the horn was the appropriate automobile sound signal. "As concerns warning signals, the horn is the only device permitted, and every car must be provided with one. However, outside of built up districts the use of other signaling devices will be permitted which are in accordance with the regulations and the customs of the respective countries."[31]

Though the resolution was nonbinding, it reflected an ongoing transnational debate about how best to regulate automobile technology. In Britain, writers weighed the promise of the automobile as a marker of progress against the safety problems caused by its relative quietness for a public unaccustomed to its sonic presence in the soundscape. "Rapid communication," wrote John Scott Montagu in the *Fortnightly Review*, "is not a bad test of a nation's civilization that we should judge by its means of communication, by the excellence of its roads, and generally by the freedom of access to and from every part of the country." The automobile promised to improve all these areas, to alter habits and have an impact on "our modern life."[32] Streets, he proposed, would be cleaner and towns would be quieter. When new conveyance technologies emerged, there was always a "unreasoning fear of speed and a natural distrust of new machines of which the public understand little and upon which they look as revolutionary and dangerous." Yet once proper modes of communication and governmental control were understood and enacted, speed was not to be feared, even in London's overcrowded streets. Speedy automobile technology might be more dangerous, Montagu conceded, but it also allowed workers access to cheaper, quieter lodgings by allowing them to travel farther faster, making it a "potent engine of social amelioration."[33] All that was needed was better signaling technology that would allow users to communicate in traffic. "The present century is the era of the engineer," he noted. Surely engineers could solve the problem of speed by inventing better technology, making good on the promises of modernity.

The debate over how legally to control speed and require better signaling devices spread internationally along with the automobile. Yet the laws governing the usage of the new technology piggybacked on discourse surrounding sound signals on older forms of conveyance such as trains, trollies, omnibuses, and carriages. Sometimes, they struggled to fit. The problems raised by the automobile generated new questions about how to regulate, standardize, and institutionalize the acoustic signals and modes of communicative action used to negotiate traffic. Different countries had different responses. The Paris motor vehicle law of 1893 made it obligatory for vehicles to "give warning of their approach when necessary by means of a horn [trompe]." It required that horns "must not make a noise similar to that of a steam whistle."[34] Yet aside from that directive, the term horn was extremely ambiguous. Indeed, there were hundreds of different pneumatic squeeze bulbs on the market, each trying to brand itself as having a distinct sound. What exactly did—or should—an automobile horn sound like?

Beyond the question of representational sound, the question of when a driver should sound the horn also had different answers. In 1901 the French government determined that the ubiquitous and constant signaling called for in earlier laws was untenable and decreed that it was not to be used except for "the purpose of giving notice of approach in dangerous places and for the purposes of avoiding accidents. It is not to be used, as it has been, for the purposes of clearing the way for an unlimited distance ahead."[35] Laws had to be updated to deal with the changes in technology.

Other countries developed similar statutes to respond to the problems of automobile signaling, yet always with inconsistencies between localities. For example, the Irish rules of the road in 1900 indicated "the approach of a vehicle should be announced by a horn or other signal,"[36] yet the city of Dublin required bells, which its officials deemed "less aggressive than the horn." The English Locomotives on Highways Act of 1896 was similarly ambiguous.[37] It made failure to carry a "bell or horn" and to give audible and sufficient warning of the approach or position of the motor car a fineable offense for all drivers, yet it left determination of the bell or horn up to the whims of local municipalities.[38] Inventors responded to the ambiguity. One French inventor created a signaling device that had both, combining a horn and a bell in one convenient contraption.

After the steep British toll rates that had been pushed for by train companies to make motorized vehicles prohibitively expensive were relaxed under the 1896 act, automobiles became more viable. The new law also allowed greater speed. Speed limits, which had been set at 10 mph on public highways and 5 mph in town under the Locomotives on Highways Act, were raised to 14 mph.[39] Drivers were required to use a bell and to use "lamps" (headlights) at night.[40] In 1903, Parliament amended the laws again, raising speed limits to 20 mph and creating more controls on communication and safety. But it was obvious that more regulation was needed, and Parliament charged a royal commission with creating legislation that would adequately deal with the problems caused by this new modern conveyance. The question of noise and signaling technology was central to the commission's work. One editorialist begged the royal commission to do something about the misuse of the automobile horn, a device deemed "unnecessary and intolerable. . . . The Driver who hoots everybody peremptorily out of his way is a public nuisance and should be suppressed by law." Moreover, "use of the horn should be forbidden to all vehicles except automobiles."[41] As elsewhere, the debate in Britain about automobile signaling technology was ongoing and very much unsettled.

Some members of the commission, understanding that using new forms of technology transformed the user, argued that making a communication technology mandatory would negatively affect drivers. "If there were no artificial means of signaling their approach they would be compelled to drive with much greater circumspection."[42] Some held that horns were already overused, often to drive people out of the way.[43] Though many commissioners thought that the horn alone should be compulsory on motor cars and forbidden on all other vehicles, they failed to agree on what counted as a horn. The commission left it to localities to determine this matter, while recommending that the use of "sirens or steam whistles by motor cars should be prohibited."[44]

As the horn emerged as the best answer to the question of signal standardization, other competing sounds were eliminated one by one. British MPs noted that other countries had begun prohibiting the siren. In November 1905 the departmental committee appointed by the French government suggested that the interior minister should "suppress the use of the siren altogether and limit the horn to open country."[45] Germany was different, requiring vehicles to carry a "single-toned horn (all other signals and also horns resembling sirens being prohibited)," which should be used to warn people of the approach or position of the car. However, German law forbade sounding the horn "if horses or other animals were frightened."[46] Yet within Germany—as was the case elsewhere—there were many local variations. The city of Köln, for example, required "every vehicle to carry a bell," but forbade "the use of trumpets as a signal."[47] Laws in Italy required motor cars to "carry a deep-sounding horn (other aural signals being forbidden in inhabited places or on main roads)."[48] Motorcycles were required to have a higher-toned horn so people could identify what was coming. The Netherlands, for its part, required a horn that could "be heard 100 yards off . . . that must be sounded whenever public safety demands it. Horns are limited to motor vehicles, for which bells are prohibited. Excessive horn blowing is forbidden."[49] One observer noted the confusion: "Should your horn be blown too softly you are prosecuted; but so you are if you blow it too loudly."[50]

No matter what sound the automobile horn was legally deemed to be, there was very little guidance on how much it should be sounded. Many legislatures required compulsory signaling all the time. Such legal obligations led to increased usage of the horn, which in turn provoked a torrent of complaints about its overuse. "The horn ought to be used with discretion," argued British MP Sir David Harrel. "You want to give them warning, but you do not want to startle people or get on their nerves."[51] In many cases, drivers were convinced that the only way to meet their obligation to drive safely was to constantly sound the horn. "Some motorists entertain the opinion that they are quite free from all responsibility if they only keep hooting all the time." The problem with this behavior was that it also convinced drivers that "it is the business of all the traffic in front of them to get out of the way." Future legislation about compulsory signaling, Harrel argued, "must take into consideration that there are and always will be that class of drivers."[52]

What should laws do about inconsiderate drivers? One expert, William Reed, told the royal commission that though there were always drivers who might feel that their use of technology absolved them of further social responsibility, the obligation to use the horn should be extended beyond what the current laws required. Horns should be sounded, he posited, when passing others, when approaching cross-roads, and to warn potential oncoming traffic of dangerous points in the road. In light of "the number of bends and turns in the roads" in Britain, "even greater than the danger from cross-roads," more signaling was needed to ensure safety.[53] It was when going around a turn blind, as it were, that the sense of hearing could warn drivers in sufficient time. Once again, the commission suggested that it ought to be up to localities to prohibit the sounding of horns or other audible signaling devices as they saw fit. Local contexts required different technologies and different behaviors tied to them. Indeed, in noisy urban spaces like London, filled with competing signals, horns were superfluous because they could not be heard anyway amid the general din, which compelled motorists to drive more carefully.

Signage directing drivers to proceed slowly could clear up some confusion about how and how much to signal while driving. Yet while it might be advantageous to have less aggressive audible signaling devices on cars, most on the commission agreed that when signals designed for cars were used by bicycles or motorcycles, it caused confusion since the public had already come to associate the horn with the automobile. Octavius Holmes Beatty, the vice chairman of the Council of the Cyclists' Touring Club, made the best case for the automobile requiring an exclusive sound when he testified, "I think the horn judiciously used is a very desirable instrument, because it has a distinctive note, and it can probably be heard further than any other signal, even including a bell, but I would be for prohibiting other vehicles than motor cars for using it, because I think it creates confusion, and in fact it irritates considerably. Cases are on record in which the rider of an ordinary bicycle has had a large motor horn attached to it and he has simply caused everybody to scurry from his immediate neighborhood by sounding it."[54] Confusion led to irritation, driving the cycle of social combustion; more regulation of signals was needed. Yet despite the robust debate, British law largely left the standardization of signaling devices tied to various transportation technologies up to localities.[55]

The United States had similarly confusing and decentralized legal requirements. States and municipalities were intent on regulating sound signaling practices. Most required that cars be equipped with some kind of audible signal, and most made signaling to approaching traffic compulsory. One editorialist in *The Horseless Age* gave a sense of the range of signal sounds and argued that America should standardize the sounds used by automobiles: "The available devices are the bell, the horn and, in the case of steam vehicles, the steam whistle. Of these, the bell is almost exclusively used in this country, while the horn holds sway in Europe. . . . The horn, which gives a distinct signal, deserves the consideration of automobilists. . . . The tone of the horn is more novel and penetrating than that of a bell of nearly equal dimensions."[56] For this writer, because the horn was both loud and had a sound that would not be confused with the signal of other vehicles, it was better suited as the representational sound of the automobile. As the range of laws and opinions suggests, cultures were attempting to solve the safety problem by compelling drivers to use sound technology to signal one another. Though they differed as to what kind of signal was legal and when drivers were compelled to initiate it, all required some kind of audible signal. Inventors and engineers stepped up to meet the growing demand.

The Technology Market Responds to the Call

At the dawn of the twentieth century, scientists, inventors, and engineers became avatars of progress, creating machines that would lead humanity to a brighter future. As such, writers and politicians often framed the new consumer technology that emerged from their work in the automobile sector as the best way to respond to the problems caused by automobile technology. In the growing automotive accessory market, the pneumatic horn, which worked by forcing air against a reed, was the most common product. While these devices usually utilized a squeeze bulb to produce air, there were many other kinds of horns. Indeed, each country experiencing the growth of automobile culture had dozens of companies offering competing products. One problem associated with the squeeze bulb horn was that it required a free hand for operation; this was somewhat complicated because the steering mechanism on early automobiles was a lever that functioned like the tiller of a boat. With one hand on the tiller and the other on a lever that controlled the speed, a driver did not have a free hand to sound the horn.

Such utilitarian concerns led inventors to come up with innovative solutions that allowed drivers to keep their hands on the levers or on the newer steering wheel. The Gilson-Peters foot horn, for example, freed the hands since drivers stomped on a piston air pump pedal. The Riley-Klotz horn engineered a different solution to the problem by attaching the air balloon to the elbow so that an operator had only to thrust the arm back to sound the horn.

Along with functionality, the volume of sound emerged as another problem with the squeeze bulb horn. As the number of cars on the roads grew, so too did the need for horns that were loud enough and clear enough to be heard from farther away. French inventors looked to musical instrument design to achieve volume and adapted it to the bulb horn. The "autophone horn," for example, featured a "double turn of the pipe after the cornet type producing a much greater volume of sound than the horn of a single turn of pipe."[57] One automotive journalist boasted of the effectiveness of this new horn technology: "The large horn is just what we need. One toot will clear the road for half a mile ahead." [58] Very quickly, the new French horn technology, with its instrument design and greater volume and range, grabbed the interest of early adopters in search of the newest technology. Importers rushed to bring the products to America. Just as quickly, American companies adopted the technology and produced their own models, such as the Stevens and Company's Esco horn, manufactured in New York City. The Motor Car Equipment Company of New York created the French Jericho horn consisting of two bulbs connected by two flexible tubes to the brass horn so that it could be "operated by the chauffeur and tourist at the same time, thus providing means for the occupants of the car to sound the horn at will should they become nervous or the chauffeur have both hands in use."[59]

The louder, "French" sound technology did not please everyone. Many

Figure 2. Ad for the new loud and instrumental French horns. From *Motor Age*, October 5, 1905. (Archive.org)

thought louder technology changed the behavior of drivers, making them less thoughtful of the experience of others. In a 1903 issue of *The Horseless Age,* Dr. F. L. Bartlett opined, "I have no use for an auto driver who makes his way downtown constantly tooting a French horn. It means 'get out of my way. I'm coming,' and has done more to discredit the automobile than anything else. There ought to be a law against the use of a French horn."[60] Noisy signaling technology, and the modes of social comportment afforded by its use, emerged as a contested social issue. The kind of signaling technology one used conveyed something of one's psychology and sense of sociality. In the *Lancet,* a British medical journal, one writer argued similarly that the way drivers used the motor horn "afforded illustration" of the "blindness of some motorists to the claims of others." He speculated that "the medical question may arise whether we may not have here some pathological phenomena associated with the possession of a motor car."[61] When speeding past others, drivers honked their horns to command people to move out of the way and literally left the concerns of others in the dust. Technology was changing not only the way people moved through space but also the way they related to the needs and claims of other people in a shared public space.

As automobile technology spread, so too did the antipathy toward the sound of drivers negotiating city streets with their horns. Writers returning from Paris complained that the constant clamor of tooting horns made streets even more chaotic. When the horns got louder, this problem became worse; the sounds of competing horns on streets where many shared the road made it difficult to tell where any individual sound was coming from, rendering outings less safe. In 1904, while weighing public nuisance claims against issues of automobile safety, the Chicago City Council passed ordinances limiting the amount of noise an automobile horn could make.[62] After similar laws were passed in Britain, one company, W. W. Gamage, changed the instrument design of its bulb horn to the two-tone "Tworn," making it less loud and more distinctive. "Much has been written lately on the need of an efficient warning which must not at the same time be a public nuisance." When sounded, the Tworn produced "one harmonious note which at the same time is loud, sharp and penetrating, one which can neither be ignored nor denounced."[63]

Yet with the growing sounds of honking horns, wailing sirens, and bells of all kinds ringing throughout the modernizing city, along with such devices as the "cut-out muffler" that were sold as means to increase horsepower while making noise that would alert everyone that you were coming, the increasingly automobile-centered soundscape was becoming ever louder and more chaotic.

Again, engineers and salesmen offered technological solutions, usually making the horn easier to sound and louder. They pushed a new wave of products in the mid-aughts of the new century that boasted a volume or a tone that would "cut through" the noise produced by other signals, thereby exacerbating the sonic arms race. Consumer discourse promoted the notion that safety required louder technology, and increasingly the law agreed, requiring consumers to adopt the latest designs. Laws in Kansas, for instance, required that an automobile horn "be heard from a quarter of a mile."[64] This regulation seemed to favor the exhaust horn or whistle technology, which used the force of exhaust gas to produce sound that could be heard for a long distance without drivers having to exert their own energies.

The feedback loop between legal requirements and consumer demand drove inventors to develop new designs. As laws required louder mechanical signals, inventors jumped in with new products that fit the bill. A whole range of exhaust horns based on steam whistle technology that tapped into the energy reserves of the exhaust system entered the consumer market, promising to make automobiling more safe. The marketing literature accompanying each new signal described the technological affordances and directly addressed the emerging safety discourse and legal requirements. Most framed their new designs as signs of progress.

A quick glance at a range of these products shows how the technocentric logic used to market technology as a response to social need in a technologized world was emerging as an ideology and becoming dominant. Products like the Autochime, an exhaust-driven horn launched by the Gray-Hawley Manufacturing Company in 1906, merely required the driver to push a pedal and the wires running under the floor would release the valves and sound the horn. In touting it as a "practical signal built for service" with a tone that was "clear, deep and powerful,"[65] the company tied convenience, speed of response, volume, and safety to its innovative technological affordances.

The Waymaker horn was another exhaust gas–driven horn based on the steam whistle design that, per the name, boasted that its loud signal communicated "make way" to whoever heard it. Yet it was designed to make the exhaust-driven signal appeal to consumers who were comfortable with previous technology. A driver activated the Waymaker by merely squeezing a bulb, as if it were a squeeze bulb horn, which then redirected the exhaust fumes to the whistle and created a sound that no one could ignore. Similarly, in France, another automatic exhaust whistle, the Sifflet Lucifer, linked its brand to its distinctive sound: its note was so supernaturally strange that everyone would pay attention and move out of the way.

More often than not, exhaust driven signals were billed for their musicality. The Aermore exhaust horn, whose name resonated with the all-important utilitarian desire for "ever more" volume, boasted that it emitted a "strong but pleasing signal" by diverting the exhaust into four different-sized pipes, thereby "producing a four tone accord." The Continental Calliope, with three tones, was billed as "the latest musical fad."[66] The Nightingale whistle—recalling the name of the melodic bird—also connected its brand to notions of politeness and aesthetic musicality with its multitone "bird-like trill." Yet at the same time it promised utilitarian functionality with its volume and capacity for soundscape penetration.

The Tubaphone, another exhaust-driven technology, tried to connect its sound to musical horn instruments like the tuba and the saxophone. It allowed consumers to choose the number of tones that suited them best, all the while providing the volume and functionality necessary for safety. The Exhaustophone, another standard multitone exhaust whistle, boasted that its three-tone signal was more than a horn, giving the consumer the volume that other competing products "robbed" them of.

Of the exhaust horns, the Gabriel horn was one of the earliest and most successful. Gabriel advertised horns that, while extremely loud, were also "a pleasure to hear," aesthetically speaking. "Each horn is tuned to a musi-

Figure 3. Ad for the Nightingale whistle, one of the musical exhaust horns. From *Cycle and Automobile Trade Journal*, March 1, 1910. (Pennsylvania State University Library)

cal key—no discordant screeching note—is easily blown, and is strong and durable." It was also much more effective than the bulb horn in cutting through the background noise that made car horns hard to hear against competing signals. Its volume and novelty made it stand out. *Motor Age* writer and transcontinental tourist Percy Megargel wrote in 1905 of the public reaction to its sound: "Our Gabriel Horn is still an object of great curiosity. . . . Teams that refuse to pull out to one side at the approach of the automobile and the sounding of our bulb horn usually give us passage room at the first notes of the Gabriel's trumpet. They seem to read the name by the sound and show their respect immediately, while the small boy and his little sister stand in open mouth wonder at the musical notes ejected from the exhaust of our muffler."[67] Its sonic novelty attracted attention, not its aggressive sound or sheer volume. Since the tone was aesthetically pleasing, it was perceived as a polite request instead of an imperative demand. The company secured two patents on these devices and waged vigorous campaigns against competitors.

As the company tried to capture consumer demand by promising both volume and "musicality" (as opposed to mere noise), Gabriel went so far as to create models of its horns that could be played like an organ from the dash. Wrote one American observer, "It will henceforth be possible for the owner of a Gabriel horn to call for the right of way with a few bars from 'Home Sweet Home,' 'Tammany' or 'Go Tell Aunt Nancy.'"[68] Indeed, using horns like this attracted public attention, and the company used celebrities who yearned to be noticed to promote their product. Such was the case with a British actress

Figure 4. A cartoon mocking the new "musical" exhaust horns. From *The Motor-Car Journal*, January 1, 1910. (Pennsylvania State University Library)

named Vesta Victoria, whose car was fitted with a "multiplex horn sounding four notes of the 'common chord' in rapid and perpetually varied succession . . . this car had a playful habit of making its presence heard wherever it went, so that the people soon grew to know it, and smiled broadly at the musical vivacity with which it heralded its approach."[69] Even if one was not a celebrity, the musical affordances were available to all. One British article in *The Motor-Car Journal* playfully argued that the musical horns were getting so sophisticated that any breakdown could be accompanied by a musical interlude.[70] Yet there was more to this framing of the signaling technology as polite and aesthetically pleasing than meets the ear. First, one can hear the obvious analogic connection to notions of politeness, linking the sounding of automobile horns with speech acts between people negotiating shared space in a civil life: the polite request of "excuse me" rather than an imperative demand to "get out of the way." By associating "musicality," aesthetically pleasing sound, with capturing the attention of others, Gabriel linked its branded technology to the all-important idea of safety.

While safety and signal volume were clearly associated through repeated use in international legislative language and marketing copy, another antithetical assertion was now increasingly heard, namely, that the horns that were too loud, imperative, and rude. This dialectic continued to play out with each new product that promised its innovative technology could solve the problems of drivers needing to signal to others while operating an automobile.

Automobile Signals on Trial

Despite the growth of available signaling technologies, none of them actually solved the many safety problems associated with automobile technology. "Of all the menaces of today," opined Woodrow Wilson in 1906, "the worst is the reckless driving of automobiles."[71] The numbers, though unofficial during this era, lend context to Wilson's growing concern. In the United States, automobile fatalities grew from 297 in 1907 to 1,291 in 1911.[72] In Britain, automobile numbers grew from 15,895 in 1905 to 89,411 in 1910, and that year the number of accident-related deaths tallied 1,277.[73] The number of legal cases connected to accidents also grew, testing the effectiveness of signaling technology and providing anecdotal evidence of its ambiguous relation to safety. Indeed, there was growing evidence that the compulsory signal sounding increasingly required by law made loud signaling technology a new problem on its own, especially on streets where horses still outnumbered cars. Dozens of court cases in the United States alone tested the viability of compulsory signaling laws as drivers who followed the laws spooked horses with their signaling devices, leading to injuries and fatalities.

One Iowa court case, for example, inquired into the liability of the dutiful driver after a horn-frightened horse caused a fatal accident. Had the law that compelled the driver's honk contributed to the accident, thereby mitigating his liability? The Iowa court decided that each situation was unique: "Whether a signal from an automobile horn is necessary in the exercise of reasonable care was held to be determined by the circumstances of each case."[74] Several states required that devices should be audible from three hundred feet away. Yet in Indiana, courts determined that drivers who used overly loud horn technology were liable if their noise spooked horses and caused accidents.[75] Language in a Kentucky statute shows the murky nature of the law: "A person operating a motor vehicle shall give warning of its approach by signaling with a horn, bell or other device not calculated to frighten such animal."[76] Signaling devices were engineered to be heard from a distance, yet they were also not supposed to frighten the animals that automobilists had to share the road with.

Court cases tested this blurry fine line. In Boston, courts blamed drivers who chose and deployed signaling technology that was too aggressive. In a series of cases that involved bolting horses frightened by a horn that killed the riders, the loud horn blowers were arrested on charges of manslaughter.[77] The compulsory signaling laws were confusing and the judgments involving horn signal technology varied widely; the laws designed to make citizens traveling in traffic more safe often seemed to make them less so.

New York City and Pennsylvania, for instance, had laws that required drivers to sound their horns not only when approaching another vehicle but also at every intersection or alley crossing. Yet judges responding to the effect of horns on horses and pedestrians routinely ruled that strict interpretation of this legal requirement was excessive. Moreover, courts disagreed whether merely blowing the horn limited the liability of the driver who had to share the roads with pedestrians and horses. In one case involving a child killed by a driver who had blown his horn, a New York judge wrote that "no blowing of a horn or of a whistle nor the ringing of a bell or gong without an attempt to lower speed is sufficient if the circumstances at a given point demand that the speed should be slackened in the exercise of ordinary care and caution."[78]

If signal laws varied widely depending on local ordinance, so too did their enforcement. While some municipalities had lax enforcement, others used strict fines to discipline citizens. Boston police set up traps at blind alleys to arrest and fine noncompliers without warnings being given: "All who fail to blow their horn are arrested."[79] Police in one New Jersey county raised signs that ordered all drivers to "blow your horn here."[80] Those who failed to comply with the sign's command or who did not have the requisite signaling technology were fined. In a similar fashion, after the city of Philadelphia required cars to use only horn technology in 1906, city police put up "blow your horn" signs and fined drivers who used alternative sounding technology.[81]

Compulsory signaling was more the rule than the exception. In Maryland, for example, laws dictated that if the lights on a car failed, the driver had to sound the horn every two hundred feet. Such laws were not unique to America. A similar range of laws existed in England, Scotland, France, Italy, and Switzerland, and, as was the case in the United States, courts in each country were constantly forced to weigh the letter of the law against pragmatic necessity as the soundscape filled with more horns. For automobile tourists who traveled between areas with different enforcement regimes, the result was confusion and chaos.[82] Attempting to alleviate the confusion for drivers, international consortiums of automobile clubs began to work toward standardizing sonic signaling technology and laws. They recommended two solutions: standardized technologies that were adequately loud and standardized signaling laws to ensure that people used them.

Despite ongoing complaints about too loud technology, public and legal debates framed the safety problem as one of horns not being loud enough. Almost all legal statues in countries with automobile laws included the requirement that a vehicle have, to quote the British motor laws of 1896, an "instrument capable of giving audible and sufficient warning of the approach or position of the carriage."[83] Driven by such discourse linking audibility and safety, a whole range of innovative signaling technologies emerged in the second half of the aughts designed to appeal to consumers' imagination purely by virtue of their ability to create more volume and be heard from farther away. Siren technology, for example, was sold as the "safest" available. Unlike exhaust horns, often marketed for their multitone polite musicality, hand-cranked sirens produced a constant sound that extended the range of their signal. The Sterk Manufacturing Company's Long Distance siren, for example, touted its "penetrating reverberant roar that warns every living thing for miles ahead that you want the right of way." The aggressive sound design brought safety to the user. Yet though sirens extended the range of the signal, the hand crank technology had the same problem that older bulb horns had: it required drivers to release their grip on the wheel and levers. Several companies turned to inventive engineers who solved this problem by using the friction generated by the engine flywheel to generate sound; though it freed the hands of the driver, it made the sound even louder. The National siren, invented by William Jones of Philadelphia, was operated by a foot lever that brought a friction pulley against the flywheel. By applying more or less pressure to the pedal, the driver could vary the tone of the siren from a soft hum to a loud blast.

The Leavitt siren horn, also driven by the energy of the flywheel, boasted that its volume equaled safety because it "can be heard above the din of traffic, steam cars, whistles and all other signals." As the loudest, it also claimed to be the safest. Because it could be heard above the bulb horns, the marketing copy boasted, it "prevents accidents and Saves Lives."[84] Of course, more volume also meant more frightened horses and more angry residents raising noise complaints; courts were forced to weigh in on the viability of siren technology. As they did, a legal framework for regulating automobile signaling technology continued to take shape.

In New York, the legal liability of individual automobile drivers and signal technology consumers was not the only governmental concern; unwanted sound or noise was also a question for the ordinance law. Indeed, as the number of cars carrying increasingly powerful signal technology soared, automobile noise become a matter of political importance. As sound studies scholars have noted, the outcry against noise as a feature of modern life emerged all over the world in the final decade of the nineteenth century, accompanying the automobile as a feature of social life.[85] Citizens claiming the right to a reasonable level of quietness and repose were increasingly acting to curb

LONG DISTANCE SIREN

THIS NEW INVENTION is unquestionably the greatest warning signal ever devised. The volume of sound is absolutely at the will of the operator at all times.

A slight turn of the crank-handle produces a soft and gentle sound, or, if desired, a penetrating reverberant roar that warns every living thing for miles ahead that you want the right-of-way — and you get it.

Write for Illustrated Booklet.

STERK MANUFACTURING COMPANY, 69 Wells St., CHICAGO

Figure 5. A suggestive ad for the Sterk Long Distance siren, which the operator could crank while driving to warn pedestrians from miles away. From *The Motor Way,* October 18, 1906. (HathiTrust)

the noise produced by automobiles, which, despite what early promoters had promised, were turning out to be noisy indeed.

One organization at the vanguard of this political action against noise was the New York Society for the Suppression of Unnecessary Noise, founded in 1907 by Julia Barnett Rice. The society, which became the model for an international movement, used publications and public hearings to generate ongoing discussions about car noise. In 1908, New York City police commissioner Theodore Bingham took the antinoise crusade to the streets to win the support of voters. He issued a general order directing the police to stop all unnecessary noises because quiet, he said, "was essential to the health and happiness of the people." He made "the unnecessary use of horns, sirens, etc, on autos or motorcycles," which he called "a public nuisance," a fineable offense.[86] Honoring the "quiet zones" pushed for by Rice and her society, he declared that automobile signaling devices could not be used within five hundred feet of schools or churches during school or church hours, and within a like distance of hospitals and asylums. Moreover, signaling devices could not be used in public places before 9 a.m. and after 7 p.m. on Sundays. The public soundscape needed to be protected from unnecessary noise. In England, antinoise societies railed against devices like the siren and called for them to be banned. As one article in *The Autocar* stated, "There can be no hardship in dispensing with the miserable, irritating, nerve-shaking, blood-curdling howl of the siren, which should not be found on the car of anybody who has the smallest regard for the feelings of others, and which adds an unnecessary terror to the lives of roadside dwellers."[87]

During a speaking tour in London in 1909, Julia Barnett Rice, now the "Queen of Silence," singled out traffic noise as the next frontier of global legislation against unnecessary noise. In Paris, where she had just spoken, she noted that "there are absolutely no restrictions on street noises. . . . In New York, we have less traffic than you have in London, but our trolley-cars which run on practically every avenue are much noisier. . . . The worst feature of London streets is the unrestrained use of motor-horns."[88] Rice was not alone in her concern about the results of the technological sound war driven by inventors and producers of sound signals in search of market share. John Stowe, in *The Motor-Car Journal,* protested "against the wailing, piercing shrieks and groans . . . by which the way is cleared for the passage of the car." Manufacturers were to blame that the "toot-toot or pip-pip" of the simple squeeze bulb horn was being "silenced by the aggressive sounds that are belched forth from devices which have their only utility in securing the circulation of money." Their horrific sounds "have added to the terrors of the street." In a culture witnessing the "triumph of the car," he appealed to the motorist to be moderate and "not render the great towns hideous by their inartistic decoration of vehicles nor by the emission of unmusical sounds from the horns."[89]

Yet as the governmental framework for automobile signaling devices grew, so too did the number of available technologies, which seemed to multiply by the month. With the question of representational sound for the automobile unanswered, the soundscape remained chaotic: "What shall be the distinctive sound to distinguish the approach of a motor car?" queried one author. "In the early days the horn had a monopoly so far as the automobile was concerned."[90] Now, with the number of cars and the noise of the street both increasing, things had changed. "Motorists are not so universally favorable to the motor horn as was formerly the case, and the penetrating sound of the whistle now awakens sleepy carters and calls the drowsy carman to get to their own side of the road. Is the utility of the whistle partially due to the novelty of the note?"[91] Whether using the horn or the whistle, drivers needed more and more sound to make themselves heard, to be noticed by others sharing the same social space.

By the end of the first decade after the emergence of the automobile, it was certain that the individual's relationship to space would be forever transformed by this speedy mechanized technology, allowing a freedom and mobility not experienced before. It was also certain that automobiles were extremely dangerous. In a growing consumer market, more responsive and louder signals were called for. Heeding that call, a generation of engineers stepped onto the stage, offering new solutions made possible by harnessing the power of the electrical impulse. The klaxon horn was about to be born.

2

FIRST ENCOUNTERS

Sound in the Age of the Electrical Signal

In the early days of the automobile era, few things inspired as much excitement as the periodic automobile salons. Part trade show, part exposition, they helped sell the public on the automotive lifestyle and on the newest technologies designed to improve it. First started by the French automobile industry in Paris in 1897, these gatherings spread rapidly to other industries and cities. The American automotive industry started staging them in 1900, and they quickly became a popular institution.[1] At the salons, inventors, engineers, and entrepreneurs displayed their latest products to the press and an excited public, hoping to capture the imagination of people fascinated by the new technology. At the 1907 Importers' Automobile Salon in New York City, the Lovell-McConnell Manufacturing Company revealed a new electrical signaling device invented by the electrical engineer Miller Reese Hutchison and called the klaxon. Lovell-McConnell, whose business involved making electric motors and finding innovative applications for them, hoped that the klaxon's distinctive sound and improved functionality might solve some of the problems that plagued automobile signaling devices and capture the attention of the automobile accessories market. From the moment the klaxon's distinctive aaOOgah sounded from Lovell-McConnell's ribbon-draped display booth and echoed across Madison Square Garden, it did just that. The rest, as they say, is history.

Yet that history is complicated, and includes how the public was primed for the klaxon's arrival. The story of the development, introduction, and marketing of klaxon technology reveals much about how industrialized societies embrace new technologies and integrate their use through a wide range of cultural conversations. As discussed in the previous chapter, manufacturers, advertisers, and commentators increasingly presented technology products to the public as responding to perceived needs, thereby establishing a feedback loop that helped solidify a growing technocentric culture. In this cultural context, inventors and technology entrepreneurs became crucial figures, positioning themselves as outright heroes who could manage the problems that arose in a modern culture dominated by new technology. The problem of vehicles communicating with each other through the noise of an ever busier and more chaotic traffic space led to a spate of technical innovations. Lovell-McConnell capitalized on these ideologies and cultural trends, drawing on innovations in the emerging field of mass media advertising. In the subsequent commercial mythology promoted by the Klaxon Company, Lovell-McConnell's specially branded subsidiary marketing division, klaxon technology was a product of this engineering mode of cultural change, the product of a dialectic that analyzed need and then invented technology that promised to fulfill that need.

Even though the "horn" had become the recommended instrument to announce the approach of an automobile by 1906, the term *horn* was ambiguous, and it was clear that the available technology did not remotely solve the functionality issue. The horns that used levers and pulleys, even the ones that tapped into the moving parts or the exhaust of the engine to transform energy into sound, were complicated and unreliable. The steering and operating mechanisms of automobiles of the era suggest how difficult it must have been to abide by the compulsory signaling laws, now mandated in most places. It was only a matter of time before inventors would turn to electricity and the affordances of electrical technology to engineer an easier way for drivers to produce an audible signal.

In the new century, electrical engineering promised modern solutions for all kinds of everyday problems. The biggest advances in automobile signaling technology were connected to the application of electricity, an innovation that carried with it a range of ideological associations. People increasingly associated electricity with the future and saw in it manifestations of the technological sublime, a transcendent form of ideology in which technology would help transform the environment and lead to a techno-utopian future.[2] From Emerson to Edison, the rhetorical connection between technological progress and spiritual symbolism created and affirmed a kind of hope for the future, a false consciousness exploited by the purveyors of consumer technology. Marketers and salesmen heralded each new invention or device as a means to help society transform humans' relationship to the environment and communicate with one another. Most important, as the inventors and promoters of the telegraph had emphasized, electrical technologies were fast, allowing immediate connection along the telegraph wire or electrical circuit.

Like the telegraph, electrical automobile signaling devices were operated by haptic push buttons instead of cumbersome bulbs, levers, or cables. Since they responded as fast as a nerve impulse, they responded immediately to any safety situation. The klaxon tapped into the transcendental rhetoric of the age of electricity, embracing and exploiting its preternatural potential. Every push of the button helped recharge the modern hope that everyday life would be rendered easier and safer through better technology.

Engineers of all stripes went to work developing means for drivers to use electricity to signal immediately—the Tallyho horn, for instance, though it was an older air horn mechanism based on a bagpipe design that stored air in a bladder under the seat. Pushing an electric button released the air instantly to produce a sound. The Columbia Electric Coaches and Carriages produced by the Pope Manufacturing Company in Hartford, Connecticut, not only offered an electric signal bell that drivers could operate by stepping on a floor pedal (bells still being the representational sound associated with electric cars) but also featured a bell for back-seat passengers to get the chauffeur's attention.[3] Every push of the button to ring the bell reinforced the notion that electrical technology was transforming everyday life.

The same magnetic alternating currents that could be used to drive a bell could also be used to drive a vibrating mechanism on a tympanum, which could be amplified and projected as an electric horn. The Holtzer-Cabot Electric Company, located in Brookline, Massachusetts, offered a horn based on the vibrator and diaphragm design that produced the sound of a reed horn. Because of its watertight design, the company boasted that the horn had been adopted by the US Navy. The Crack Unicum electric horn, also based on the buzzer and diaphragm design, connected to a tube instrument to amplify the sound. It produced a penetrating blare that lasted longer than the regular "toot-toot" and was immediate.

Even in France, where the bulb French horn was king, the "corne électrique" gained a following because of its utility. As one 1905 ad in France stated, "The most practical warning signal [avertisseur] that exists is certainly the electric horn, which is used more and more. With this apparatus, one no longer needs to squeeze a cumbersome bulb, a simple button suffices."[4] Indeed, the introduction of electricity into the accessory market led to a wave of invention that all but promised to solve the signaling problem with the touch of a button. It was safe, it required no extra movement, and it was loud. With their push-button functionality and responsiveness, electric horns piqued the interest of automobile owners, becoming not only features of international automobile shows and salons but also a constant presence in the soundscape as the number of vehicles continued to grow.

Such was the environment when the Importers' Automobile Salon opened

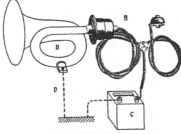

Abb. 176. Elektrische Huppe.

von der Mechanofix-Jndustrie-Gesellschaft fabriziert wird, ist die Be-
triebsfähigkeit ohne Unterbrechung vorhanden. Jn kritischen Mo-
menten, wo ein schnelles Signal ausschlaggebend ist, kann die elektrische

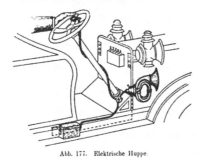

Abb. 177. Elektrische Huppe.

Figure 6. German opera-
tional description of electric
horn technology, showing
how the push-button could
be mounted on the steering
wheel. From *Automobil und
Automobilsport.* Germany:
R. C. Schmidt, 1908. (Hathi-
Trust)

in Madison Square Garden on December 28, 1907, featuring 1908 model foreign cars and a host of electrical signaling devices ready for market. Those
in attendance heard Lovell-McConnell's new electrical sound signal loud and
clear. The device's simple design addressed the problems of volume, range,
immediacy and convenience. The klaxon quickly captured the attention of
the automobile public and created a buzz in the press. The *New York Tribune*
reported that New York mayor George B. McClellan Jr., who "has the loudest automobile in New York . . . and wants everything that has to do with his
car to be distinctly 'up to date,'" had purchased a strange new signal there.
Those present on its introduction "on New Year's Eve," the *Tribune* continued, "heard the remarkable quality of noise that the klaxon produces. It not
only drowned every other noise made by the various alarm signals that were
let loose on that occasion but reverberated with ear-splitting vibrations above
the combined dissonance."[5] Immediately, people noticed. How could they
not?—Being noticed was the whole point. Indeed, at a trade show at which
all signaling products competed for attention, from the new electrical push-
button devices to the exhaust horns and older instrument bulb designs, the
klaxon noise cut through the din.

Figure 7. Humorous cartoon by Sis Hopkins, depicting responses to the sound of the new horns. "'She (*sighing*)—'Pedestrians are getting too foxy to be run down any more.' He—'Yes: but I've got a new horn that sounds so awful it scares 'em to death.'"From *Own Book and Magazine of Fun*, May 1909. (Billy Ireland Cartoon Library & Museum, Ohio State University)

As early drivers embraced the technology, a whole new kind of sound was being heard in city streets as Lovell-McConnell's publicity men tried to promote its technology. Cartoonists lampooned the smug drivers who were willing to use their electric horns to drive other motorists out of the way with sound. Yet this was precisely what its inventor had had in mind.

Miller Reese Hutchison (1876–1944) was already an established engineer tinkering in the world of electricity and its application to sound when he invented the klaxon. Like many Americans who came of age at the dawn of the electrical age, he had idolized Edison while growing up in Alabama. He was said to have confided to his father, "Someday I am going to be Mr. Edison's engineer, so I must study and work to get ready for the position."[6] His interest in applying electricity to sound and telephony technology first yielded results when he won an award in 1904 for the installation and operation of the first commercial wireless telephone. As a young engineering student at Auburn University, he began experimenting with a device that would enable the deaf to hear, the "acousticon."[7] He went on to study the anatomy of the human ear at Alabama Medical College to better understand the mechanics of hearing so that he could come up with better designs for his applied electrical technology. His work in the realm of sound and telephony led him to design a dictograph to help record speech, and he received recognition from Queen Alexandra of England for his acousticon. It was during this time, and by applying his thinking about sound reproduction and acoustic design, that he came up with the idea for an automobile signaling device that would sound immediately and be heard through the ever-growing din of automotive traffic.

The moment of inspiration that led him to come up with the klaxon is steeped in commercial hagiography, one of the ways in which technology companies hyped the engineering ethos in American culture. "Realizing the limitation of existing signals," read one of the promotional articles pushed to dozens of newspapers and automobile journals by Lovell-McConnell soon after the product reached market, "he set himself the task of devising one which would make many times the noise of a horn and yet be free from both complication and tone variation."[8] The engineer, according to company mythology, set out to find a way to produce sound using electricity that would have sufficient utility. The standard electric horn design, as Lovell-McConnell was later quick to point out in its marketing literature, used a soft diaphragm and electromagnet buzzer, but this paradigm had certain problems: the platinum contacts burned away too fast, making the device less durable, and the volume of sound it produced was not a significant improvement over that produced by the old reed bulb horn. Hutchison solved the problem by inventing a mechanism that utilized a large steel diaphragm that was sounded by a lobbed wheel driven by a shaft attached to a 3,000 rpm electric motor, which ran on one of the new six-volt storage batteries that Edison had developed at Menlo Park.[9] Each time a point on the lobbed wheel hit a steel button in the center of the diaphragm, it made a noise. As the motor attached to the lobbed wheel initiated, the pitch of the note rose in tone, falling as soon as the current was closed with the release of the push-button, creating the distinctive aaOOgah sound. Since it did not require the circuit to be broken, unlike the electromagnet that drove door buzzers and electric horns, it was more durable. A sound projector in the shape of a bullhorn spread the "peculiarly metallic Klaxon," directing the sound waves laterally while sending them directionally ahead. As one of his biographers noted, "The completed apparatus, after many tests and refinements, was the press-the-button Klaxon of today, claimed by its inventor to be the most efficient converter of power into continuous noise in the world."[10] Indeed, Mark Twain—whom Hutchison met after Edison made Hutchison chief engineer of the Edison Laboratories, as well as his personal representative—once jestingly accused Hutchison of "inventing the Klaxon to make people so deaf that they would have to buy his Acousticon!"[11]

It made sense that Hutchison brought his product to F. Hallett Lovell Jr., an entrepreneur from a wealthy family dating back to the *Mayflower* whose new company was also tied to the electrical revolution in consumer technology.[12] "An inventor dropped in to see me," Lovell would later recount:

> In six seconds he pressed an electric button which produced the wildest, most startling noise I ever heard. It made me jump as I had never jumped before.
> "I see it makes you jump," smiled my visitor.
> "Who wouldn't jump?" I demanded.
> "Ah that's the answer!" he exclaimed. "You've said it!"
> Again he pressed the button, again I jumped. Nor did he have to talk much to convince me that it would make anybody, everybody jump. So I decided to take over the invention, to become a merchant of racket. I saw tremendous possibilities in the thing's uncanny screech. It said "Danger. Look out." In a way that was irresistible.
> I called it the "Klaxon" from the Greek word *klax*—to shriek. I made up my mind to put the word Klaxon in the language—to make it mean automobile horn, just as pianola means piano and kodak means camera.[13]

A perfect apparatus for conveying the ideology of the technological sublime, its main utility was the way the incredibly loud sound prompted an immediate reaction from anyone who heard it, as immediate as the sound produced by the electric push-button. Lovell bought the patent from Hutchison and set to work trying to figure out how to make consumers *want* a machine that emitted a sound that made everyone who heard it jump and recoil. Turning an annoyance into a convenience meant the company had to change the way people heard the sound, a flight-inducing strident shriek. Lovell-McConnell had to accustom people to the klaxon noise so they would hear it not only as something positive that they *needed* but also as a sound they wanted to associate with themselves, a sign of who they were in relation to modernity.[14]

Lovell-McConnell set to work, laying the proprietary ground for a marketing campaign that would shift consumers' perception of the klaxon sound. Soon after securing the patent on Hutchison's technology, along with previous patents for the technology that had implications for the klaxon design, the company also patented the language and graphics that would accompany the technology. It filed a class 36 patent, "musical instruments and supplies," for the product under the name Klaxon in March 1908, officially registering the orthographic KLAXON trademark as part of the copyright in July 1908. Seeing the quick growth in automobile sales, the company recognized the potential for an international market for its communication technology and patented the klaxon in Great Britain, France, Germany, Italy, and Belgium.[15]

Lovell-McConnell registered the brand in France in April 1909, and soon thereafter in countries where it legally controlled the application of the technology.[16] The marketing literature it began to send out through its distribution company, named Klaxon International, with an address listed as 1 Madison Avenue, New York City, reveals that company officials knew just how powerful the sound was that they were bringing to market and just how important modern marketing techniques would be in its international dissemination. "It is the only signal ever built," read the direct mail brochures that the company sent to automobile accessory marketers and jobbers, "which enables the owner of a high-powered car or motor boat to obtain a fair percentage of the right of way, without which he might just as well be driving a carry-all or navigating a brick barge."[17] The power of the sound made it an investment in wear and tear on the car and in safety. "No slowing up on hills or sudden stops to avoid collision at the last moment—the KLAXON gives you a clear road."[18]

Other signaling technologies, Lovell-McConnell's marketing literature insisted, just couldn't compete with the power of the klaxon's sound. "A command lies in every note of its sharp strident blast, very different from the easygoing lullaby of the auto horn or chime whistle. Its voice penetrates through the rattle of loose backboards and hoof-beats on the roadway, cuts the fog bank on the water and carries far enough ahead to let others know that you are coming and to act accordingly."[19] Yet it was not natural for people to embrace an automobile technology that made those who heard it involuntarily recoil. Klaxon technology had to be sold to consumers through the emerging science of consumer advertising.

Going Native

The first advertising campaigns to reframe the powerful sound of klaxon technology utilized a genre of ads, known as "native advertising," that went hand in hand with the new automobile culture. Native advertising was an established genre of commercial speech that blurred the boundaries between journalism and commercial copy and was a common feature of the automobile industry's promotional practice. These pieces, which read like announcements of technological innovation for a public that was being trained to keep up with technology, were usually pushed out by sales and marketing departments through a variety of publication venues that masked their commercial origin and advertising intent. The articles that Lovell-McConnell placed in prominent automobile journals and newspapers introduced the unnatural sound produced by the klaxon and connected it to the sense of wonder associated with modern electrical technology. The early native stories on the klaxon, usually around three paragraphs long and illustrated with a schematic diagram, were pitched to the tinkerer and new adopter of the technology. One syndicated newspaper piece focused on Hutchison, the inventor of "the most effective noise producers in the world." It emphasized the klaxon's immediate functionality, which made the shriek audible "at a distance of five miles" and permitted "the direction from which it comes" to be immediately ascertained.[20] While laying out the affordances of the technology and its potential applications, these pieces included rhetoric celebrating the engineering ethos of a technocentric modernity, the hallmark of a culture whose teleological sense of itself—and of how this new mode of interacting with the world could lead to a better life—was tied to the electrical sublime.

The native advertising stories were most often connected to an event, such as an automotive show, that gave the journals' "reporters" a reason for discussing the automotive technologies on display. For example, a 1909 special edition of *The Horseless Age* dedicated to the American Motor Car Manufacturers' Association Show at Grand Central Palace, in New York City, was effectively one long advertisement for the growing automotive industry and the technocentric lifestyle it had begun to connote.[21] Not only did such trade shows attract men who were fascinated by automobile technology and interested in seeing the latest products, they were specifically designed to grow automotive culture by including things for the "novice who has got his first touch of the fever" and for "ladies" attracted to the automobile lifestyle. "A good many ladies visit an automobile show chiefly to get a line on the different styles of dress, both for evening and automobile wear."[22] *The Horseless Age* December 1909 issue gave a lengthy report on new accessory technology, including a rundown of "signaling devices." The description of the klaxon repeated language and framing identical to that in the copy pushed by Lovell-McConnell to newspapers. Native advertising works by laundering the commercial intentions of the communicant, presenting puff as objective journalism. Here the description presented the sound produced by the klaxon as a technological marvel:

> In sound and operation, the Klaxon is unlike any other warning sig-nal for automobiles. It is operated by an electric motor running at 3,000 r. p. m. and using current from the ignition battery. At the top of the motor shaft is a toothed wheel which strikes a hardened button in the centre of a 5 1/2 inch steel diaphragm, producing 500 double vibra-tions per second. The effect is a bass toned roar, loud enough to be heard a half mile away, and of a characteristic attention-compelling quality which distinguishes it from all other sounds. The Klaxon comes in many different sizes, suitable for every signaling purpose for automobile, motor boats, etc.[23]

The native advertising emphasized utility: the ease of use of the klaxon, the distance its sound carried. The advertisement not only presented the klaxon as a specific accessory promising to solve the safety problem of automobiles, it also cast the entire automobile market as a site where the dream of tech-nological progress and of the transformation of everyday life was being real-ized. Similar language found its way into native advertising in other auto-motive journals, such as *Motor* and *Motor World,* and in *Scientific American,* which emerged as a popular bible of the increasingly technocentric Ameri-can culture.

The *Scientific American* writers echoed the ready-made copy, pushing the promotional language and rhetorical frames offered by Lovell-McConnell that emphasized the "attention-compelling" utility of the sound to deemphasize aesthetic concerns and help frame the noise as desirable: "An automobile horn can hardly be classed as a musical instrument. Its office is not to pro-duce a soothing tone, but to emit a loud sound so startling and ear-piercing as to excite immediate action on the part of the pedestrians in the path of the car. . . . The [Klaxon] produces a sound so entirely new that it is very dif-ficult to describe. The sound resembles a growl or roar, but as the speed is increased the sounded ranges up to a shriek or yell."[24] As would continue to be the case, words like "startling" or "ear-piercing," which in other contexts would immediately connote unwanted or uncivil noise, came to signify sonic qualities tied to utility in this context.

In addition, Klaxon found ways to associate its sound brand with the idea of car racing, one of the growing varieties of cultural events designed to pro-mote the automobile as a lifestyle.[25] For example, at the February 1909 New

Orleans Automobile Club's Racing Carnival, Klaxon sponsored a race and used its horn to start it. The winner received a gold-plated klaxon and the runner-up a silver-plated klaxon.[26] The company had pursued a similar strategy when it gave a horn to McClellan, mayor of New York City, for him to use on his car. Klaxon expertly promoted the idea that sophisticated and adept car users, as pioneer adopters of automobile technology, used klaxon horns. Every driver who used its signaling technology daily served as an embodied advertisement for the company.

Sounds of the Automotive Lifestyle

As a result, in popular culture representations of automobile usage, honking the horn came to be associated with joy riding, as a kind of sonic marking. A Tennyson-derived poem by G. E. Bird, "Honk, Honk, Honk!," in *Automobile Topics* conveyed this sense.

> Honk, honk, honk.
> Sounds a horn across the lea,
> And I would that my tongue could utter
> The joy that it brings to me.

> Honk, honk, honk.
> Is the merry tune for me.
> Since I bought this car not the finest horse
> Do I ever care to see.[27]

Popular songs of the era also promoted the association between the joy of riding and honking the horn, as if that was what it communicated. The waltz "In My Merry Oldsmobile," for example, first recorded in 1905 by Bill Murray without any horn, quickly incorporated the honking sound into the recorded sound (a "honk honk" at the end of phrases), a trend that continued into the 1930s in subsequent recordings.[28]

But was the sound of the klaxon truly that of a horn? Was it a honk, or something else? The Klaxon people themselves did not know how to answer the question. They wanted to find and expand the market for the technology by branding its louder, unique sound, but they also wanted to be in line with the emerging legislation requiring "horns." They tried to have it both ways. Though some city ordinances, such as the 1903 Cincinnati law that defined "horn" as a bulb-driven reed horn, were specific, Klaxon went to work associating its technology with the word "horn." A local ad in the Charleston *News*

Figure 8. Gabriel's twenty-eight-note horn, on a car driven by inventor C. H. Foster. From *The Motor,* October 1907. (Pennsylvania State University Library)

and Courier from June 5, 1909, for example, touted "The Klaxon Horn. . . . The Best signal horn for a motor boat."[29]

Moreover, the company's competitors were also still trying to convince consumers that their push-button horn technology signified something other than sheer fright. The Gabriel Horn Manufacturing Company, for example, continued to expand its offerings, centering the brand on musicality, retaining, perhaps, an association with gentility tied to class distinctions. The company started offering more and more elaborate models with multi-octave ranges that could be operated from the dash by way of push-button keys, including a flashy twenty-eight-note version of the automotive organ that the company gave to Mayor Sherburn Becker of Milwaukee in advance of an automobile show in that city. Like Klaxon, Gabriel tried to capture the attention of the public at automotive shows, as it did at the Automotive Dealers' Association Show in Pittsburgh in March 1909. In between sets of the Third Regiment Boys' Brigade Band, the horn manufacturer played music on the thirty-six-tone Gabriel, "this year heard at frequent intervals."[30] Gabriel echoed the debate about tone and social contract in its advertising, linking the musicality of its horn to the device's refinement and "politeness." Indeed, the company's ads from 1909 associated the sound with royalty. Capitalizing on the company's success in European markets, the Gabriel ads bragged that the technology was being used "exclusively on the personal cars of King Edward of England and Emperor William of Germany, and other crowned heads of Europe." Another ad claimed "The King of Signals is also the Sig-

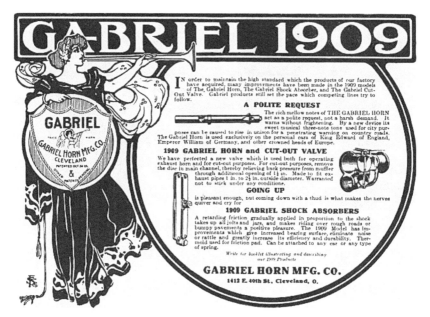

Figure 9. Gabriel Horn Manufacturing Company's 1909 promotion of horns that resonated with class distinction and politeness. From *Cycle and Automobile Trade Journal,* January 1, 1909. (Pennsylvania State University Library)

nal of Kings." Gabriel wanted to associate its device with aristocratic refinement and class.

Since it could not compete on the level of class refinement by associating the tone of its horn with musicality, Klaxon had to appeal to the utilitarian sensibility of consumers. It had to present the "racket" produced by the klaxon as a desirable sound and reframe the criticisms of the horn's noise as pointing up a positive aspect of the technology. This active reframing through native advertisement resounded across the Atlantic, with *The Motor-Car Journal's* description of the 1909 Olympia Motor Show in London reproducing the language used in American publications. The exhibit, the editors wrote, was a sign of the speed of technological progress in modernity, and of the constant technological improvement in the automotive industry. "We are entering on a period during which every part of the automobile is undergoing revisions."[31] The klaxon, which cut through the sound of the auto show to attract attention to the display by its importer, the Motor Accessories Company, made a particular splash. The native advertising repeated the language of the advertising copy, designed to foster a phenomenological framing. It now contained an important catchphrase designed to help people understand the implications of the klaxon's unique sound. "It can be operated from half a dozen dry cells, or a six-volt storage battery, and provides a tone and penetrating note that will entitle it to the description of being the X-Ray of sound, so clear is the tone."[32] Associating this innovative communications technology with an innovative medical technology that helped doctors save lives was an important step toward invigorating the Klaxon brand.

The X-Ray of Sound

Klaxon's first major marketing slogan, "The X-Ray of Sound," shows Lovell-McConnell tying its new signaling device to a growing cultural fascination with electricity and its applications in everyday life. By 1909 the still new X-ray technology (X-rays were first discovered in 1895) had charged the imagination of a wide public of hobbyists, tinkerers, photographers, physicists, lecturers, and doctors. At first it was seen as a physics experiment and was not widely used by clinicians. Many were fascinated by its implications as a technology that enabled people to "see through" matter. Over a ten-year period that came right before the klaxon's emergence, the technology was widely adopted by physicians, who had to overcome their concerns about sudden fires and costs.[33] As inventors like Nikola Tesla and Thomas Edison worked to solve these problems and publicized their inventions in newspapers and on the lecture circuit, which in Edison's case involved developing brighter fluorescing screens for fluoroscopy, the discourse surrounding X-rays helped the public accept the technology as a necessary part of modern medicine.

The Lovell-McConnell Company intentionally created the analogy with the klaxon horn. The klaxon was to the soundscape and traffic-filled roads what X-rays were to the human body, a technology that allowed the operator to penetrate things normally thought to be impenetrable, to transcend the normal material confines of matter and space. If seeing inside the body was a problem that modern electrical technology had solved with the X-ray, then klaxon technology had solved the problem of cutting through the noise of modernity and warning the listener.

Like the X-ray portrayed on the lecture circuit and in newspapers, Klaxon tied its product to the aesthetics of engineering and invention. The new, sophisticated advertising campaign that pushed the analogic slogan achieved this through graphic choices in the company's illustrative material and through the use of associative language. The ad campaign began in 1909 with the announcement of a special release of a seven- by ten-inch lithograph of a schematic drawing that allowed purchasers to "see" inside the invention. Each new installation of the "X-Ray of Sound" campaign added associative layers with which Klaxon was signaling the arrival of a new Madison Avenue advertising culture, selling the modern consumer a picture of him- or herself signified and reified by every toot of the horn.

The first ads with the "X-Ray of Sound" campaign, which described the klaxon as the "most original, unique and effective automobile signal ever devised," followed the "see-inside" aesthetic design. As was the case in the trade journals where the ads primarily appeared, the ad was graphically centered on the schematic drawings of the chrome-vanadium steel diaphragm, reflecting an ethos of electrical invention and innovation. It described how the sound was created by the vibration of a hard ratcheted wheel against a steel diaphragm run by an electric motor. The sound produced, according to one ad in the *Automobile Blue Book*, the American Automobile Association's annual touring guide, was a "sudden, sharp, metallic howl, audible a mile or more ahead in still air, and effective a quarter to half a mile under driving conditions." It had, according to a variation of the ad that ran in *Motor*, a completely "unique quality . . . utterly unlike any other created sound. . . . We could not hope to convey an idea of it to the man who has not heard it." This was a new technologized sound for a new technologized world. Just as the X-ray had proven itself as an emerging technology that could transform the way medicine was done, so the klaxon would transform automobile culture. Both could save lives.

One exemplary campaign ad told the reader to associate the klaxon sound, "the best protector of both horseman and motorist," with safety. This association was, the ad insisted, officially endorsed by the US government. Unlike other "musical signals," the klaxon was safe precisely because it was the loudest and most caustic horn on the market. It produced an immediate physiological response in the hearer to the sound: "a true warning quality, to which the hearer responds involuntarily and at once."[34] Here the scientific resonance of the X-ray contributed to an analogic understanding of the sound. Just as the X-ray passed through skin and flesh to reveal the skeleton beneath, the klaxon sound had a similar transcendent or penetrating function in the urban soundscape. It cut through the background noise to reach the ear of the pedestrian, carriage driver, or automobilist, bypassing the aesthetic sensibilities, projecting a warning that penetrated to the involuntary response location in the brain, creating a reaction similar to a physiological reflex. Klaxon used pseudo-scientific language to push its sound nostrum, an effect graphically conveyed in its description of the klaxon's "sound wave," which the company's ads claimed had a distinct "saw-tooth" shape. The function of this sound wave, which, like the X-ray machine, the advertising graphic helped the public visualize, was very different from that of a musical sound wave.

Figure 10. Ad from Klaxon's "X-Ray of Sound" campaign. From *The Motor Boat*, May 10, 1909. (Pennsylvania State University Library)

Whereas one could be ignored by not listening, the other cut straight to the central nervous system, demanding to be heard.

The "rough, jagged" sound wave, the ad claimed, gave each individual "vibration an explosive snap." Klaxon was not designed to "please" the ear, as a horn with a musical sound wave might, but rather, since the "function of a warning signal is to warn," the brain "does not pause to translate the pleasing sound into a warning—the first thrill of [the listener's] auditory nerve IS a warning." But more important, "Those violent saw-tooth waves CUT THROUGH AND KILL musical sounds." This pseudo-scientific discourse linked discussions of the electrical signal to thinking about neural networks.

Just as the interior of physical objects could be laid bare by X-rays, Klaxon's ads allowed the reader to *see* the guts of the horn's technology, in this way

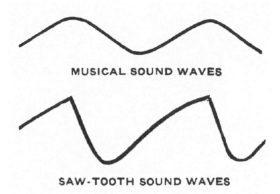

MUSICAL SOUND WAVES

Figure 11. Close-up of Klaxon's "X-Ray of Sound" campaign ad showing a pseudo-scientific representation of different sound waves. From *Motor Age,* May 26, 1910. (HathiTrust)

SAW-TOOTH SOUND WAVES

evoking and activating the technological imagination. This mode of thinking, one that embraced emerging technology because it saved lives, was imperative for the modern world of the automobile—or at least an idea of what automobiling would become as cities quickly filled up with faster and faster cars. In this sped-up culture, time was of the essence, and klaxon technology decreased the reaction time, allowing the driver to maintain speed without sacrificing safety. The "X-Ray of Sound" ads embodied the technocentric logic of modernity: with each sounding of the horn, klaxon technology was solving problems created by automobile technology.

Like the sound itself, which advertised both the product and the corresponding identity of the consumer each time he or she pushed the klaxon button, the ads increasingly popped up everywhere, sounding the commercial note in all kinds of lifestyle publications. A native advertisement in the pages of *Field and Stream* arguing that the automobile made it easier to retreat from urban environments into nature pushed the early adopter mantra and the utilitarian pragmatism it conveyed. "If it is a Klaxon you can let people know you are coming. No slowing up to avoid collisions."[35] The effectiveness of the technology, the copy read, was due to the uniqueness of the sound. "Its voice cuts through fog, drowns other noises or goes through them, and always makes folks hear."[36]

As these types of cross-platform ad campaigns progressed and Klaxon International found its marketing voice, the design of the ads moved beyond schematic drawings. They began to portray everyday situations—where the noise passed through competing sound signals as an X-ray passes through flesh—through graphic dramatization that put potential consumers into a situation and asked them to imagine how the technology would help. Savvy marketing sold the idea of a savvy consumer who knew how to negotiate the modern world by choosing the right technology.

When it came to this new mode of selling product association and consumer identification, imagination was everything. For example, as part of an early blast of the "X-Ray of Sound" campaign, Klaxon ran a full-page colorized ad campaign in several magazines and trade journals in 1910 that, with slight variations, featured a well-to-do couple driving in a car with the man's hand on the klaxon button. Behind them the reader saw a lurching horse with blinders on. Framed analogically, because the horn's sound cut through the background noise of a busy soundscape filled with cars and animal bodies, honking horns, bells and whistles, the klaxon allowed the male driver to protect his wife. The ad stressed that the involuntary or natural response of the listener to the sound was what made it a perfect safety device. In the same way that the blinded horse next to the vehicle would be warned, the startle response would clear the way for the driver and his charge: "The KLAXON is the most effective safeguard against collision ever devised. The penetrating Klaxon blast is audible to another driver a quarter to half a mile ahead, and on water from one to two miles. It resembles no other created sound. It is purposely harsh and startling, for a harsh note has a natural warning quality lacking in musical notes. The driver who hears a KLAXON does not stop to think: he turns to his side of the road involuntarily and promptly." With the mere push of a button, the driver utilizing klaxon technology could clear the road, extending the range of communication between signaler and receiver by extending the range of the senses. The visual representation of the klaxon user is also a striking reminder that most early adopters of automobile technology were members of wealthy social classes.[37] Here the new electrical technology, operated by a push-button on the steering column, allowed the well-dressed individual consumer to negotiate traffic, to safely manage modern public space with his automobile *and* keep his mink-stole-wearing wife safe. The mode of utilization—one hand firmly on the button at all times to signal to those ahead—was a much more efficient way to operate the automobile. With little motion required, the technology and its electrical impulse would tie into the operator's nervous system, linking the haptic sense to the sense of hearing.[38] This version of the ad, from the March 1910 issue of *Motor,* emphasized how pushing the button instantly sent an electrical signal that produced five hundred vibrations per second and threw the sound forward by way of a "scientifically formed projector."[39]

At a time when other auto accessory producers were merely advertising the product and a price by describing the technology and its function, Klaxon's advertisements were constructing roles that the technology consumers could

Figure 12. Ad depicting an early adopter of klaxon technology protecting his mink-stole-wearing wife from a possible collision with the push of a button. From *Life,* April 7, 1910. (Library of Congress)

occupy by presenting a situation they could identify with, one in which they could imagine how safe they might be with or without this modern invention. Moreover, the ads associated a kind of social and ethical comportment as part of a safe society with the utilization of the signaling technology.

Safety thus came to be associated with emerging electrical technology and was absorbed into a mechanized view of perception, wherein the driver operated a machine that extended and augmented the body's senses, both driver and machine responsive to electrical impulses. Those who heard the klaxon sound were ostensibly rendered machinelike as well; it created an autonomic reaction that bypassed thought and moved the hearer as agent out of the way. For instance, the July 10, 1909, ad included copy that described the "violent vibration" created by the mechanism that allowed the user to "wake the dead. . . . It commands attention among dozens of other noises, where a horn or air whistle would be lost."[40] Indeed, many of the early "X-Ray of Sound" ads explained the mechanics of sound production and the science behind it, presenting the klaxon's sound as "mechanical clatter" rather than as a "musical note" and tying the characteristic pitch of the invention to the engineering ethos and the modern way of life it conveyed.

Though Klaxon was not unique in associating its technology with safety, especially in relation to a range of sound and the horn's penetrating power, the company's ability to reiterate and creatively reinforce the message it was sending was unparalleled. The company followed up the message in glossy graphic ads with echoes that ran in smaller media markets. In other words, on the heels of publishing the graphic ads in national automotive journals, Klaxon ran local ads in newspapers across the United States, repeating the association between safety and the physiological, almost precognitive reaction caused by the klaxon's uniquely caustic sound: "It is the loudest of automobile signals. . . . It is the only warning signal whose note truly expresses its purpose. A musical note is no more rational for warning purposes than a song would be as a cry for help. The KLAXON note is harsh, vibrant and metallic— not by chance, but purposely! The driver who hears a Klaxon knows instantly what it means. His brain does not pause to translate an agreeable sound into a warning—the first thrill of his auditory nerve IS a warning."[41] Of course, the assault on the sensorium had long been a rhetorical feature used by anti-noise activists and editorialists. Yet the blending of technology and physiology in Klaxon's ads shifted that frame of perception in the reader, associating the noisy sound not with annoyance but with safety.

Klaxon Expands

When the klaxon entered the French soundscape, the attention-capturing sound was similarly dissonant, and Klaxon set to work reframing it as a useful and transformative technology. As one native advertising story in *Comoedia* queried, "What is the klaxon?" It answered, "The klaxon is better than a siren or a phonograph speaker. It's an original thunderous [*tonitruant*] device."[42]

This book began with a story from *Harper's Weekly* about the arrival of the "the half-terrifying" klaxon in France featuring an apocryphal count who was an early adopter. The klaxon's sound, which reached "the ear of everyone who may possibly be in the way long before the car arrives or is even in sight,"[43] frightened the count and his wife even as it compelled the count to put one on his car. His half-frightened attraction to its sound—"I must have it—Now!" he cried. "Quick! How much is it?"[44]—dramatized the strange attraction of French motorists to the "necessary power" of the uncanny technology. This klaxon attraction was not uniquely French. In cities all across Europe and America, the bossy and brusque klaxon shriek captured the attention of drivers, who spread its sonic brand as quickly as they could get it on their cars. The native advertising and the growing presence of graphic advertising across different media platforms helped the public understand its utility, representing the ear-capturing noise as a desirable signal.

Lovell-McConnell, with its patented mechanism and aggressive marketing campaign, continued to try to shape people's perception of the sound by framing its harshness as a safety feature. The company launched an ad campaign to counter the Gabriel horn's royal and genteel association, boasting that "the President of the United States uses Klaxon on his official white steamer" and likening the use of the klaxon to "insurance against collision" that allowed drivers to sustain speed, a crucial feature of mobility associated with American modernity.[45] Celebrity association had long been used by merchants to pique the desire of consumers. If the genteel royalty of Europe had embraced the musicality of the Gabriel horn, then America, the new country tied to invention and technology at the vanguard of the cultural world, had embraced the automobile and the klaxon. This was a fact that President William Howard Taft himself had described in a letter. Taft had broken with the tradition of riding in carriages, and the White House had even released the photograph that ran in the ad as part of the story. After the klaxon ad appeared, the White House had to address complaints from other automobile makers that Taft was endorsing the White Steamer. After Lovell-McConnell began sending out postcards of the ads as part of an innovative mail campaign, the White House released a statement claiming that "general knowledge" of Taft's automobile preferences was not the same as endorsement. The White House requested that the ad not be run again. "We will, of course, respect your wishes," Lovell wrote, "although it is a matter of sincere regret that we cannot use the letter as it would make a very strong ad."[46]

Yet more and more consumers were identifying with the subjects of Klaxon's ads, both imaginary and presidential, and sales of automobiles continued to climb. One 1910 article estimated that the number of vehicles in America had grown from 6,000 in 1902 to over 130,000 by 1910, at which point Britain's total exceeded 85,000 cars. Germany saw growth from 10,000 cars in 1903 to 50,000. France's numbers grew from 3,000 in 1900 to about 45,000 a

THE PRESIDENT OF THE UNITED STATES
USES THE

KLAXON

ON HIS OFFICIAL WHITE STEAMER

To the motorist who has not used a KLAXON, its harsh, metallic blare often seems unnecessary. But the motorist who has used one knows that no other signalling device ever used on an automobile compares with it as an insurance against collision and an aid to sustained speed.

To the KLAXON user, blind crossings and hidden turns are virtually non-existent: his approach is heralded in ample time for unseen traffic to make way. Heavy vehicles going the same way are signalled long before they are overtaken, and turn out in season to require no slackening. On steep, winding hills a KLAXON may be the sole protection against disaster.

The value of the KLAXON as a safeguard and a time-saver for the conservative motorist was never better attested than in its adoption by President Taft on the White House automobile.

LOVELL-McCONNELL MFG. CO., Manufacturers
NEWARK, NEW JERSEY

THE KLAXON COMPANY, Sole Distributors for U. S. A
1 MADISON AVENUE, NEW YORK,

Figure 13. Klaxon ad leveraging use of its device by President William Howard Taft. From *Life*, January 10, 1910. (Pennsylvania State University Library)

decade later.[47] Lovell-McConnell, which had built a "machine shop, a foundry, a power plant, a storage building and a garage"[48] in Newark, saw all these car owners as potential consumers. The company was poised to manufacture and sell its technology to automobile users wherever it could reach them.

Media theorist Marshall McLuhan helped expand our understanding of media beyond the paper and wires that transmit information to include objects whose embedded messages are strengthened through a feedback loop every time they are used. The automobile was such a medium, one that repeated its message whenever an auto passed by. McLuhan once said of the disruptive "power of the car medium": "The motorcar ended the countryside and substituted a new landscape in which the car was a sort of steeplechaser. At the same time, the motor destroyed the city as a casual environment in which families could be reared. Streets, and even sidewalks, became too intense a scene for the casual interplay of growing up. As the city filled with mobile strangers, even next-door neighbors became strangers. That is the story of the motor car."[49] As the car medium continued to spread its disruptive message, the klaxon would emerge as the dominant communication technology for it, pushing its aaOOgah into soundscapes all over the world. And as automobile technology continued to refashion, in McLuhan's words, "all of the spaces that unite and separate men,"[50] Klaxon Ltd., 1 Madison Ave, would realize the potentials of technology advertising as it worked to mold the perception of users and to convince the public that the disruptive sound produced by the device would make driving safe. The next chapter explores the groundbreaking narrative advertising Klaxon used to spread the sound brand from sea to shining sea.

3
KLAXON AND THE RISE
OF MODERN ADVERTISING

At the close of the twentieth century's first decade, the automobile industry was expanding rapidly. New companies were entering the market constantly, hoping to make it big. In the United States, 485 companies gave automobile manufacturing a try between 1900 and 1908, and some 250 of them remained active at the end of the decade. With hundreds of companies competing for market share, it was difficult for the hopeful entrepreneur to capture the attention of potential buyers. Increasingly the new auto companies turned to the emerging field of mass media advertising to do so. By 1910 the US automobile industry was spending over $1 million per year on advertising. Lovell-McConnell was at the vanguard of this movement.

Raymond Williams, one of the founding voices of cultural studies, famously proposed that modern advertising as a form of communication emerged at the end of the nineteenth century and became dominant by about 1930. Advertisements before this paradigm shift generally let people know what products were and what they cost. But the Industrial Revolution introduced a wider array of consumer products, and merchants needed to appeal to the imagination of consumers beyond mere cost to create demand for their products. So advertisers had to develop rhetorical means, such as catch-phrases, purple prose, and puff, and find ways to apply them in print media using eye-catching technological innovations such as lithography. The most significant development in modern advertising, Williams said, was the appeal to the "personality" of consumers, which worked on and molded their anxieties and fears. Modern advertising emerged as an "organized system of commercial information and persuasion" and became the leading mode of public discourse during the very time that the klaxon came to dominate the urban soundscape.[1]

One of the most significant moments in Williams's brief account of modern advertising is his description of the development of narrative ads that put the reader in the psychological position of having to make a moral decision by presenting a hypothetical situation that the reader is forced to think through. In that moment, he said, the reader buys not only an object but also a "structure of feeling" that brings along with it "social respect, discrimination, health, beauty, success [and] power to control your environment."[2] By making the consumer identify with the narrative, the advertisement molds the consumer's psychology. And this, Williams said, is what makes modern advertising as a system so distinctive and so powerful. "True psychological advertising," he wrote, "is very little in evidence before the First War."[3] If badly drawn and poorly written advertisements belonged to the old paradigm of advertising, "such a poster as 'Daddy, what did YOU do in the Great War,' belongs to the new" because it exploits the anxieties and personal relationships of its viewers to persuade.[4] It asks implicitly, "What kind of person are you?," and provides a means for the consumer to answer this question by making a moral choice.

Klaxon's ad campaigns started putting potential consumers into such moments of moral decision-making years before the start of World War I, waging the kind of psychological warfare that Williams associates with modern advertising and assembling a structure of feeling crucial for the solidification of techno-utopian ideology. The point is not that Williams was wrong in dating this type of situational advertising to World War I but that the situational advertising techniques that the US War Department and the British War Ministry drew on during the war were already being used widely in the advertising world. Klaxon's advertising campaigns were at the vanguard, heralding the emergence and eventual scope of this now dominant form of communication.

Our modes of listening, as part of our communicative repertoire, are a product of our communication culture. We live, think, and perceive within the linguistic frames that cultural discourse provides us with, and in our modern world, advertising plays an outsized role. The klaxon, as a technology and a cultural phenomenon, is proof that advertising shapes how we have come to listen to and negotiate our modern lifeworld. First heard and described as dangerously noisy or physiologically disquieting, the klaxon's shriek came to be heard as a necessary noise, a sound that signified safety. This was possible because advertising taught people how to perceive the sound they heard; it taught them what the signal meant within a structure of feeling increasingly conditioned by the aspirational hopes associated with the automobile. Moreover, through its advertising campaign Klaxon helped promote technology consumption as a response to the challenges of everyday life, a way to deal with the world by purchasing consumer technology, an action that Henri Lefebvre described as an "internal" critique of everyday life.[5] Rather than searching for different and more fulfilling ways to live outside consumer culture, people increasingly dealt with the perceived problems of everyday life by opting in, by choosing among the ready-made solutions that a consumer culture produces.

As Lovell-McConnell expanded its star product's market reach across the United States and from there abroad, the company wanted consumers to opt into automobile culture and to choose their horn because it made driving feel safe. The company used the power of modern mass media messaging and creative—and penetrating—advertising. Its innovative multimedia and multisensory advertising campaign, one that Klaxon scaled to a global audience, gradually shifted how the public interpreted the sound of the klaxon horn. Employing sophisticated situational psychological narratives supported by beautiful full-page graphics, techniques that would soon became standard advertising practice, the company turned the noise that critics decried as an assault on the human sensorium into a "safety signal." More broadly, its advertising campaign marked the arrival of a new era of consumer culture and the ascendance of the techno-utopian consumer ideology underpinning Lovell-McConnell's message.

Madison Avenue and the Logic of Situational Advertising

The difficulty of effecting a shift in apperception, of turning an unwanted noise into a desired sound, is highlighted in the ads that Klaxon provided to local distributors to use in local newspapers. For example, the Gibson Automobile Company, a distributor of the klaxon, ran this ad copy in the *Indianapolis Star* on March 2, 1910: "The Klaxon note is a concentrated extract of noise and its note, well termed 'The X-Ray of Sound,' contains that quality of unusualness which obtains for it immediate attention among dozens of other noises."[6] Making this "unusual" sound, which the company itself wanted consumers to hear as an "extract of noise," seem natural in everyday life required that consumers imagine how this sound would make them feel safe, and then choose the klaxon because they preferred this structure of feeling.

Of course, selling noisy technology as a response to the increased noise of modern life was a discursive feature of advertising for both bulb and exhaust horn devices as well. Yet Klaxon came up with ways to cut through the noise of a cluttered marketplace, differentiating itself from other brands by characterizing its noisy technology as a sign of utility that could be understood in

the context of real-life scenarios. Serious situations demanded serious technologies. Whereas ads for most horn technologies talked about safety in
a general way, Klaxon invited its imagined consumers to see how it would
protect them in a series of ads presenting hypothetical situations. No matter
the situation, klaxon technology would protect drivers and pedestrians.

In *Understanding Media,* Marshall McLuhan posited that the car itself
should also be understood as a media technology that transformed the pattern
of modern life because it invited greater movement through and exploration
of the city and the countryside. As it did, it made both more dangerous for
the "casual interplay of growing up."[7] Klaxon's situational advertising dramatized this transformation of rural and urban spaces whereby the automobile
made any situation potentially deadly. In the face of this transformed landscape, Klaxon offered its innovative technology as a safe solution. A motorist could explore the landscape at dizzying speeds while remaining safe and
keeping others safe as well. Situations fraught with danger could be tran-
scended through proper consumption.

Klaxon's glossy situational advertising, first deployed in the fall of 1909
in multiple national publications, invited the motorist to see the countryside as a space for exploration just as it provided a way for the motorist to
feel safe while exploring. Employing an innovative technique of representing anxiety-provoking situations that weighed on the imagination of the individual, Klaxon introduced the situation presented in the October 1909 *Motor*
with the headline "You Can Trust the Klaxon." Inviting the reader to compare
and contrast, the colorful lithographic ad showed two similar situations on the
road with tragically different results. In the first situation, a car is confidently
driving down the road, while the sound rendered as a growing "KLAXON"
and the graphic "sawtooth" sonic waves project the car's presence as it comes
to a blind corner. In the foreground, two horse-drawn wagons have already
pulled off the road, showing the effectiveness of the "peculiar and penetrating" sound of the klaxon that warns a "quarter mile away." Sounding the
klaxon extends space and time: it increases the space of communication by
extending the range of the senses, and thereby grants the time needed to
avert collision without losing speed. "Owing to the Klaxon's range, its owner
can travel at uniform speed, saving time, brakes, gears and tires. On narrow, winding hill roads, where a quick stop is impossible going up or down,
the Klaxon may be the sole protection against collision." Indeed, in the second situation, which represents the cause-and-effect scenario associated with
"toy horns"—that is, non-Klaxon signaling devices—an automobile without
a klaxon technology is about to collide with a horse-drawn carriage and people

Figure 14. Situation portrayed in "You Can Trust the Klaxon" ad campaign. From *The Motor,* October 1909. (Library of Congress)

are being thrown from both. The message is clear: if you want to be safe, get a real warning signal commensurate with the transformative power of the automobile, not a toy. This way of associating the klaxon's push-button sound technology with safety continued to transmit the idea that the road to safety in the increasingly dangerous world of automobile traffic was paved with the latest technology. Having seen the imaginary situation, the consumer is led to choose the simple technological solution: buying a klaxon horn.

As Klaxon's ads emphasized a mode of repeated loud signaling to other drivers and pedestrians, the company continued its narrative subjectification through an expensive graphic multiplatform media campaign. One ad theme, that of being trapped in fog, began as a series of text-based ads in the nonautomotive journal *Motor Boat* in 1909, targeting yachtsmen, a similar demographic of technology consumer, who were making the jump to motorize their vessels. Once again the klaxon's "peculiar" sound technology solves an anxiety-provoking safety situation in which the line of sight needed to navigate is unavailable. "In a fog the KLAXON is worth more than all the other sound signals put together."[8] Problems that had plagued voyagers for eons could be solved through modern technology and "acoustic science." While "musical signals"—again, non-Klaxon signaling devices—had "smooth" sound waves, the klaxon's harsh note had a "saw-tooth form" to "cut through the Fog." Modern technology, backed by science, kept the user safe. Moreover, by owning a klaxon, the user fulfilled a kind of social contract, albeit one constructed by commercial discourse. Once again, the safety situation communicated through the ad led the consumer to the proper choice.

In 1910 the campaign changed its graphic design and began to lead with images depicting dangerous situations. The campaign reran the fog theme ad in *Motor Boat* several times, as well as in general publications such as *Life* and *Collier's*. Each variation reiterated the discursive association between safety and the klaxon, appealing to the reader's situational imagination. The January ad in *Motor Boat* described the "mirage of sound" created by fog, which disperses ordinary signals, but not the klaxon: "Its harsh 'sawtooth' sound waves *cut through* a fog bank by reason of their greater acoustic energy."[9] They ran variations of this graphic ad, paying for an entire page in prominent national weekly magazines, because its ideas connected with an audience beyond the motor boat aficionado. Though the copy was different, the image—sometimes in color—helped establish a structure of feeling about a dangerous situation that was managed through klaxon technology. Each time, the klaxon's "sawtooth" sound waves, cutting through and managing the space, protected the user from danger in a life-or-death situation.

Klaxon blasted variations on this graphic narrative note—anxiety-provoking safety situations solved by using klaxon sound technology—again and again as the campaign extended throughout the year across different publications. In the 1910 *Life* Easter issue, readers were placed on "steep winding hills"—a dangerous and frightening place for touring drivers owing to the lack of visibility—already shared by a car and a horse carriage, the whole seen from the point of view of an omniscient narrator. The graphically rendered "sawtooth" sound of the klaxon, tied to the kinetic logo, moves as part of the sound wave, visibly projecting from an unseen klaxon owner. The scene concretizes the hypothetical cause-and-effect situation and invites readers to imagine themselves in a dangerous situation. By pressing the but-

A WHISTLE in a fog may be called "the mirage of sound." A fog bank disperses ordinary sound, much as it does light. Smooth musical notes are thrown hither and thither by the moving masses of vapor, and no man can tell where they originate.▮

It is the peculiar merit of the KLAXON that its harsh "saw-tooth" sound waves *cut through* a fog bank by reason of their greater acoustic energy. The note of the KLAXON is like a succession of small explosions, too rapid for the ear to separate. Its direction of travel and the source of the sound are perfectly definite.

In a fog, the owner of a KLAXON is safer than if he had a steam whistle aboard. Even before he has located an approaching steamer, the navigating officer of the latter is apprised of his whereabouts.

THE KLAXON COMPANY
SOLE DISTRIBU-
TORS FOR U. S. A.   1 Madison Ave., New York City

LOVELL-McCONNELL MFG. COMPANY
Manufacturers   NEWARK, NEW JERSEY

KLAXON

Figure 15. Klaxon's sawtooth sound wave cutting through fog on water. From *The Motor Boat,* September 10, 1909. (Library of Congress)

ton, the klaxon user immediately causes the drivers of both the automobile and the horse carriage to pull over, even though they cannot yet see him or her. Because of the signaling technology, which penetrates physical and social space by extending the senses, no speed is lost, and safety and security are gained.

Again, Klaxon challenged the reader to think of this safety situation as an ethical one. "The greater the inherent risk," the copy states, "the more evident is the need for an effective distance signal. . . . In such a situation, the *conservative* motorist is the one who adopts the best-known safeguard: The *reckless* motorist is he who takes a chance with an inefficient horn, and thereby jeopardizes the property of others besides himself." Crucially, the ad invites the reader to think of him or herself in this situation, asking the question, "Which sort of motorist do you aspire to be?"[10] Indeed, just as Klaxon imaginatively

Figure 16. Situation depicted in Klaxon's "X-Ray of Sound" ad campaign suggesting the horn extended the range of the senses to keep the driver safe. From *Life*, March 3, 1910. (Library of Congress)

flipped the perception of its horn from caustic mechanical noise to pleasingly safe sound, the company was creating a narrative according to which, through technology, the user did not need to reduce speed: according to Klaxon's messaging, the driver who chose the correct signaling technology could see the purchase of a klaxon itself as an ethical act that also increased the pleasure of driving. There was no need to slow down and drive more deliberatively; one merely needed to be a better consumer of technology.

Another situation that might require the use of a klaxon while driving in the countryside involved the situation ad-headlined "Overtaking Cars At Speed," a situation that had legal implications along with safety concerns as most state and municipal laws required warning the driver ahead of one's

Overtaking Cars At Speed

It is even harder, using ordinary means of signalling, to get past an overtaken automobile than it is to get past a farm wagon. The driver ahead
simply does not hear a horn above the noise of his own car. Yet he must be
made to hear, for it is not safe to run abreast of him without his knowledge.

The KLAXON has the peculiar merit over all other sound signals that
it is instantly heard *and noticed* by drivers of other automobiles. Its sound
is not only louder, but more distinctive—it does not resemble any other sound
in the world. Because of the peculiar saw-tooth form of the sound waves,
it is also more "penetrating."

From the growing preponderance of automobiles
over horse vehicles on the roads, ability to signal
effectively from auto to auto is of the first importance in choosing a sound device.

All dealers carry the KLAXON.

LOVELL-McCONNELL MFG CO.
Manufacturers
NEWARK, N. J.

THE KLAXON COMPANY
Sole Distributors for U. S. A.
1 Madison Ave., NEW YORK

Figure 17. With Klaxon's sawtooth sound wave and carrying power, "No need to slow down
when you've got a klaxon." From *Motor Age*, January 6, 1910. (Pennsylvania State University
Library)

approach and intent to overtake. Klaxon technology, the ad claimed, *made*
the other driver hear you coming above the noise of his or her automobile
because it was louder than any other horn. And with more cars on the road
every year, adopting this sonic technology made you safe.

Klaxon ran dozens of iterations of this serial campaign over the next fourteen months across the American mediascape, in automobile trade journals like *Automobile Topics* and *Motor*, mass circulation national magazines
like *McClure's* and *Collier's*, and publications specially targeted for their
upscale demographic, such as the *Harvard Lampoon*. Each presented anxiety-
provoking situations that klaxon technology solved. Each sold the idea that
Klaxon's cutting-edge signaling technology allowed conscientious drivers to

warn other drivers far down a winding country road. It increased the user's capacity to communicate by extending the link between sender and receiver beyond the line of sight. These ads routinely placed the consumer in a specific subject position. Sometimes, as in the "Overtaking Cars At Speed" ad, the perspective of the reader was tied to the car with the klaxon, and sometimes the imagination of the prospective consumer was captured by putting the consumer in the position of the other driver, wherein he or she could appreciate the unseen klaxon user announcing his or her presence around a blind corner.

These were "real situations," which Klaxon did its best to convey visually by emulating photographic realism, highlighted by the sawtooth klaxon sound wave extending the senses of the user. An ad that appeared in the January 20, 1910, edition of *Motor Age* not only evoked photographic realism with its lithography but also named the place, a "Culvert near Hewitt, N.J., Greenwood Lake Road," where a driver appeared grateful to be warned of an approaching vehicle coming around a blind turn and about to go through a railroad underpass. In this ad, the reader and potential consumer was asked to think of the other person whom driving put at risk, and to adopt an ethical attitude toward technology—using it to signal your fellow motorist—that would make all motorists safe from the hazards of automobiling. Owning a "real signal," one that let the "other fellow" and the driver know the other was coming a quarter mile away, was aiding both self and society. The ad cast owning a klaxon as the only truly ethical choice.

The same sentiment was repeated in an ad showing the view of the klaxon signaler extending the senses around a corner where a barn blocked the line of sight. Here the sense of hearing imparted safety. Although privileging hearing in relation to traffic safety, the ad augmented the sense of *seeing,* and this type of graphic design not only allowed the Klaxon admen to insert text to describe the safety situation more fully to the reader, it also allowed the reuse of graphics as needed. The April 14, 1910, ad on the same page in *Motor Age* that Klaxon bought every month reused the same graphic content as the barn-blocking-the-view ad but shifted the resonance to make the reader imagine the unsafe situation of *not* having a klaxon horn, making the late adopter of klaxon technology analogous to the increasingly vulnerable horse-drawn vehicle. Those who could think in advance, the "prudent" and "long-headed motorist," would never be caught in such a situation.

Since klaxon users were not only using their cars on country roads, the company also created variations of hazardous safety situations in urban situations. It ran the first in the *Saturday Evening Post,* a glossy weekly American

Figure 18. Ad from Klaxon's "X-Ray of Sound" campaign using photographic realism to convey real situations in real places. From *Motor Age*, January 20, 1910. (Pennsylvania State University Library)

magazine with a circulation of over one million that understood and exploited the power of graphic illustration to capture the reader's imagination through wonderful serial lithography.[11] Klaxon ran an ad that was on par with the imaginative appeal of the Norman Rockwell images that frequently graced the magazine's cover. This ad, which first ran in the August 13, 1910, issue and was located on expensive space inside the front cover, where full-page ads got the most notice, moved away from the rural situations that had dominated the campaign to this point. Here, instead, it represented a decidedly more literal and urban situation with metaphorical appeal to the imagination of those who negotiated urban space shared by drivers and pedestrians. Of course, one of the greatest social problems of automobile technology as a feature of everyday

Figure 19. Ad from Klaxon's "X-Ray of Sound" campaign emphasizing the signaling power and therefore utility of the device. From *Motor Age*, May 12, 1910. (Pennsylvania State University Library)

urban life was the dramatic increase in pedestrian accidents linked to it. In fact, New York City—represented in the ad's image—started keeping statistics on accidents in 1910, and of the 471 traffic fatalities that year, 95 percent were pedestrians struck in the street.[12] This was the anxiety that the ad tapped into. Here the very same idealized children that Norman Rockwell often featured at play on the magazine's cover were placed at risk by the automobile, yet kept safe by the klaxon. The safety discourse being associated with the sawtooth sound wave of the klaxon was thus doubly potent. In this ad, which also ran simultaneously in *Collier's* (circulation 500,000), Klaxon appealed to the worried urban mother and the urban driver, promising that children playing in the streets would be safer with the klaxon because the attention of children, who were absorbed in their Rockwellian state of constant play, could

NO MOTHER NEED WORRY–
If the Auto horn is a KLAXON

Children hear its sharp blast, no matter how absorbed they are in their tag or "One Old Cat." It is audible for blocks, even above the roar of elevated trains and the noise of traffic, and its note has a peculiar warning quality which compels attention. The romping boy and girl, the absent-minded man crossing the street with his nose in a newspaper—all are warned in ample time for safety.

If a child is struck by an automobile, it is because he did not hear the horn, or because he heard it too late. The horn is blown, but he darts from the sidewalk unheeding—and the tragedy occurs before brakes can be set.

A soft-toned horn attracts no attention, even from adults. Against children it is useless, as every motorist knows. Yet it is the motorist's duty to protect the children, because they have not learned to protect themselves.

The peculiar rasping tone of the KLAXON is intentional. It warns where no other horn is heeded. It safeguards children and pedestrians, and it lifts a weight from the motorist's mind and nerves. It is a long-range signal for warning unseen horsemen at bends and blind corners; but it is equally useful for emergencies anywhere.

Your children are SAFE if the automobile uses a KLAXON :

LOVELL·McCONNELL MFG. CO.   THE KLAXON COMPANY

KLAXON
"The X Ray of Sound"

Figure 20. Urban children protected by klaxon technology in the "No Mother Need Worry" ad, part of Klaxon's "X-Ray of Sound" campaign. From the *Saturday Evening Post*, August 13, 1910. (*Saturday Evening Post* Archive)

be captured by its "sharp blast," audible for blocks, even above the roar of elevated trains and the din of traffic.[13] Klaxon's unique signaling technology was so loud that it compelled attention, almost as if eliciting a physiological reflex.

The blame for traffic accidents, the ad implied subliminally, lay with people who used non-klaxon horns that could not be heard above the din. The klaxon's "peculiar rasping tone" made it impossible even for children absorbed in play to ignore because it cut through the other noise of the city. Traffic law had established that it was the motorist's "duty" (a point discussed in the next chapter) to warn pedestrians adequately, and Klaxon extended the situation to moral law. By using a horn that warned unseen pedestrians, horsemen, and children, Klaxon's "safeguard" technology could "lift a weight from the motorist's mind." With automobile accidents and fatalities a constant feature of urban life, the ad reiterated the ideology that more effective communication technology was the best response to the modern human condition increasingly determined by technology.

Moreover, the ad relieved the motorist from having to forgo the prime benefit of automobile technology, namely, speed, in managing the vicissitudes and contingencies of sociality and urban life. Children might be playing or a man might be absent-mindedly crossing the street in a densely populated urban area, but the klaxon owner could barrel down the road sounding the horn, warning those not paying attention that he or she was coming. The purchase of the product relieved the consumer of the legal and ethical burden of using an automobile carefully, and the ad subtly showed society thanking the klaxon user for it. It relieved the mother who might worry about her children playing in urban streets that were increasingly dangerous because of the growing number of vehicles. The structure of feeling these ads created, by placing the reader in a situation he or she could identify with, alleviated anxiety by nurturing faith in the right product. No matter the situation in each ad, the answer was always to trust the best and latest consumer technology, the very structure of feeling underpinning the emerging techno-utopian consumer ideology.

The consumer (and, more important, the potential future consumer) who imagined herself in this situation is kept safe by showing faith in emerging technology, a circuit of belief completed through the purchase. The ad promoted good technology as the glue of society. Ethical concern for fellow urbanites is conveyed through proper technology consumption, and this social contract becomes reciprocal with the gratitude of the other, imagined as the reward. The implied sociality expressed through the choice of the right product was a constant feature of the Klaxon Company's sophisticated anxiety-evoking narrative ads. Another of the X-ray situational series, titled "The Other Man Thanks," foregrounded the association between purchasing klaxon technology and meeting one's social and ethical obligations.

Like the imagined mother of the *Saturday Evening Post* ad, who thanks the driver shown in the advertisement for choosing a technology that keeps children safe, the "other man"—in this case an old horse-drawn grocery delivery wagon driver who has stopped his cart after hearing the klaxon's warning coming from the other side of a one-lane railway underpass—thanks the driver for keeping him safe. Not only does the klaxon's note help avert "an accident in close quarters," but using it also "promotes natural good feeling."[14] Again, proper consumption of technology helps mend the social con-

Figure 21. "The Other Man Thanks": ad honoring the social contract through use of better technology. From *The Motor*, December 1909. (Library of Congress)

tract. Throughout these ads, Klaxon's advertising team was designing scenarios that pulled the reader into a mode of consumption psychologically linked to a desired identity and tied to a structure of feeling. One's choice about signaling technology communicated not only one's presence as a driver in space to other drivers but also a klaxon user's social commitments and sense of responsibility. In short, Klaxon was signaling the arrival of a new psychological mode of advertising that produced the structure of feeling tied to consumption that so intrigued Raymond Williams.

Of course, Klaxon was not alone in a mediascape where automobile and automobile accessory companies competed for consumer attention and market share, but it was in the vanguard. The rest of Madison Avenue was watching and learning about this new mode of consumer persuasion. Just as other horns got louder and louder to compete over urban traffic, Klaxon's competitors began to shift their mode of advertisement to get noticed amid the increasing noise of print advertising. They too began associating the sounds of their products with safety, selling a structure of feeling grounded in the industry-wide belief that ever-improving technology would continue to make the automobile safer to drive.

Sound Technology and Ad Wars

The growth of the automobile industry led to a dramatic growth in automobile advertising. By 1910 the industry was reaping upward of $300 million from consumers per year. That same year, US banks tied to the industry started financing automobile purchases, which meant that the lifestyle could be purchased on the installment plan.[15] Advertising was the key to igniting the desire for products in this growing base of consumers.[16] As the practice of selling the automotive lifestyle spread throughout the mediascape, so too did advertisements for sonic signaling products. Once push-button electrical signaling technology came to dominate the horn market, the klaxon's main competitors were technologies that harnessed exhaust gas (horns and whistles) and those driven by electricity. The manufacturers of these devices all were using advertising to make their sound technology appealing to the potential driver.

Though the number of exhaust-driven signals had dropped off as electric horns got more popular, the producers of those that remained were using advertising to get the attention of consumers. The Nightingale whistle, an older product that remained a presence in the trade journals, distinguished itself by its musical sound, described in advertising copy as a "chromatic scale of bird-like notes" that could be adjusted to be "a low, melodious, attractive town signal, or to make a noise that penetrates a mile or more." By 1911 the Nightingale's producers had introduced a puff slogan in their advertising, boasting that their product was "the Signal that can be heard in Heaven" as a way to differentiate its musical connotation from the more devilishly aggressive signaling devices.

The Randall-Faichney Company of Boston, Massachusetts, manufacturer of the Jericho horn, with its noisy biblical association, did not change its organ-pipe-meets-steam-whistle design but did start shifting the focus of its ads and increasing its advertising presence in response to Klaxon's graphic campaign. Whereas the earlier ads had merely featured descriptions of the product, by 1911 Randall-Faichney had begun associating the noise of its product with safety discourse *and* pleasant musicality. It was the "perfect motor signal," the company's situational ad copy boasted, because it (as well as the company's "chime-tone" product the Jubilee) allowed the user to get the "greatest pleasure out of motoring, free from anxiety as to the safety of the occupants of your car—and of the public." The Jericho afforded this experience because of the technology—a loud sound device operated by a hands-free pedal on the floor—and because the musical tone "warned without offence."

The anxiety created here was that of being a sonic nuisance by bothering the neighbors with your poor choice of noisy technology.[17]

As Klaxon increased its advertising budget and made its presence more pervasive in the mediascape, Jericho's ads worked to differentiate its technology. Jericho's producers framed their choice in signaling technology as an index of an automobile consumer's sense of ethical obligation, a sign of the consumer's commitment to respecting the right of his or her neighbors to not be bothered. While Klaxon framed its noise as a desirable safety feature, Jericho rejected noise and appealed to the consumer's sense of social comportment. Whereas the sound of the klaxon was so noxious that people pulled over immediately—or at least Klaxon's ads so claimed—by 1911 Jericho's ads were featuring the tagline "The Signal of a Gentleman—Warns without Offence." Unlike the klaxon, which sacrificed or perhaps exchanged auditory pleasure for safety, the "Jericho saves Trouble" and "saves controversy" by being pleasant. Different iterations of the advertising copy for the Jericho horn proposed that its technology fulfilled its utilitarian function by being loud. Indeed, one Jericho ad campaign used the tagline "It's a Road-Clearer" but promised it did such road clearing without the rudeness of the klaxon by communicating more "melodiously." As such, the Jericho's sound was presented as a warning signal that was safe yet "not a nuisance" and did not "cause offence."

Although Randall-Faichney's message and brand association differed, by 1912 it had begun to catch up, and adopted for the Jericho horn the situational narrative advertising strategy that Klaxon had pioneered. One exemplary Jericho ad that ran in *Motor* depicted two men, one of whom had just been in an accident, chatting next to the wrecked car. "Well, what more should I have done?" the first asks. "I was going carefully. I sounded my signal time and again." The other responds, "You didn't have the right kind of signal. . . . If you'd had a Jericho Horn on your car, the teamster would have heard you above the din of the street and the noise of his own wagon, and would have pulled over for you to pass. . . . Because it is so different."[18] Just as with the Klaxon ads, the anxiety-inducing situation could be solved by purchasing the proper technology.

Another exhaust horn, the Gabriel horn, was a big klaxon competitor in the ad wars. Gabriel too sought to position its technology in the market by framing its horn's sound as more "agreeable." It too gradually moved from reason-why ads and adopted situational advertising strategies that stressed that different devices had different sounds, and that the technology one chose as a consumer said something about the kind of person one was. Whereas

MAKE EVERYBODY HAPPY

You are likely planning an Auto Tour for this summer. You get more fun out of a week's touring than a year's riding around town. Out in the country where nature is at its best — viewing new scenes — meeting new people — stopping at quaint old inns. Before starting, insure your safety by equipping your car with a

TRUMPET HORN

the horn which multiplies your pleasure a hundred fold, which revives the memories of good old coaching days with its bugle and trumpet calls. It's sweet, far reaching notes warn without frightening horse or pedestrian. No danger of trespassing the laws of any state by using a Gabriel. The Gabriel Trumpet Horn has become very popular with Auto Clubs and cliques who have their own private code of signals for saluting each other on the road.

WRITE FOR BOOK

GABRIEL HORN MFG. CO.
Office and Factory: 1414 E. 40th St., Cleveland   New York Branch: 1926 Broadway

Figure 22. Gabriel's musical Trumpet Horn, which "offends no one." From *The Motor*, June 1910. (Archive.org)

Klaxon went for a signal so loud it produced an involuntary reaction, Gabriel tacked toward musicality, appealing to the kind of person who wanted to be associated with pleasantness. As the copy in a June 1910 ad in *Motor* phrased it, using a Gabriel kept you safe and would "make everyone happy." According to one of its later British ads calling out klaxon technology (British magazines eventually caught up with American advertising techniques), its sound should be heard as "a polite request for a clear road. Instead of a spasmodic noise, which alarms only by reason of its irritating jar, the Gabriel produces a soft, resonant chord."[19] Musicality implied an expressive act of communication by way of the aesthetic sense. This branding of musical signaling technology as "not noise" became increasingly important as states and localities contemplated legal restrictions on signaling tones in response to noise complaints.

Gabriel continued to position itself and its technology as musical to differentiate its brand. Its horn had all the safety affordances without causing a nuisance, a point the company emphasized repeatedly in its advertising. If one wanted more than the one-, two-, or three-tone varieties of "the Agreeable Signal," the deluxe edition Gabriel "trumpet horn" consisted of four single tubes that either could be operated individually from a keyboard or could sound together. If consumers really wanted to personalize their courteous signal, they could purchase a special ten-tube "musical horn" in the key of G operated by way of a keyboard resembling a typewriter situated on the passenger-side dash.[20] Yet the exhaust horn, though more musical, was more complicated to use than the push-button electric horn. It broke down more as a result of tailpipe corrosion and rust in the wire mechanism, which made the device less reliable and immediate. Klaxon exploited these functionality problems in its ads.

More and more, to capture the imagination of potential consumers and compete in the growing automotive signaling market, signaling technology had to be electrical. Although Klaxon used patent law, exclusive licensing agreements, and other competition-squelching business practices to corner the market (see chapter 4), a number of loud electric buzz horns and sirens managed to compete in the market for signaling devices. The full-page color ads for Monoplex, a buzzer horn, though they lacked situational images, did appeal to the consumer's psychology by claiming that "the mental strain on the man at the wheel is lessened by his knowledge that he controls—without moving either hand or foot—a signal whose warning note is instantly responsive to the slightest movement of one finger."[21] Producers of the Typhoon electric horn, also emphasizing its instantaneous push-button design, ran a colorful half-page ad in *Motor Age* giving the reader a picture of a "lumbering truck a quarter mile up the narrow road that requires time to get out of the way, and the heedless school boy at the crossing who has to jump, all know of your approach if your horn is a Typhoon." Though the ads lacked imaginative appeal, Typhoon's producers joined the chorus of competitors who used the space they purchased to frame the sound of the klaxon as rude, stating that although their horn's sound was "instantaneous and penetrating," it nonetheless was the most "dignified warning obtainable—it never insults."[22]

Klaxon responded to the negative framing of these competing ads from the dozens of electric horn manufacturers by making sure its media presence was bold and constant, running ads for the smaller Klaxonet, which, as an early example of fandom and social networking in advertising campaigns, had been named by users as part of a contest, with a cash prize for the winner. The ads were editorial and pedagogical in their design. They showed schematic diagrams of each kind of horn to educate users about the differences in technology, drawing a distinction "between an 'Electric Horn' and a Klaxon," emphasizing that "the Klaxon is not an 'electric horn.'" The electric horn, the ads explained, used a diaphragm vibrated by means of a "buzzer"— the same technology used for doorbells or for communicating with servants or office workers—which required a battery-draining spark between two platinum points that would quickly wear off. "The Klaxon," on the other hand, "is a noise machine." Its steel diaphragm and "glass hard toothed wheel" driven by a motor meant that it would not wear out. "The Klaxon note is loud. It is sharp and clean-cut—totally unlike the nasal buzz of the 'electric horn.' One Klaxon 'tiger' (a short abrupt note made by lightly touching the klaxon push button) is more effective than a dozen 'buzzes;' yet it makes less actual noise. Klaxon noise is concentrated—not drawn out."[23] Whereas its competitors sought to blur the distinction between the technologies while echoing the structure of feeling, Klaxon drew sharp contrasts.

While some competitors differentiated their horns by characterizing them as comparatively pleasant, others tried to outdo the klaxon, boasting that the sheer volume and tone of their products could extend the range of the senses even farther. Sirens were the biggest early competitor in this domain. Where Klaxon's copy claimed the range of the horn's unique sound wave extended to a quarter of a mile, the SirenO Company copy from 1909 described its device as the "only faultless electric horn," and loudly proclaimed that its horn "clears the road for a mile ahead." The company ran pictures of the Indianapolis Speedway, where SirenO was the official horn. Its "Mile Ahead Electric Signal" graphic campaign of 1910 boasted that the SirenO's uniquely loud signal protected the consumer without taking away from the "pleasure" of speed. "The motoring public are fast coming to realize . . . that a harsh, nerve-racking, ear-splitting signal is unnecessary." The SirenO, by contrast, "insures the comfort and safety of all, and spares from unnecessary wear and tear, on one's nerves."

In response to Klaxon's sneaky brand association with President Taft (see chapter 2), SirenO ran an editorial ad that, like the ads for the Gabriel horn and the Jericho horn, linked its product to European aristocracy. Titled "Noblesse Oblige," the ad featured a photograph of Prince and Princess de Sagan of France in their Panhard coupé. SirenO claimed that its sound signal could be heard from afar, yet the horn's appeal to the idea of aristocracy was different from that of the exhaust horns, which boasted a more melodious gentility. Drivers let the world know they were coming by being necessarily "shrill" without being "low and harsh."[24] It was the sense of social obligation associated with European nobility rather than the musicality associated with exhaust horns that made the SirenO the choice of aristocrats.

Over time, Klaxon's biggest rivals were the horns that used slightly modified, cheaper copies of its motor-driven lob-wheel technology, the Newtone and the Long Horn. Like Klaxon, Newtone began running full-page ads in *Motor*, the *Cycle and Automobile Trade Journal*, *Motor Car*, the *Automobile Trade Directory*, *Motor World*, the *America Motorist*, and other media outlets where automobile industry ad wars were waged. Like Klaxon, Newtone transitioned from ads that displayed and described the technology and price to ads that turned to editorial and narrative forms of communication. In 1910, Newtone ran ads that exemplified the "reason-why" ads, ads featuring an image and copy explaining why the consumer should buy, which were common in the industry.[25] Headlined "The Mile-Away Electric Motor Warning Signal," the ads touted its "deep, penetrating, clear, powerful, yet pleasing sound." The horn was differentiated from electric horns in that it "consumes only one third of the current, yet it gives a louder and more agreeable note."[26] Most important, Newtone took on Klaxon directly, undercutting Klaxon's price and denying that it infringed on any patents: "The 'Newtone' is now recognized as the most powerful and pleasing Motor Warning Signal of the class, and, as it sells for one half of the price charged for similar horns, it has met the favor of the trade." Very quickly, the ads for the "Mile-Away Motor Horn" got more sophisticated. One full-page inside cover ad from *Motor Car* claimed that with "a touch of the button, the warning note is spontaneous, powerful, clear, abrupt—a perfect danger signal."

Whereas Klaxon continued to emphasize that its horn's harshness was the sound of safety, Newtone borrowed copy ideas from its exhaust horn competitors and trumpeted its "powerful, melodious note, that never fails to warn, yet still retains an air of courtesy; that harsh, rasping sound so obnoxious to the refined motorist is entirely eliminated." The company continued to hit this note, differentiating the horn's "penetrating and melodious" tone from the "rasping sound" of the Klaxon in an ad for its "Torpedo type" model, priced at $20 to Klaxon's $35.[27]

As the noisy ad war continued to promote emerging technology as the means for negotiating social space in the automobile, cultural critics increasingly sounded off about what the klaxon's growing presence in the soundscape implied about modern Western culture. In *Harper's Weekly*, Steven D. Thatton opined that the new, stronger warning signals spoke to the tenor of the automobile-centric times. Whereas the first bulb reed horn signals communicated "'Please look out!' in mellow, musical tones. The latest roar discordantly or bray hoarsely. Their warning is far-flung, convincing and says plainer than shouted words: 'Car coming! Out of the way!'" Yet, showing just how effective Klaxon's marketing language had become at shifting the cultural conversation, Thatton suggested this overbearing technology was necessary. "Without devices of the present sort, automobiling would not have progressed nearly so rapidly. For the car in rapid motion needs its warning sounds far ahead of it." Because of the emerging signaling technology, "automobiling has now attained a measure of safety that could have been reached in no other way."[28]

Volume was not the only safety affordance that signaling technology contributed to automobile culture, according to Thatton. "Much scientific study and investigation has been put into making just the proper sort of warning sounds. The first problem was to invent a noise that should be sudden and decisive and should mean to everyone 'Automobile!'" The push-button ease of electric horns also allowed a "man or woman driving a car at high speed" to emit a sound "very nearly automatically." The "necessary power of the half-terrifying" klaxon, he said, also reached "the ear of everyone who may possibly be in the way long before the car arrives or is even in sight."[29] Again, in an echo of Lovell-McConnell's marketing copy, the social situation created by the speed of automobiles made the klaxon's immediate "terrifying" sound a safety necessity.

Around the globe, antinoise societies were singling out the klaxon as a sound icon, a symbol in their fight against the noise. After completing a speaking tour of European cities during which she counted the number of horns she heard in each, noise suppression activist Julia Barnett Rice told the press that "she would not rest until the Legislature restricts the size of the horn" so that horns could be heard only in close proximity "instead of five miles, as now, vide the latest manufacturer's advertisements."[30] Klaxon was well aware that critics used language from its marketing copy against it, to describe and rail against the sonic rudeness of its noisy technology. Through its contacts at trade journals, the company pushed back against detractors and tried to reinforce the association of its loud sound with safety. In a section of *Motor Age* titled "Manufacturers' Communications," the company characterized the steady drone of complaints from antinoise societies as unsafe; in their urge to suppress "unnecessary noise," antinoise crusaders too hastily condemned "anti-danger devices" without understanding their utility. Any signaling device, the pro-klaxon voices argued, could be "misused." To be sure, some drivers "seem to take keen delight" in abusing their warning signals, which created the "wrong impressions" about the technology. "The wrathful public, in order to end the nuisance of the erring chauffeurs, now and then, urges the abolition of everything except the soft noted and inconsequential warning signal."[31] Yet continued investigation, Klaxon argued, proved that "the warning signal necessary to prevent loss of life and limb and to avert collision is one whose harsh and menacing note can be used in small as well as large volume." Previewing later debates about technologies, it was not the technology itself that was the problem but the users who abused a technology that was an absolute necessity in the modern age.

Klaxon had shown the power of advertising to capture the attention of a rapidly expanding market and to position its noisy horn as uniquely suited to respond to the safety problems of the automobile age. Its innovative situational advertising strategy cut through the noise of the market and helped separate its technology from that of other signals. In turn, Klaxon's competitors began expanding their media presence both to appeal to consumers and to attack klaxon technology for being overbearing, noisy, and rude. Klaxon responded by leaning in to the criticism, turning the negative criticism into a positive by associating its horn's necessary noise not only with safety but also with social responsibility.

The Public Safety Signal

To maintain its advantage over a growing tribe of competitors, often marketing cheaper horns, Klaxon pivoted from its "X-Ray of Sound" campaign, which emphasized its innovative technology, to one centered on a structure of feeling linked to consumers choosing technology that conveyed a sense of social responsibility. For the 1911 market year, it launched a massive serial campaign under a new slogan, "The Public Safety Signal," that, in addition to associating the company's product with safety and security, presented its unique sound technology as a public good. Every time a consumer sounded a klaxon, which acted as both medium and message, Lovell-McConnell wanted the public to associate the sound with the ideas of the campaign and hear it as the favorite horn according to public opinion.

The slogan worked like an editorial headline linking together the expensive serialized full-page ads, each of which repeated normative ideas about public safety tied to early adoption of the company's technology and emphasized the individual consumer's responsibility as an automobile user to purchase a communication device that would protect others. In many ways, this ad campaign was as much about selling the technology to the consumer as it was about shaping the public debate over automobile safety. In an era in which legislatures all over the world were deliberating how to regulate automobile usage—with the number of cars on the road growing every year—through legislation and ordinances, Klaxon pushed to have its product received as the answer to the safety problem and to be perceived as the consensus industry standard.

The campaign sought to create the appearance of consensus in public opinion about klaxon technology in several ways. Taking a page from the celebrity endorsement model that the company had used with photographs of President Taft, the campaign gathered endorsements from real or symbolic characters from across society, from the famous to the iconic everyman, all of whom testified to the multifaceted importance of the Klaxon horn's unique sound. Typical of this strategy, one prominent narrative ad in *McClure's* included a testimonial from an imagined "traffic officer," an iconic figure associated with safety, law, and order. The Klaxon "saved lives every day,' opined the policeman with his hand on "his best friend," the horn. Appealing not only to the driver's sense of safety but also to his or her desire to avoid costly accidents—and to have cheaper insurance rates—the copy also claimed that "insurance adjusters," all of them, "pronounced Klaxon the only warning signal that positively protects."[32] The paradigmatic traffic officer spoke to the social issue of increased automobile use, the aggregate number of accidents every year, and growing safety concerns. From his unique perspective, the klaxon emerged once again as the best solution to the problems of an automobile-centered world. Indeed, a similar ad that ran in *Collier's* and *Cosmopolitan* included a testimonial from an "insurance adjuster" who, like the traffic officer, read accident reports every day, which gave him perspective.[33] The message was clear: whatever claims the Klaxon Company's competitors might make, those who knew the scope of problems caused by the automobile knew that the klaxon was a superior technology.

As Klaxon moved to construct an imaginary public safety consensus, the advertising community quickly took notice of this revolutionary strategy. In *Printers' Ink*, the established trade journal for the advertising profession, where admen talked shop, William Allen Johnston reported on Klaxon's innovative and successful communication technique, which was effectively helping to tie its brand to the "aaOOgah" sound and linking both to the idea of public safety. "There are some advertising lessons to be found in the advertising campaign on the Klaxon, the automobile warning signal." Though the company was in the "enviable position" of dramatically expanding production and increasing factory space, Johnston noted that Klaxon had decided to expend "an advertising appropriation larger by far in amount, and much more comprehensive in scope, than any in their history."[34] But the massive scope of the full-page advertising campaign, echoing throughout national weeklies and monthlies, was only part of Klaxon's innovation:

> Still more seemingly unconventional is the intent of the advertising in itself. . . . It is directed wholly at the public at large, at the pedestrian, the

Figure 23. Ad from Klaxon's "Public Safety Signal" campaign, which associated trusted public safety figures with the sound of the horn. From *McClure's*, October 1910. (Pennsylvania State University Library)

999 who do not own automobiles, the 999 who perhaps never will. It is the purest kind of "editorial" publicity. Advertising space, purchased at highest rates, is used to put before the reading, thinking public that which many people think. . . . It shows other manufacturers and many corporations having a public issue to tackle and a public sentiment to create, just what can be done with "editorial" display advertising rather than depending wholly on a campaign of "press stuff" to editors.

Just as there exists to-day a feeling against the automobile upon the part of a portion of the pedestrian public, so there has also been expressed an antagonism against the powerful warning signal and its distracting noises.

It is probable that sooner or later the governing bodies of the cities and country in general will demand that autos carry a fully adequate signal, just as they now demand adequate lights. The Klaxon is offered as the kind of signal that will fill the bill. . . . The advertising states [that] the manufacturers themselves do not find it agreeable, but such a signal is essentially a safety signal and public safety demands its use.[35]

Anyone who did not use this "necessary noise," the article noted, was lacerated by the campaign as an "irresponsible motorist" or "disorderly person." Johnston believed that the industry could learn from this model, not only in relation to the ideas that Klaxon was associating with its product but from its commitment to selling technology through massive advertising budgets to help the company cut through the noise.

Johnston lauded Klaxon for continuing to spend $3,000 a page to deluge print media with editorial interpretation of public discourse about the soundscape. This was the way, he believed, to make the purchase of the company's product a case of "human interest." "Offhand one would say that there could be little human interest appeal in an automobile accessory. As a matter of a fact there is human interest in everything that humans touch, and that human brains conceive and that human minds want. All that is necessary is to dig it out and then humanly portray it."[36] Klaxon did so, and the company did it well. Its ads, Johnston noted, used typography, illustrative art, and the most accurate portrayal of "life's realism," photography, to link the sound of the signal to the pedestrian and the concerns of everyday life.

Each ad throughout this campaign, even those that did not have images, told a story "sharply, concisely and with a catchline of direct human appeal. It is my opinion," wrote Johnston, "both from the standpoint of magazine writing and practical advertising experience that few, if any, pages in the entire magazine were more generally read than this Klaxon page."[37] The lesson to be drawn in relation to this carefully and expensively conceived modern advertising was crucial: "If you advertise at all it pays to do it in the best, even if the most expensive, way. Largest obtainable space, best mediums, preferred position—these first of all, and then on top of this appropriation all the extra expense, however great, to make this costly space count for all its possible worth."[38] Without overtly selling the product at a price, this editorial publicity strategy, the way in which the Klaxon campaign shaped public opinion about its signaling technology as a necessity of modern life, paid off in the long run. As Johnston concluded, "It is absolutely certain that this one advertising page will secure as much attention as the most interesting page in the regular reading matter."[39]

Indeed, Klaxon's expensive weekly page ads, each of which had different copy that spoke to a question of human interest and the safety of the public, dominated the American mediascape. Klaxon outspent its competitors, realizing that the key to selling technology was communicating the idea that consuming technology was a necessary feature of, and an appropriate response to the challenges of, modern everyday life.

No matter what method they used in the "Public Safety Signal" campaign, Klaxon made sure to reiterate and reify the structure of feeling highlighted in its campaigns. An ad in *Motor World,* for example, used celebrity endorsement to build the idea of public consensus. It featured the inventor and automobile maker, Hudson Maxim, whose persona was aided by a colorful portrait next to his words, praising the Klaxon: "I have carefully considered the comparative value of the automobile warning signals, and I think the sharp warning sound made by the Klaxon incomparably better than the musical, groaning, wailing, or siren sounds made by others." In nature, Maxim declared: "Warning sounds are harsh and untuneful, they are not pleasant to the ear. The warning growl of the dog, the cry of the fowl that voices danger, the warning snarl of a pair of tigers fighting over a piece of meat, are not pleasant, nor musical, nor wooing sounds. . . . All animals are repelled by repellent sound and attracted by attractive sounds. . . . There is nothing like the Klaxon with its harsh, untuneful warning."[40] Having an engineer hero tied to the automobile revolution endorse klaxon technology as a necessary solution to automobile safety problems helped the consumer hear the sound—and the competing musical signaling sounds—the way Klaxon wanted them to hear it. Another similar ad from February 1911, quoting an editorialist from the influential general publication *Harper's Weekly,* hit the same utilitarian notes: "The sound of the signal-horn must be *short, harsh, sharp.* Its tune must not be musical, because musical tones lull and soothe."[41] Only the Klaxon fit this bill. A week later, on the same page in the magazine, with the regularity of an editorial columnist, a brightly colored ad proclaimed that the "best cars are equipped with Klaxon warning signals" and that the "owners of these cars represent the most conservative and best citizens of the community."[42]

The March 16 installment, again on the same page, went one step further and listed "some users of the 45,000 users of the Klaxon," including William H. Taft, Thomas Edison, and George Westinghouse. The ad characterized Klaxon horn users as "men whose lives mean most to themselves and to others. Men who are most anxious not to injure others, or others' property. Men who by standing, conservatism, responsibility, represent the best citizenship—these men—the country over—carry Klaxons on their automobiles."[43] The normative claims here are an important feature of this consensus-building endorsement as a form of advertising because they demonstrate the extent to which these ads were creating subject positions along a binary axis. Klaxon users were linked to ideas (often the headlines of the weekly editorial ads) such as "protection" or "quality" or "conservatism" or "reputation" or "service" that had important ethical and social implications. Klaxon was creating a social identity for its brand clustered around notions of safety and concern for the public good.

One ad dramatized this emphasis particularly well by linking it to a real-life urban situation. If the "No Mother Need Worry" ad described above was the shot, this was the chaser. Titled "A Vital Need," it referenced an actual event, displaying a photographic copy of a news clipping from the *New York Sun* about a young boy, Julien Metz, who had been tragically killed because of outdated technology. Because he could not hear the car with an "inadequate bulb horn" coming above the noise of an elevated train passing overhead, he had dashed out in front of the automobile and was killed. On the other side of the page, the ad laid out the problem before offering the technological solution: "There are some people who do not realize this . . . who maintain that for city use the bulb horn is entirely ample. . . . The Klaxon would have prevented this accident. It would have been heard above the noise of this train: it would have been heard and *heeded!* It is in just such an emergency that the need of the Klaxon is *vital.* Its note is instantaneous; its command irresistible."[44] The message was clear: proper technology saved lives and promoted public safety, and only the klaxon was more than adequate as a consumer-ready safeguard for an automobile-centered world.

As a result of the success of the advertising campaign to build public consensus about the sound of the klaxon, a number of car companies wanted their brand to be associated with the structure of feeling that Klaxon was building and made reciprocal agreements with the horn company beginning in 1912. Klaxon would repay them for their endorsement by cross-promoting their products in the ongoing serial editorial campaign. In an era that witnessed the rapid multiplication of automobile companies producing cars, Klaxon used advertising power to portray itself as a common denominator, an industry-wide standard and a consensus sign of quality. The Matheson "Silent Six," for example, was cross-promoted in a full-page ad because the manufacturers amplified the Klaxon brand by connecting it to their own, asserting that the sound quality was particularly important for a car whose main selling point was its silence. "The Matheson Company not desiring to abandon the silent operation of their car have decided to adopt the Klaxon horn as a part of their regular equipment, and which will effectively notify the pedestrian that the 'Silent Six' is coming, even though they may not otherwise hear its approach."[45] Twenty-two motor car manufacturers—much like the "experienced motor car buyer" who realizes that an "adequate signal" is as "necessary to his safety—and to the safety of the pedestrian ahead—as are adequate brakes"—tied their brand to Klaxon's. More, the ad claimed, "must follow."

The cross-promotional campaign serialized, with Klaxon releasing another installation every time the number went up. The companies included King, Kissel, Locomobile, Matheson, Peerless, Oldsmobile, Packard, and Peugeot. One ad focusing on the Simplex explained why it, and "nearly every high-grade car," came regularly equipped with a klaxon. "The predominating factors in the design, construction and equipment of the Simplex automobiles are safety, quality and efficiency. In accordance with that principle, we have adopted the klaxon horn as part of the equipment."[46] Even foreign carmakers like Mercedes and Fiat, influenced by the global expansion of Klaxon, regularly equipped their cars with a klaxon for the US market. They were rewarded with expensive cross-promotion. Because of the "finish" of the horn, the level of electrical current consumption, the reputation, and because the "tone penetrates distinctly over a greater distance," the klaxon "assures Fiat buyers maximum satisfaction and liberal service should any unforeseen troubles ever arise." Klaxon, in short, "is strictly in keeping with the high standard of quality and maximum efficiency it is our unfaltering aim to maintain."[47]

Lovell-McConnell's campaign sensitizing consumers to the need for klaxon technology was not limited to using elites to model pro-klaxon beliefs and behaviors but also showed how everyday people were adopting the technology because of its association with public safety. The company once again turned to focusing on the opinions of ordinary consumers, launching another naming contest for its newest model with a cash prize. It also solicited essays from consumers by offering cash prizes for essays on why the bulb horn was insufficient technology for the modern age. The winner's essay became a full-page ad. The company ran ads touting the thousands of klaxon users, creating the idea of a cultural movement of everyday people adopting klaxon technology as a way of life. Long before brand-name fashion, as Umberto Eco famously observed, turned the consumer into a form of media, Klaxon was using its users as media to amplify its message.[48]

In a modern automotive industry that embraced modern advertising as a communications strategy to create demand for its products and to promote an identity and way of life tied to them, Klaxon was out in front. The company realized that technology purchases were more than just choosing tools for their specified function; they were about consumers expressing something about who they were—their values, hopes, and dreams—through the technology they bought. Klaxon used innovating advertising to provide consumers with a structure of feeling they could be proud of when they sounded their horns.

Yet as this brief chronicling of the ad wars related to sound signaling technology has shown, Klaxon had many competitors that were also trying to gain a foothold in the market. F. Hallett Lovell always wanted his technology to become generic, to be to sound signals what Kodak was to photography. Though its advertising strategies helped it capture the imagination of consumers' marketplace of ideas, Lovell-McConnell dreamed of market dominance. To achieve that goal, Klaxon Ltd. needed more than clever advertising strategies. The next chapter shows how Klaxon turned to the law, and to modern anticompetitive business practices, to solidify its status as producer of the paradigmatic signaling technology for the modern world.

4
KLAXON AND THE MUTABLE LAW OF THE TECHNOLOGY BUSINESS

From its very beginnings, automobile culture has been intricately tied to governance and regulation as various societies tried to come to terms with the impact that automobiles were having on people's everyday life. Different cultures have generated regulations on safety features, ordinances on what could be used where, rules about how cars must be used, and a myriad of public and juridical conversations. At the vanguard of modern business practices, Klaxon recognized early that its product would be tied to ways in which governments regulated the market. Just as Klaxon did with its advertising budget, it leveraged its growing capital to mold the law and make government control of automobile culture serve its interests.

As the last chapter showed, Klaxon's innovative sonic and graphic branding, combined with its pioneering strategies in modern advertising, quickly transformed both the modern soundscape and people's perception of it. Yet market innovation and sophisticated communication strategies were only part of the design for growth as the company worked to corner the market for sound signaling technology. The company knew that the modern soundscape would be increasingly determined by juridical discourse and governmentality, and it went to work trying to control the boundaries and reach of those debates. To understand Klaxon's success in a new technologically centered sound-world, it is necessary to explain how the company used the law—patent law, contract law, ordinance law, and traffic law—to consolidate and corner the sound market.

Roughly from 1910 until late 1914, Klaxon used patent law to control the production of technology and limit its competitors, contract law to control the pricing of its products and bar competitors from distributing competing products, and ordinance law to reflect its commercial interests and standardize the industry to solidify its hegemony. The company's virtual monopoly during this period ensured its profitability, which gave it the capital to wage ever more aggressive legal battles and coordinated national and international lobbying campaigns to shape traffic law, heralding the arrival of modern business practices that would come to be the norm as the West entered the age of consumer culture.

Klaxon achieved this conquest of the soundscape by pushing into the sphere of governmentality, an effort exemplified by its campaign slogan, "The Public Safety Signal." Both "public" and "safety" were normative ideas underpinning growing conversations about the public responsibility of those who operated automobiles. These conversations served as the foundation for attempts in legal and juridical circles to normalize and governmentalize automobile technology. Yet the definition of *public* was very much about the sound environment that benefited the private interests and profits of the Lovell-McConnell Company and its shareholders. The power it held over these conversations about "publicness" is an example of the phenomenon Jürgen Habermas pointed out long ago:[1] private interests have tremendous power over our cultural conversations about the public good. The law as it applied to automobiling was a site of contestation, and Klaxon spent enormous sums on lobbying and strategic communications to mold the law to benefit its private interests, which it equated with the public good. Indeed, when Klaxon lost the ability to impose its heavy hand on the market for sounding devices by controlling the juridical conversation, it began to lose the battle of defining what counted as "necessary" noise, the signaling technology required of automobile drivers in various countries.

Binding the Competition: Patent and Contract Law

By 1910, Klaxon had established itself as offering the most innovative and effective signaling technology on the international market, leverage that allowed its device also to be by far the most expensive. Klaxon's profitability was the key to its constant expansion, and to maintain this competitive advantage the company had both to limit competitors from offering similar technology and maintain its ability to keep prices high. Indeed, Lovell-McConnell created what amounted to a franchise model to distribute its products domestically and overseas, expanding into England and France in 1910. It took care of the advertising for its distributors. As such, the business model depended on Klaxon maintaining the prices it set in its ad campaigns and catalogues. When distributors or salesmen engaged in price cutting, or selling the technology at rates below those advertised in Klaxon's strategic communications, this caused the company all kinds of problems. So Klaxon sought remedy in the law.

In 1910, Lovell-McConnell began systematically suing any competitor or retailer that infringed on its patents or sold its patented products under price. That summer the company sued Kaufman Brothers of Pittsburg, Imperial Automobile Supply Company, American Auto Supply Company, Empire Auto Supply Company, Moto Bloc Import Company, National Trading Company, National Auto Supply Company, Lowe Motor Supplies Company, and several others in the United States to send a message to the automobile industry. Companies that distributed Lovell-McConnell products were forced into new, iron-clad agreements. *Motor World* hailed the two-pronged strategy as "setting [the] pace of the accessory trade in regard to price maintenance."[2] The licensing contracts were crucial. "The keystone of the Lovell-McConnell plan is the comprehensive and rigid license form," the language of which gave the company the ability to sue anyone "who has been notified that he is objectionable to makers."[3] Anyone who distributed Klaxon technology had to respect the terms of the contract.

Speaking on behalf of the company and its shareholders, F. Hallett Lovell Jr., president of Lovell-McConnell, defended the need for the unprecedented legal aggression against "cut rate houses," which sold horns cheaper than they were listed in Lovell-McConnell's catalogues and nationally circulated advertisements. "Price cutting," Lovell argued, was a "serious menace to the regular dealer, whose business has been built up steadily through fair dealing and regular methods."[4] Just as Klaxon ensured the safety of drivers, Lovell said, the "manufacturer ought to be responsible" for protecting distributors who entered into legal agreements with the company and agreed to its standardized pricing. The company had a "duty" to ensure that the "dealer makes a legitimate profit and is given the same protection." Even more, it was in the interest of all manufacturers and distributors of patented technology to stop price cutting "to protect their trade and themselves."

Indeed, protecting its patented technology was central to the business model of the Lovell-McConnell Company. All distributors licensed to sell the company's technology in the United States were legally bound to comply with the standard pricing established in the national advertising campaigns. With its powerful legal team, Lovell-McConnell enforced these binding contracts over its flexible sales force, referred to as "jobbers," which included auto shops, parts stores, casual salesmen, units of sales to auto clubs, and anyone who sold its product. Injunctions were issued to those who failed to comply, which shut down the business of the accused pending trial. And as with its aggressive advertising practice, the industry took note of Lovell-McConnell's innovative business practices.

Motor Age declared that Lovell-McConnell's push toward legal standard-ization of contract law "blazes the way for a new business method." This method meant that jobbers could not sell horns individually or in bulk for anything less. "No other manufactures, so far as known," *Motor Age* noted, "places such a restriction upon jobbers."[5] All those who sold the klaxon were legally bound, through patent law and contract law, to sell the device at the price set in the national advertising campaigns, which was the highest price of any horn on the market.

In return, jobbers were effectively given the kind of advertising campaigns that are associated with franchises today: coordinated communication of stan-dardized messages in the national, regional, and local press, all centered on a brand and the sound associated with it. Winning the advertising game, using the local franchise jobbers to amplify the message, and using the legal arena to control production and dissemination of the klaxon, Lovell-McConnell saw the profits roll in. Not only could the company afford mas-sive national and international advertising campaigns, effectively drowning out competitors in the marketplace for signaling technology, but it could sue anyone who dared challenge its dominance or tried to undercut its profit. This new practice of forcing jobbers into exclusive and binding sales agreements was known as "sewing up." Jobbers hated it and pushed back, but it would take them years to get remedy. It was not until 1917, long after Klaxon's legal dominance over the market had slipped, that the US Department of Justice took note: "Sewing up jobbers as a means, not merely of distributing your product, but of preventing competitors, is a business expedient that has lately found disfavor with the United States Department of Justice."[6] Until then, Lovell-McConnell's legal stick kept jobbers in line.

The company also used incentives to sew up its distributors. Lovell-McConnell promoted exclusive sales relationships and kept jobbers faith-ful to their contractual obligations by utilizing a bonus structure known as "Christmas presents." The company claimed it was a reward for loyalty, but it was effectively a prearranged rebate or bonus pegged to how much a job-ber sold. And sell the company did: in 1915 alone, at the height of Klaxon's dominance, it increased its presence in the American soundscape by close to 900,000 horns. Of those, 209,000 horns were sold directly to automo-bile manufacturers and 283,000 directly to retailers. The rest, some 372,000, were moved by jobbers.[7]

The legal stick was key to Lovell-McConnell's anticompetition business practices. Its lawyers were busy taking on jobbers, retailers, and manufactur-ers who tried to create cheaper models of klaxons in violation of patent law governing the technology. For example, when Joseph W. Jones and United Manufacturers, makers and marketers of the Jones electric horn, brought their horn to market, Klaxon sued them for patent violation. United Manufacturers backed down and settled in March 1911, acknowledging the validity of the Klaxon patents. As part of the settlement, United agreed to a permanent injunction that would prevent it from manufacturing a similar warning signal.[8]

One case, a December 1911 suit against American Ever Ready Company, sent a signal to everyone. Not only did Lovell-McConnell sue Ever Ready for infringement of seven Klaxon patents, it also sued Ever Ready for "unfair competition" because it sold these patent-infringing technologies at a cheaper price than the price set by Lovell-McConnell. The case established precedent that gave Klaxon a near monopoly on signaling technology. Judge Charles Hough, of the US District Court of the Southern District of New York, rendered the decision. Because the patented technology afforded a particular sound, Hough's ruling made it illegal for another signaling device to sound like a klaxon. "It must be a very little distance indeed within which anyone can distinguish a Klaxon horn from an Ever Ready." The defense claimed that the mechanism of the Ever Ready horn technology differed slightly, which rendered the patent violation moot: "Undoubtedly a critical examination shows divergence in position of fastener arms, variations in at least one curve." Hough rejected this argument and determined that if a horn looked and sounded the same, even though its mechanism had slight alterations, this amounted to violation of the patent and the trademark: "What strikes the beholder even when his attention is directed to distinctive parts is not the difference but the general, unnecessary and apparently intended resemblance of the alter to the earlier device. . . . Does this sort of conduct need the restraining hand of equity? I am inclined to think it does."[9] This decision gave ownership of a type of sound or tone legal cover for the generic association with signaling technology that Lovell had long strived to achieve.

Ever Ready appealed, but the decision was sustained by Second Circuit Court of Appeals judge Emile Lacombe, who wrote that "the resemblance between complainant's horns and defendant's horns is very great." The Every Ready horn, he declared, was "a manifest imitation in details of construction, with the consequent likelihood of confusion" for those who would hear it.[10] Legally speaking, the sound quality was deemed to be part of the public understanding of the product, and anything that could be confused with a klaxon violated Klaxon's patent because it aimed to deceive. Ever Ready responded to the decision by seeking relief from the injunction that had halted production, claiming that "a sample of its horn was given to the Lovell-McConnell attorney, and had been tampered with so as to make it more closely resemble the Klaxon horn." Relief was denied.[11] Thus Klaxon was now free to grow its monopoly over signaling technology with protection under the law. It exerted its powerful leverage by continuing to target like-sounding technology for suit. The Henry Phillips Rubber Works Company was next, in a patent infringement injunction that was sustained on January 10, 1912.[12]

The legal strategy of using injunctions gave Lovell-McConnell the power not only to squash its manufacturing rivals; injunctions also helped the company go after retailers who sold "illegal technology." Following a suit against Automobile Supply Manufacturing Company for selling the Newtone horn, Klaxon warned all dealers "that handling the 'Newtone' horn will render them liable to similar suits, dealers in their licensed Klaxon horns being especially advised that—by reason of the conditions of the Klaxon restricted licenses—the sale of any horns infringing any Klaxon patents will render them liable to a preliminary injunction."[13] Moreover, Klaxon's lawyers used an injunction to prevent the Newtone makers from defending themselves in the court of public opinion, halting the publication of any written literature that defended Newtone's position or tried to interpret the case for concerned dealers.[14]

This legal protection was central to Klaxon's near monopoly on the sound market, not only because it prevented competition but also because the device's brand name became legally tied to the klaxon's aaOOgah sound. This branding strategy, whereby even slight variations of the sound were legally negligent, was crucial as the company developed different sizes and models of horns to work with different cars. By law, it "owned" the peculiar tone since US courts had now stated that if a horn produced the aaOOgah sound, even if it was a slightly different design, selling such a horn amounted to patent infringement.

Klaxon set out to further its court-protected control over signal technology, buying up the patents of any new inventions with possible application for different models of cars. Klaxon's lawyers also enforced the company's market dominance without mercy, ensuring that any sounding of similar technology would echo and reiterate the frames presented by its strategic communications. When people heard that aaOOgah sound, the law stated, they were hearing Klaxon. And the horns rolled off the assembly line: in May of 1912, Lovell-McConnell announced it was enlarging its plant as part of a plan to double capacity.[15] The stock price soared.

Klaxon's legally protected market dominance was not limited to America, and its aggressive push into patent law and enforcement of its contracts became part of its international business strategy. In Canada, the Knowles Company found itself at the wrong end of a suit after failing to comply with the dealer contract that granted it sole right to deal Klaxon in Canada. Knowles countersued Klaxon International in Ontario High Court in February 1912, but Klaxon's contract was upheld.[16] In Europe, Klaxon was able to gain access to French markets without the high tariffs associated with imports by licensing its patent to Blériot and registering it in France, a move that made the horn the talk of 1912.[17] While the industry took note of the new product, Klaxon used the fourteenth annual Salon de l'Automobile in Paris in 1913 as a high-profile way to communicate its intent to enforce its patent ownership in France the same way it had in the United States. At the height of action on the first day, the police descended on the Salon, seizing all other signaling devices "falling under the jurisdiction of the Klaxon Blériot patent." As *Le Figaro* reported, "By law, the owner of the patent has, in effect, the power to exercise its right against all venders or buyers . . . to have seized everywhere any device which was a violation of the patent [*appereil resultant de la contrefaçon d'un brevet*]." With this action, Klaxon International sent a signal: any motorized or hand-cranked horn on the market that was not an official "Klaxon Blériot" would be silenced through the power of the law.[18]

Knowing that patent protection was the key to its monopoly in America, Klaxon began aggressively buying up any emerging technology. Klaxon bought the remaining shares of its patent from Miller Reese Hutchison in May 1913. It quickly bought the work of other inventors that same month.[19] Its market dominance led its legal strategy; the company used its profits to buy the patents of those it sought injunctions on, thereby solidifying its hold on the market for electrical signaling devices.

Transnational Deliberation on Horn Regulation

Wherever the klaxon was sold, in cities, states, and countries, the sound was a source of intense public and juridical deliberation and increasing regulation. The question of what signaling technology could be legally sold under patent and contract law continued to be intricately connected to the juridical definition of a legal horn, as defined by statutes requiring drivers to sound them. What exactly, legally speaking, was an "adequate" warning signal or an "adequate" horn? What did the law require of drivers? Such legal questions related to the function of sound as a signaling mode within a modern sound-scape were settled in different ways, depending first on municipal rules and later on laws standardized within and between nations. Klaxon, as it sought to retain its control over audible signaling technology, was at the center of these social and juridical debates and the ongoing negotiations of ordinance law.

Compulsory sounding laws emerged along with automobiles in the last decade of the nineteenth century, piggybacking on other statutes tied to other forms of transportation. Yet they did not quite fit, and vigorous conversations grew up over what kind of signaling should be required of drivers.[20] The answer was usually local, resulting in a shifting patchwork of laws that was as confusing to drivers as it was to carmakers. At the dawn of the automobile age, drivers had to signal constantly, letting anyone in the environment know they were coming, going, or about to do something.

Though local laws worked out car-specific rules of the road, the problem was international in its scope. French law, article 15 of the 1899 decree, required all vehicles to have "a horn [*trompe*] to signal their approach." When the klaxon entered the signal technology market and Blériot began manufacturing the klaxon in France, new questions arose as to what sound was legally implied by the word "horn." Did it have to have a "honk honk" sound, a representational aesthetic established by the once dominant French bulb horn technology in the car's early years, or could other signal tones produced by newer technology satisfy the requirements of the law?

Klaxon paid vast sums to have its technology promoted in the trade press with native advertising wherever its product was sold. Just as in the trade press in America, Klaxon's ad copy in French automobile journals linked the peculiar sound its technology produced to utility and necessity. A 1910 editorial in *La Revue d'Automobile,* for example, made the case that "the guttural cry of this American device is an effective warning. As cars today get more and more silent, we are required to signal our presence with a more powerful device."[21] To help normalize that sound for French ears, Klaxon once again paid to have it used at important events by influential people. It arranged to have the horn equipped on the official car of the Tour de France, and by 1913, as Blériot's coproduced klaxon gained market control, on the car of French president Raymond Poincaré.

The klaxon was now heard throughout France, but was it legal? Once again the question was asked and answered at the local level. Many municipalities in France wanted to bar noisy technologies that disturbed citizens. Boissy-Saint-Léger, for example, decided in 1907 that the siren—a huge cause of nuisance complaints—was not a horn, by law, and that it was illegal to use one instead of a horn.[22] This was a constant complaint in small rural towns because touring *automobilistes,* bourgeois converts to the motoring life, were often required by law to sound their horn whenever they saw a house on the horizon or passed another car. The number of cars on the roads grew year by year, from 44,796 in 1909 to 76,771 in 1912,[23] and with it the number of accidents and fatalities, which seemed to call for such compulsory sounding; yet the complaints about noise rose in tandem. Municipalities everywhere had to cope with the presence of these sounds, and they often sought legal relief.

Not all rural municipalities rejected modern electrical technology. In 1913, Nantua, a quiet lakeside community in eastern France that grew up around a Benedictine monastery, reversed the notion that a *trompe* had to sound like a bulb horn. Instead, it decided that the electrical machinelike sounds of the siren and the klaxon both fell in the category *trompe* under the law. "It follows that the klaxon and the siren, which are frequently used by automobilists can and should be considered to be a derivation of the horn [*trompe*]."[24] Yet there was another legal question that needed to be decided as well. Was it necessary to compel people to honk their horns, as was currently required by law? The writer reporting on the municipal ruling asserted that since "these instruments emit a sound that is powerful enough, and has a sound that is bizarre enough, to frighten animals that pull vehicles, it appears that municipalities should create laws surrounding its use, and even to forbid them."[25] Until that point, however, klaxons should legally be considered horns.

Once Blériot started manufacturing the hand klaxon as *"le klaxon mécanique,"* making the sound available to cars that did not have an alternator to produce electricity, the number of klaxons on the roads increased. As was the case in the United States, klaxon users, working with automobile associations, pushed for liberalization of the legal statutes. In one precedent-setting Parisian case, a man who had been "arrested for using a klaxon, considered 'susceptible to frighten horses,'"[26] was acquitted after the court found that the language "susceptible" in the police chief's decree was too vague a legal determinant.[27]

In Germany, wherever the klaxon entered the soundspace after Strasbourg's Auto-Bestandteil Company acquired distribution rights for the Klaxon-Blériot device, the legal parsing followed.[28] Laws dating to 1910 required drivers to have a low-toned warning signal and, if the signal had multiple tones, to sound them simultaneously.[29] As was the case in France, drivers had to sound audible warning signals before passing anyone on the road, but German law required drivers to stop signaling if animals were frightened. Horns were required to produce short notes and not long sustained ones, so as to not be confused with the sirens used in Germany by fire brigades.[30] In cities, the low-toned signal was required, but outside municipalities, drivers were allowed to use "fanfare signals" or other musical devices. Per clause 21 in the

Reichsgesetz (Reich law) of May 3, 1909, anyone who violated these rules could be fined up to 150 marks or punished with imprisonment.[31]

As they had in France, German distributors of klaxon technology pressed for the klaxon's tone to be considered legal under the law so that the franchise would be more valuable. They were successful. A 1912 decree from the German kaiser himself established ranges of sounds that were legal for different vehicles: "Motor-cars here must have a deep-noted horn or klaxon, and motor bicycles must have a high-noted horn. For the horns, chords are allowed, but not tunes or short refrains."[32] This was similar to the ranges of sound signals required in Italy, where a 1910 law stated, "All motor vehicles must be equipped with a one-toned horn. The tone must be low note for automobiles, and of high note for motor-cycles. All other signaling devices are forbidden, except that within the open country sirens may be used in a 'subsidiary' way."[33] Sirens, or other long-duration signals, were restricted to emergency vehicles.

Despite these laws, several scenarios emerged in Germany that tested the klaxon's legality. One case that worked its way to the *Reichsgericht* (Supreme Court) involved a man who had used a klaxon (defined as a "*Signalapparat*") and had frightened an animal. Since the klaxon made a "powerful noise capable of frightening animals," leading to the death of a horse carriage driver's wife in an accident, the prosecution argued that the man was liable. The *Reichsgericht* ruled in favor of the defense in relation to the question of liability but suggested that signaling devices like the klaxon, capable of frightening animals, should be forbidden in all circumstances.[34] Legal commentators called this decision "sensible," as frightened animals were capable of destroying life and property, yet the legal question was far from settled.

Cases like this showed the legal bind created by signaling laws. On the one hand, laws required drivers to "draw attention" (*Aufmerksam zu machen*)[35] to themselves and their passage; on the other hand, the law waived the legal requirement that they signal if there were "shy animals around." As a result, German law, like the laws in most other countries trying to regulate automobile usage, was vague as to which exact situations required signaling. Drivers were obliged to make others aware yet were expected to do so in a way that did not frighten animals or startle other drivers. The sound made by klaxon technology—which the company's marketing began calling *Klaxonhuppe* rather than *Signalapparat* to characterize it linguistically as a horn, per the legal statutes—was somewhere right in the middle. If used quickly and abruptly, the signal was legal. If long and drawn out in duration, it was not. Indeed, the gray areas of German law were revealed in several decisions that reached contradictory conclusions, a fact that observers of the *Oberlandesgericht* (higher court) admitted put drivers on the "horns of a dilemma."[36]

There was no regulation in Germany against unnecessary honking per se, but there was a general regulation against unnecessary noise that created a public nuisance. This legal dilemma for Klaxon was later complicated by cases that sought to set precedent as to what counted legally as a horn, and in which the klaxon tone was tested to determine whether it could be considered "low" per the legal statutes.[37]

Amid the testing of horns and case law, the older bulb horns were deemed to be "insufficient" as signaling devices: "[The bulb] is not sufficiently protected against the effects of weather and dust, and therefore often fails in crucial moments such as accidents."[38] The court agreed that the klaxon was a better sound technology "because it is especially necessary in hazardous traffic situations where there is intense street noise. The bulb horn, even if it does not fail, is not powerful enough." As a result, though the *Klaxonhuppe* was not strictly a horn under the law, it was considered a legal and necessary signaling device.

Cases continued to work their way through the German courts through 1914 involving the klaxon and other electric motor–driven horns, testing the right of German authorities "to forbid the use of these signals because of the harsh sounds they emitted." The law was finally settled in the high court in Bavaria, setting precedent for all federated German states. "Motor cars," the court ruled, "should be equipped with a deep-toned horn, free of annoying, screeching and squeaking noises." The court decided that the klaxon, because it was not any of these sounds, was "admissible in cities and towns in the German Empire." The judges' decision, as reported in *Automobile Topics*, gave Klaxon the victory it needed.[39] In America, Klaxon touted the decision in advertisements as well, adding to the perception that Klaxon technology was winning the consensus of global public opinion.[40]

Great Britain also had laws on the books requiring signaling devices for automobiles. The legal debate about the use and abuse of the "hooter" began to get louder as the number of cars increased. Indeed, by 1912 there were 207,468 licensed cars and motorcycles on British roads.[41] As it had done in France, Klaxon International concluded distribution agreements with British manufacturers, the latter of which gained exclusive control of the British production of the patented technology. The franchised distributers of these "British-made" klaxons were racing to keep up with the demand. Yet, as was the case elsewhere, klaxon users were increasingly the subject of legal complaints, as were other sound technology devices. Noise ordinance laws

Figure 24. Ad assuring the British public that the Klaxon warning signal is British-made. From *The Motor,* January 2, 1912. (Pennsylvania State University Library)

designed to curb sonic nuisances rendered illegal "cut-out" mufflers, or silencers, as the British called them. The same fate befell exhaust horns attached to tailpipes before the exhaust had passed through the muffler, meaning that many of the exhaust horns in use were illegal by 1912.[42] Yet most complaints about horns had less to do with specific technology than with older statutes that required constant signaling.

A lively discussion about the relationship between the social contract and the law emerged in the British press. Many legal commentators likened the behavior of motorists communicating on the road to any other form of negotiating public space. "Why should noisy hooters and horns be allowed?" asked E. H. Hodgkinson in a 1911 book titled *The Tyranny of Speed, or The Motor Peril and Its Remedy.* "As far as possible motorists should not be heard." Compulsory "hooting" laws on the public highways, as such, were a "gross breach of manners. The raucous horn practically snorts out at the pedestrian, 'Get out of the way, I am coming.' If an accident ensues it is assumed that the latter is in the wrong and has merited his fate."[43] This led to social breakdown. A hearty public debate about the normative ethics of signaling in traffic led to a vigorous dispute in Parliament over how best to regulate "the hooter," especially those used by taxicabs. According to one writer, "The taxi driver hoots as energetically as though each blast of his horn meant another two-pence in extras."[44]

Members of Parliament had much to debate as they worked to craft law on the hooter. "It is incumbent on all drivers to give audible warning," read a circular from the Commissioner of the London Police. "Especially at corners and at points where streets cross each other, so that vehicles approaching the junction may be apprised of each other's advent."[45] Because of the statute, the first question the police asked after any accident was always "Did you blow your horn?" Those who did were not liable; those who did not were. As police did in the United States, British police enforced compulsory signaling laws with police traps, fining those who did not comply. Such surveillance and governmental disciplining, by design, created a structural problem of excessive hooting. Yet, as in other countries, British law was somewhat arbitrary as to when hooting was necessary and when it was excessive.

The *Evening News* of London weighed in on the debate, offering a potential "reasonable" check on excessive hooting. Automotive associations, motor unions, should come to a consensus on the best horns to use, banishing "the more discordant" technologies. Moreover, they should help standardize compulsory signaling rules and communicate proper behavior to their members so that horns would be heard as more "polite to the general public." If automobilists did not self-regulate, the writer cautioned, it was only a matter of time until more rigorous laws were passed.[46]

In the conversation about legal standardization and public understanding of the use of horns, some British columnists proposed that particular types of vehicles carry their own representative sound, as they did in Germany, Italy, and Spain. That way, pedestrians and drivers would know what was coming. The editors of the *Irish Times,* reporting on the debates at the International Road Congress convening in London in 1913, advocated "the use of deep-toned horn in towns and populous places, and the reservation of whistles and klaxons for long-distance signaling on country roads." All agreed that those who used "piercing and raucous signals in populous places" jeopardized the ability of all to use "appliances that have a material use in proper circumstances."[47]

Yet as klaxon users became more numerous and the American technology spread internationally as a legally sanctioned sound linked to an American brand, antipathy toward its presence grew in Britain. As Parliament debated the Street Noises Bill in 1914, written "to amend the Law in respect of warning instruments on motor vehicles," speakers frequently discussed the klaxon. Captain Arthur C. Murray, the bill's presenter who had also introduced the 1911 Motor Traffic (Street Noises) Bill that the new bill was trying to improve upon, put it this way: "The klaxon positively sweeps the street. The horn may sound the hint polite; the klaxon is the blast imperious."[48] In 1911 the Royal Automobile Club had suggested that "excessive use of noisy warning devices at night" should be prohibited. But three years later, the problem remained. The 1914 Street Noises Bill now contained specific language restricting the klaxon.

H. E. Shaw, general manager of Klaxon in London, responded to the legal danger with an editorial in the *Times*. Echoing the strategies used in Klaxon's American commercial lobbying campaign, Shaw argued that Klaxon was a "proved necessity" for safe driving. The "bulb horn" that many in Parliament called for was "already known by motorists, taxicab and omnibus drivers [to be] inadequate." The problem was not the technology but its abuse by the user: "We have always maintained that it is not the use of klaxon horns, or other loud warning signals that is objected to, but their abuse, and we would welcome the punishment of those who take a delight in making day or night hideous by prolonged pressing of the push button. The klaxon horn is not intended as a noise maker pure and simple, but as a warning signal. We have always advocated that it should never be used in crowded streets or cities, except in cases of emergency."[49] Conveniently ignoring years of "clear the way" advertising that promoted precisely the opposite, he argued that klaxon sound technology was only a problem when people used it excessively. He noted, and repeated, "Some 'don't s' for Klaxon Users"—language included in catalogues, owner's manuals, and increasingly in Klaxon's international communications strategy—and suggested that if the technology was used correctly, there would be no need for legislation against it. "Observance of these simple suggestions will make your klaxon warning signal all the more effective when its use is necessary; it will indicate consideration for the safety and comfort of householders, and other road users; and will do much to overcome any lingering prejudice in the minds of the public against motor-cars and motorists."[50]

Several *Times* readers responded to Shaw's endorsement of the klaxon as the only adequate and necessary signaling technology, noting that it was only because motorized horns were so loud that the klaxon sound was necessary. "Of course the bulb horn will be 'inadequate'," wrote a "London Rector" in the *Times*, "so long as less 'polite' and more 'imperious' sounds are permitted. The sound which for the moment is most imperious rules the road." Things would only get worse: "Unless we deal summarily with the matter at the present stage, we shall soon find that the klaxons, sirens, buzzers, whistles, screechers of today are being superseded by some more horrible and more imperious instruments tomorrow."[51] The writer suggested that English law should follow the lead of some municipalities in France that had limited motorists to using the more polite bulb horns within city limits. "I submit to your readers that the bulb horn is the motor-car's way of saying 'By your leave, please,' and that the screecher in all its forms is the bad language of the road, and ought to be surpassed by public opinion, if not, by the law."[52]

"Dash those klaxons," cursed another writer annoyed by unwanted intrusion of noise in his garden. "I suspect hundreds of others living in quiet country roads say something similar every day." Defenders of the klaxon, he charged, were "ignorant of road courtesies," and unwilling to slow down. They showed "scorn of the comforts and rights of those who reside near the roads." For the klaxon user, safety was merely an excuse to "become another road hog. I have noticed that it defeats its object by arousing the resentment of carters and waggoners who feel bullied by its arrogant blast. 'Clear the road,' indeed. If I hear one coming up from behind and ordering me to clear the road, I do what I can to hold the road."[53] Of course, the klaxon had its defenders, especially in the British trade journals, where Klaxon could force its not so invisible hand into the debate. In *The Autocar,* automobile enthusiast and Welsh baronet John Owen defended the klaxon against its critics. He wrote that having a "klaxon" was "more necessary than any other accessory on a car. What I might call 'kid glove' horns are of no use at all."[54] He recounted hitting a motorcycle with a side car while driving a Studebaker, equipped with a "mellifluous and soothing electric horn. . . . The driver failed to hear me and I failed to hear him. . . . If I had had my Klaxon it would not have happened, because the cyclist would have heard that I was coming and acted accordingly."[55] Volume, range, push-button reaction speed, and convenience, he said, made the klaxon the safest warning signal technology for a motorist to own. Following the user-abuse linguistic frame promoted by Klaxon, one meant to sidestep government legal regulation and put the onus on consumers, Owen wrote that "although I praise noisy instruments, I deprecate their abuse, and in towns at night they ought to be kept silent." Klaxon technology was good when used correctly; abuse of the horn was not the fault of the technology.

Owen called for commonsense laws to regulate automobile horn use along with the growing sound of motor culture in everyday life. Commonsense laws, he wrote, would not condemn the klaxon as a sign of the "American invaders." Klaxon technology was "too valuable to be abandoned. The proof of it is that hardly any motor drivers who have once used them are to be found without them." Prohibition of klaxons was foolish, as was the call to "unify horn notes and sanction melodious instruments only. . . . One might as well make it compulsory to carry always on one's car that fearful thing: a tenor."[56] While aesthetically pleasing sound signals might seem less odious, they failed the test of utility. Adequate sound technology, properly used—an argument echoing the by now standardized discursive regime constructed, repeated, and reified by Klaxon's lobbying and marketing in all countries where it distributed its technology—saved lives.

In the United States, the debate over the legality of the louder automobile horns and the necessity of compulsory signaling laws was remarkably similar to that in Europe. As cars increased in number, so did the complaints about noise to police and legislatures. Nationwide, American municipalities were coming to terms with the ever-increasing number of klaxon horns in their soundscape. As was the case in Europe, legal responses varied depending on local and state government. The increasing presence of electric horn technologies caused states such as Massachusetts to revisit the signal laws requiring constant usage. In 1910 the Massachusetts legislature discussed the need to eliminate laws that led to "needless arrests [that] were made for not blowing a horn at every crossing."[57] According to a writer in *Motor Age*, though the proposed legislation was designed to address the sound complaints about automobile signaling noise, the law had dramatic implications for car horn makers: "Here [the bill] strikes at one part of the accessory business, the makers of some of the horns on the market. The changes make [horns] all right in the open country so the operator has no need to slow up except where the view is obstructed, but the provision for cities and towns simply says that no horn shall be sounded, except the ordinary reed horns."[58] If the law passed, Klaxon and other electric horn makers would be legally barred from the market; the company's technological advantage and the basis of its market success, producing a signal loud enough to cut through any other noise, would become illegal. Klaxon quickly countered this legislative push through aggressive lobbying of legislators and advertising meant to sway public opinion.

Indeed, municipalities all over the country were coming to view compulsory signaling laws and the misuse of "adequate" signaling devices as a serious nuisance. In San Francisco, with its echoing, narrow streets and winding hills, citizens complained about police enforcement of compulsory signaling. Writing in the *San Francisco Chronicle*, W.H.B. Fowler suggested that it was time "to enforce a reasonable use of horns and other warning signals at night." While most drivers respected people's need for sleep, there were "unfortunately, persons who drive automobiles who have little regard for the personal feelings of others." Fowler complained:

It is their idea that the klaxon or sirens on their cars are to be used indiscriminately, and it would appear that they do not hesitate sometimes to use them for their own amusement rather than for public warning purposes. It is not an uncommon thing for some brainless driver to turn loose an air-splitting noise producer on Sutter Street for several seconds, when a mere touch of the button produces all the warning signal that is necessary for a warning. . . . It is not questioned that the only effective type of warning signal is the klaxon, and its use should be encouraged and the inefficient bulb horn abolished. At the same time, the misuses of the klaxon type, especially during the night, should be very quickly checked.[59]

While conceding that the klaxon was the most effective horn at communicating with others, indiscriminate and constant use of the full klaxon was, indeed, too much. Proper and measured use of the technology was the only safe choice.

As was its tendency in America, Klaxon turned to advertising to educate users and the public about how to use the klaxon properly. In its manuals and in a series of ads and native advertorials that appeared in various large markets, the company taught users about the "tiger growl," a short burst of sound created by a quick push of the button.

To draw the user community into the debate and help shape public opinion in Massachusetts, where the legislature was debating the issue, Klaxon also announced a prize for the "best suggestions as to the proper use and regulation of motor car warning signals." Communicating the company's commitment to legality, Klaxon saw that the judges of the contest would all be connected to automobile policy in some way; they included former Massachusetts governor William L. Douglas, James A. Gallivan, chairman of the board of street commissioners, and Daniel F. Gay, director of the Automobile Legal Association and director of the American Automobile Association.[60] Wrote the *Motor* editor, "A contest of this sort is extremely valuable from its educational effect on the general public and also in teaching motorists how properly to use a vital portion of their accessory equipment and a portion that is liable to great abuse unless used intelligently."[61] By acknowledging the potential problems with the klaxon's technological affordances and working to improve how its technology was used, the company got out in front of the public relations problem, setting the agenda and taking control of the media framing.

Klaxon's transnational strategy was to respond vigorously to the growing attempts to regulate what signals could be used and when they should be used. In countries where Klaxon had extended its patent on the technology, the company used print media to try to set the tone of those debates. Back in America, it turned up the volume on this tactic once again with a brand-new campaign to make the klaxon the legal industry standard.

The Sane Warning Signal Campaign

Klaxon's American lobbing and public relations strategy expanded in 1914. The company used print media to control the debate about signal devices through advertorials, ads that read like editorials, and pushed its lobbying campaign in municipal and state legislatures all around the country. It called this multipronged communications and legal strategy the Sane Warning Signal Legislation Campaign.[62] Klaxon turned salesmen into lobbyists, who took the message on the road and hard-sold the evangel to legislatures. From courthouses to capitals, Klaxon's lobbying team cast the legal debate as one about "adequate" signaling and touted the company's technology as the only one whose affordances were suited to the safety challenges faced by a country increasingly centered on the automobile. It provided municipalities and state legislatures all around the United States with ready-made language to shape the debate and the law. Each victory was announced in Klaxon editorial ads in big red font, publicizing the growing legal standing of the klaxon as the most adequate warning signal, one that best responded to the challenges of regulating the automobile as a growing feature of everyday life.

The first prong of Klaxon's Sane Warning Signal campaign was to present the older bulb horn technology as inadequate for dealing with the safety situations encountered by drivers every day. At the 1911 American Road Association's Good Roads Congress, Klaxon's lobbyists helped write recommendations about automobile laws that updated the legal definition of an "adequate signal" that favored Klaxon's proprietary technology. The company then ran ads that quoted the association's recommendations—the very ones its lawyers had helped write—as if they were an external validation of the superiority of klaxon technology. The company called for a uniform federal standard by which cars would have "an adequate warning signal . . . which should produce *an abrupt sound, sufficiently loud to be heard under all conditions of traffic.*"[63] This language, especially the emphasized text, found its way into municipal laws all over the country over the next several years as a result of Klaxon's coordinated advertising and lobbying strategy. "Men of national prominence and indisputable authority in automobile matters," read one ad, declared "the bulb horn must go." Expert opinion was amplified through serialized print ads that featured such iconic figures as the "the Mechanical Engineer" and "the

Accident Claim Adjustor." Each iteration associated words like "uncertain," "unhandy," "unreliable," "useless," "weak toned," "out-of-date," and "unsafe" with the bulb horn. In one ad, an engineer, Edwin W. Hammer of New York City, called for the law to respond. "I look forward with confidence to the time when it will be unlawful to depend upon a bulb-horn as signal device for automobiles, the only adequate device being one which is power driven and capable of giving an abrupt, harsh note which will command attention and thereby prevent accidents."[64]

The Sane Warning Signal campaign had its first big success in Chicago, whose city council had long wrestled with the question of legal horn technology. Over the years, Chicago had enacted ordinance laws against whistles, the cut-out muffler, and the siren. Eventually everything except the bulb horn was made illegal. In September 1911, Klaxon representatives met with Chicago's chief of police to demonstrate the klaxon and to persuade the department that the horn did not fall into the category of the prohibited siren. The chief decided that "reasonable use of the Klaxon warning signal as a warning danger is entirely proper and not in violation of the terms of the ordinance."[65]

In November 1911, Chicago alderman Charles M. Thomson submitted legislation to solve the problem. Known as the "father of the ordinance forbidding the use of the muffler cutout," he utilized Klaxon's strategic language: "That an automobile warning signal must be adequate is plain. To be adequate it must warn instantly. Its note should be harsh, abrupt, effective. The shrill, screeching signal is unnecessary. . . . We do not want a musical signal, nor one which has to be sounded a number to times to gain attention. The warning the signal gives must be instantaneous. A man who is warned needs to get out of the danger zone without stopping to think. He can think afterward, but first he must escape the danger."[66] When the proposal was adopted by the city government, Klaxon featured the triumph in its weekly editorial series, which continued to provide readers of automobile magazines with news about cities adopting the language of Klaxon's lobbying campaign. "Chicago is the first city to officially recognize the need of a more efficient warning signal than the bulb-horn."[67] Already, the ad touted, the legal pressure had convinced seventeen carmakers to follow the "trend in public opinion" and equip their cars with Klaxon technology at the factory. In an era of dramatic and dynamic emergence and disappearance of carmakers and competition, Klaxon was the first to show how a market could be cornered and consolidated by careful application of modern business practices that marshaled the power of law as a weapon against competitors.

Based on their success, Klaxon editorial ads predicted that by 1914, no carmakers would equip their cars with the bulb horn because it would be illegal and irresponsible to do so.[68] Klaxon's lobbying campaign continued to yield results as cities reversed local ordinances that had limited motorists to the bulb horn. In Denver, the police board removed its restriction against the klaxon after meeting with Klaxon representatives in November 1911.[69]

Each legal success was amplified in Klaxon's ad campaign to create the appearance of growing governmental consensus. The company lobbied the New York State Automobile Association, which then recommended that the state and city follow Chicago's lead in adopting "sensible legislation."[70] After the New York City Board of Coroners issued a statement that weighed heavily on the legal standing of the klaxon as the most "adequate" signal, Klaxon selectively reported its findings.[71] "The time is near when New York will take action similar to that taken by Chicago and other cities."[72]

Any time local ordinance legislation threatened its business, Klaxon's machine would spring into action. When Indianapolis tried to limit "noise making devices," Klaxon lobbyists and lawyers descended on City Hall. They were successful: the city's legal department reversed its bulb-horn-only ordinance, announcing that such legislation was invalid because it would be class legislation.[73] St. Louis was next. Klaxon announced that the city had adopted the "sane signal" language, which "decrees against the notoriously inadequate bulb horn." Indeed, "this practical ordinance is . . . rapidly coming to be recognized generally as the one logical solution to the warning signal problem . . . [and] provides the maximum of safety with the minimum of noise."[74]

Klaxon's weekly legal news column in *Automobile Topics*, its paid advertorial space, continued at full speed. It gave the opinions of "traffic experts" in Chicago, Baltimore, and St. Louis attesting to the insufficiency of the bulb horn.[75] Klaxon ads quoted general counsels for the Automobile Associations of Massachusetts, Illinois, Minnesota, Wisconsin, and Maryland, each calling for a ban on the bulb horn. Klaxon quoted fifty presidents of automobile clubs and associations who echoed and repeated Klaxon's campaign's linguistic frames.[76] It also quoted the chiefs of police in thirty cities where it was pushing the "sane signal" law, each demanding Klaxon technology as standard. In each of these serial advertorials, Klaxon characterized the bulb horn as a thing of the legal past, inadequate for solving the problem of communicating in traffic amid the growing din of the city. Only the klaxon, these ads argued, met this "essential" function: "The law recognizes it and experience proves it to be the very foundation of safe motoring."[77] Not surprisingly, when Klaxon's hometown, Newark, adopted Klaxon's ready-made legal language, Klaxon trumpeted the decision as part of a national trend. "One by one progressive communities are taking definite stands against the ineffective, unreliable bulb horn—as a menace to the safety of the street."[78] With its multipronged approach, designed to normalize klaxon signaling technology yet curb its abuse, the campaign resonated with the antinoise debate ongoing in the courts and in legislatures.

Indeed, antinoise legislation was on the rise in America, especially in the New York metropolitan area. In 1911, Julia Barnett Rice, president of the Society for the Suppression of Unnecessary Noise, had announced that the society would tackle the auto horn as a social problem. In 1912 the push began. The *New York Times* touted the "consistent attempt to obviate the needless noise evil and at the same time to increase the safety of the streets."[79] Meanwhile, with new municipal victories to report, Klaxon kept its advertorial campaign going month after month, trying to control the narrative and counteract the campaign against its technology by antinoise foes.

Klaxon's communications strategy set the media frames and agenda, often modeling legal debates. One ad from October 1912, titled "Is It Legal?," used an imaginary courtroom dialogue between a "Motorist" who had hit a pedestrian and a "Magistrate" to help dramatize the stakes. "Shouldn't you have given some warning of the approach of your car?" asks the magistrate. "I blew my horn immediately and applied my brakes," replies the motorist. "What kind of horn is your automobile equipped with?" queries the magistrate. "A regular bulb-horn—the honk-honk—the kind that is on most cars," answers the motorist. "Was there any other noise at the time?" asks the judge. After the motorist answers "the usual traffic roar," the case for the bulb horn, and with it the motorist's defense, goes downhill. "Clearly the responsibility for this accident rests upon the *horn*—and I believe, upon you, for failing to provide a better one. . . . I hold that the kind of signal with which your car is equipped—the bulb horn—is NOT *legally an adequate signal*."[80]

Indeed, real court cases in 1912 followed similar patterns, showing how Klaxon's push to change public opinion also changed the opinions of the courts. Stop, Look and Listen laws, originally designed for railroad crossings, required both pedestrians and motorists to do so when crossing a street.[81] Several cases decided that this rule did not apply to automobile pedestrians and drivers so long as drivers had "adequate" signaling devices to let pedestrians know they were coming.

There were laws that diverged, such as a July 1912 Maryland law that, although adopting Klaxon's "sane signal" language, also made it a fineable offense of $50 to use anything other than a bulb horn between sunset and sunrise.[82] Most municipalities, however, continued to revise their ordinance and traffic laws according to the ready-made language of Klaxon's strategic campaign. For example, cities like Des Moines, which had previously limited the use of klaxons to city vehicles, effectively making it the representative sound of official emergency, reversed course and allowed average citizens to use the technology.[83] After Seattle did the same, Klaxon took out a half-page ad in *The Star* to highlight its success.[84]

Following a visit from the Klaxon lobbying team, Cincinnati also reversed an ordinance dating to 1903 "prescribing the use of only the bulb horn," and allowed the klaxon.[85] Philadelphia, where ordinance law once prohibited anything but the bulb horn, updated its laws such that any signal was allowed, so long as it was only a single note and not prolonged.[86] Portland followed suit.[87]

After California became the "first state to legally define an adequate warning signal," Klaxon published an ad bragging that fifty-seven manufacturers—producers of "every high-grade car made in America"—were now installing Klaxon technology at the factory so as to comply with the laws sweeping the nation.[88] At a time when over 250 car manufacturers were in business and there were close to a million automobiles on American roads, Klaxon was pointing the way toward industry regulation and standardization, to governmentalize automobile culture and make it safe.

Branding Standardization: Klaxonizing the Automobile Business

In the United States, Klaxon continued to be tremendously effective at using its strategic communications and lobbying power to mold public debate and the legislation that flowed from it. With the Sane Warning Signal campaign, Klaxon pushed to ensure its market dominance by government decree. Crucially, the company also moved to tie the brand name to the growing trend toward market consolidation and standardization, using an innovative strategic communications campaign wherein it echoed the ongoing push carried out by its lobbyists and lawyers. The "Klaxonized" campaign, which repeated slogans like "A Klaxonized car is a legalized car," was a perfect synthesis of the company's multipronged approach.

Klaxon commissioned William Allen Johnston, who had written on Klaxon's revolutionary graphic ad campaigns for *Printers' Ink,* to write a safety manifesto pamphlet for Klaxon titled *A Vital Problem.*[89] The argument found its way into the pages of *Collier's,* where Johnston made the case for Klaxon technology as the industry standard: "We have made of this vehicle a national institution; an interwoven factor everywhere in our daily activity. . . . This is the situation; and out of it an alternative stands as clear as daylight. If we continue not to take the automobile seriously; if we fail to regulate it as fast as it is being extended, then it follows inevitably that the city battlefield of New York's coroner's clerk will become a national one."[90] The legal problem, Johnston argued, was lack of standardization, a "hodgepodge list—mostly of nonessentials," in which "no two states are at all alike." This chaos had consequences. "The more inadequate the State Law the more each city and village within the state feels itself called upon to pass specific ordinances." Existing laws, unfortunately, were "framed hastily, without regard to uniformity, logic, facts or legality."[91]

Johnston called for a national conference that would bring together engineers, traffic experts, automobile club officials, and elected officials to create standardized laws pertaining both to automobile and pedestrian safety in a sensible way. Germany, he offered, had undertaken a scientific study and proposed standardized laws that had reduced traffic accidents. Why not the United States? Only the enactment and enforcement of standard laws would protect the consumer from the "present chaos in the smaller cities and villages—where such action as is taken is generally due to the whim of the corner policemen. Uniformity of rule and enforcement sounds the keynote." He recognized that the "signal situation" was complicated, but it could be resolved if approached rationally.[92]

Johnston, who hid his financial connection to Klaxon, pushed a line of argument that echoed Klaxon's campaign language. In short, he argued that laws against the klaxon were the product of backward thinking. Moving forward, America needed standardized signal laws to keep pedestrians and drivers safe.

Klaxon's synergistic media and lobbying push continued to yield results. The July 12, 1913, ad in *Automobile Topics* trumpeted the new Connecticut warning signal law prohibiting the bulb horn and announced that the klaxon was now used by more than 200,000 motorists in America.[93] Similar measures directed against bulb horn technology were pending in other states and in twenty-six of the largest cities in the country. Industry standardization was following the Klaxon plan. At the end of 1913, Chattanooga joined the Klaxon train, turning against the "old-style bulb 'honkers.'"[94] The new law required that every automobile "be equipped with a klaxon or other signal sufficient in character and volume to give ample warning to pedestrians and drivers of vehicles."[95] The pressure for manufacturers to make their cars "legal," that is, to install Klaxon technology at the factory, continued to mount.

"How much longer," Klaxon asked in an ad constructed as a "dialogue" between a "Car Agent" and the "Manufacturer," would manufacturers allow their cars to be equipped with "inadequate signals?"[96] This business-to-business pressure on manufacturers and their dealers to equip the cars they sold with Klaxon technology, to "Klaxonize" their products with the standard signal of the industry, became the basis of a new ad campaign that linked the "responsible manufacturer" and Klaxon technology.

Echoing the success of its push toward the juridical normalization of sound, Klaxon began advertising which car brands had been Klaxonized, turning the brand name into a verb connoting standardization and legality. "There is no difference of opinion as to the Standard automobile warning signal," read one ad.[97] "A Klaxonized car is a legalized Car," read another in *Motor Age*. In an era before market consolidation and takeovers resulted in automotive industry concentration, the September 6, 1913, *Automobile Topics* ad boasted that fifty-eight car manufacturers believed that supplying inadequate warning signals was "short-sighted policy" and instead installed Klaxon technology at the factory. The ad warned car buyers to look for the Klaxon nameplate under the hood and, if it was missing, to ask the dealer "for a Klaxon. . . . He will do it rather than lose the sale of the car." In the October 25 serial installment of the ad, fifty-nine companies were cross-promoted for having Klaxonized their cars. These manufacturers paid four to eight times more than they would have for "cheap unknown electric horns" because they were committed to quality. Klaxon was using the benefit of synergy and cross-promotion to advocate that its horn was the "recognized standard" of the industry and of the law.[98] A month later, on the same serial ad page in *Automobile Topics,* the number of Klaxonized cars had increased to sixty-four;[99] by the end of the campaign, over one hundred brands were listed as using Klaxon technology, nearly half the cars manufactured in America. By the end of 1913, Klaxon had become the industry standard, and when automakers ran their own ads, they included mention of their factory-installed klaxons.

The Law Pushes Back

Klaxon's campaign to make its technology the legal and market standard yielded dramatic results, and its factory worked round the clock to keep up with the demand. Yet the increased sales of klaxons also yielded two immediate legal problems: now that it was the industry standard, there was a corollary increase in the number of noise complaints that singled out Klaxon technology, and Klaxon's competitors had grounds for seeking legal relief from its anticompetitive technology trust, claiming the company was monopolizing the market.

In May 1913, shortly after the Chicago city government revised its ordinance law, Alexander J. McGavick, a bishop of Chicago, called for enforcement of the prohibition against the unnecessary usage of the klaxon: "Perhaps we have enough ordinances on the books to cover the unnecessary noises produced by thoughtless and careless owners and drivers of automobiles on our boulevards. If we have, we need a more rigid enforcement of those ordinances. We want the open muffler suppressed at all hours of the day and night: we want the automobile horn used as a warning, and not as a plaything and a nuisance. Ordinances are of no good to a community unless they are enforced."[100] He was not alone in calling for laws to enforce quietness. The Cincinnati Automobile Club published a pamphlet titled *Honk Honk* that denounced "reckless drivers" who never slowed down to comply with safety and relied on their "klaxon horn to give [them] the right of way. . . . Their proper place is behind the bars, where they will not be in danger of hurting themselves and their possible innocent victims." To help remind members to restrict unnecessary usage of their klaxons, the club issued metal plates to club members to attach to the dash with the words "Safety First."[101]

The pushback was not limited to America. By 1912, France had 89,165 automobiles on the road, with a large concentration in and around Paris.[102] The growing presence of the klaxon's roar on city streets and country roads drove a legal and moral debate about what kinds of sounds were reasonable and should be legal. One case involved a touring American in France whose car was equipped with a klaxon so loud that, on hearing it, locals threw rocks at the car. "It appears that French peasants expect from visitors the same politeness that is accorded them, and construe a loud signal on the road as being so impolite as to be insulting and to warrant the retort uncourteous with stray fragments of the roadway." This was, the editor of *Automobile Topics* commented, the "experience of a number of tourists, used to blowing road hogs out of the way by the very volume of sound of their horns." When rural French peasants heard the klaxon, they did not hear the sound of public safety; rather, they heard an impolite demand. "To the French ear, the soft blast of the mild reed horn says 'Please,' while the grate of the electric horn or shriek of the siren is offensively imperative."[103]

A number of French municipalities brought the debate to the bar, and commentators continued the conversation in print. Prince Pierre d'Arenberg, the president of the Federation of Regional Automobile Clubs in France, argued that the choice of signaling device went beyond what was required by ordinances: "Very loud signaling devices, like sirens, klaxons and whistles, should only be used exceptionally on the road unless there a reason to signal the approach of one's car from a long distance away, such as going around a blind corner [*virage masque*] or a crossroads. It should never be used in town."[104] It was more courteous, he argued, to slow down when conditions made it necessary.

Klaxon's European response was to agree with these calls for reserve and provide technology that had both tones, the bulb horn and klaxon, to be used when necessary so as to comply with the law. Again, it was up to the driver using the double horn to know the law and act responsibly. At the end of 1913, the mayor of the town of Calais announced new regulations. First, the law would limit drivers to a maximum speed of 20 km/hr. Drivers were required to slow down, not just sound their horns, at intersections and corners. Cut-out mufflers (*l'échappement libre*) were strictly forbidden. But most important, the ordinance strictly defined the horn (*trompe*) as the reed and bulb French model. "Drivers of automobiles should use only the horn [*trompe*] to warn coaches, cyclists or pedestrians. The usage of all other warning signals [*mode d'avertisseur*] other than the horn (sirens, whistles, rattles, klaxons, etc.) is strictly prohibited. It is illegal to use the horn abusively, especially during the night."[105] Similarly, the town of Châlons-sur-Marne announced laws whereby "only the horn [*trompe*] is authorized in the town as a warning signal, and drivers are forbidden from abusing it, especially at night. The siren, the klaxon and warning signals with several sounds are strictly prohibited."[106] This was a problem Klaxon had to overcome.

Towns around the globe where the klaxon was heard were passing similar laws. It was also clear, as one 1912 case in Canada showed, that merely sounding an "adequate horn" as a safety measure could cause as many problems as it prevented: one Manitoba driver blew his horn at a pedestrian, who was so startled and confused by the horn that he took a step back only to be struck by the car. The judge awarded damages to the pedestrian plaintiff and required drivers to "exercise a more than ordinary degree of care for the safety of pedestrians and to anticipate the possibility of being confronted at any time in such a situation by pedestrians who for the moment lose control of their mental faculties and are overcome by a sudden panic."[107] This was one case among many where courts decided that sounding an adequate horn was not an adequate safety measure.

Just as Klaxon's control over the courts in the area of contract and patent law went through a rise and fall, so too did the company's control over traffic law. Lovell-McConnell may have been in the vanguard of using its lawyers to corner the market, but its competition learned quickly that the courts would be one of the biggest arbiters of success in the burgeoning technology business, and that was where they fought back. One of Klaxon's biggest competi-

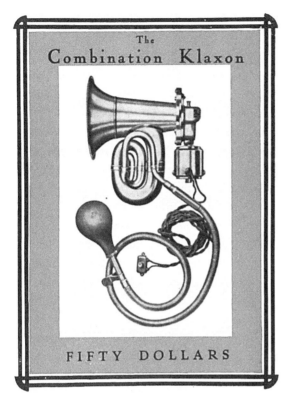

The
Combination Klaxon

FIFTY DOLLARS

Figure 25. The combination bulb and klaxon horn, Klaxon's response to changing ordinance law. From *Motor World,* September 8, 1910. (HathiTrust)

tors in the sound technology market was Newtone, which filed its first countersuit against Klaxon in March 1911.

Klaxon suffered its first major legal setback when the US Supreme Court decided, as of February 1913, that no more preliminary injunctions were to be issued in equity cases involving competing signal technologies. The new ruling, made in accordance with suggestions advanced by the US House and Senate, meant that Lovell-McConnell, as a manufacturer of a patented article, could not obtain temporary relief without being able to show "irreparable loss and damage."[108] In order to enjoin an infringing competitor, it had to establish the damage in advance, meaning it could no longer halt the production of the defendant's product during a protracted trial. *Automobile Topics* reported that this shift was foreshadowed as Lovell-McConnell's last three attempts to obtain preliminary injunction had "failed to succeed" because the company had been unable to prove "irreparable damage."[109] Klaxon could no longer use its massive legal war chest to tie up competitors in court without proof that its patented technology was being infringed on.

After the decision, Klaxon withdrew a request for an injunction against Charles E. Miller for selling the Newtone horn. Since Klaxon had a licensing agreement with Miller that contained the usual claim acknowledging the validity of the Klaxon patent, the company sought an injunction to prevent Miller from selling either signal. Yet, though the Supreme Court decision against temporary injunctions might have taken away one legal technique for controlling the competition, the lawyers merely applied a different business strategy. As part of the settlement, Lovell-McConnell instead purchased all remaining stock in Charles E. Miller. Having gained controlling interest in the company, it sold only Klaxon horns thereafter.

The shifting legal landscape notwithstanding, Klaxon continued to litigate aggressively, suing car manufacturers Jackson, Haynes, and Garland, the maker of Velie and Speedwell brand cars, and their dealers in January 1913 for equipping their cars with a klaxon-style horn—the Sparton, made by Sparks-Withington Company of Michigan—that infringed on its patent.[110] Sparton continued to be a problem for Klaxon, and with the new law in effect, it was harder for the company to use its legal muscle to limit competition through temporary injunctions. Sparks-Withington felt emboldened and announced that it was prepared to defend its dealers in any legal fight.[111] Yet Lovell-McConnell continued filing suits against dealers. It sued Brady-Murray Motors Corporation, in New York, for offering a Chandler motor car equipped with the Sparton, and the Louis Geyler Company, in Chicago, for selling the Hudson motor car equipped with the same horn.[112]

In October 1913, George Cooper Dean, chief counsel for Lovell-McConnell, devised a line of attack to replace the now unavailable tactic of preliminary injunctions. He asked for a fine of $24,100 against Sparks-Withington for falsely marking its horns with the word "patented," an offense that under Section 4901 of the Revised Statues of patent law merited a $100 fine for each separate offense. The suit claimed that Sparks-Withington had "affixed to certain unpatented articles, to wit, automobile horns, a word purporting that the same was patented, to-wit, the word 'patented,' and that said automobile horns were so marked 'patented' for the purpose of deceiving the public." In addition to filing this suit, Dean also sued Sparks-Withington for patent infringement, claiming that the "Sparton Model B, was a clear imitation of the Klaxon and Klaxet."[113]

Klaxon's legal dominance over the klaxon-style signaling technology market may have reached its apogee in 1913, when Newton's two-year appeal of the 1911 patent infringement case was finally decided and set precedent determining the outcome of Lovell-McConnell's suits against Sparks-Withington

Company and Square Horn Manufacturing, along with a myriad of legal cases against jobbers and dealers who handled Newtone horns.

Judge Thomas Chatfield's eighty-six-page ruling against Automobile Supply Manufacturing Company's Newtone and Motophone horns was fascinating as a legal grounding of the phenomenology of sound. It went beyond Judge Lacombe's ruling in the 1911 suit against Ever Ready, which had deemed a "resemblance" in tone to be an attempt to deceive the public. Chatfield also determined that the Newtone horn too closely resembled the Klaxon. Yet mechanism and engineering schematics, the usual determinant in technology patent cases, took on secondary importance. What mattered to Chatfield was the sound:

> Both the complainant's and the defendants' devices. . . . attain a sound of the same tone, power and attraction compelling capacity. . . . This sound can be heard at a great distance. Both parties advertise that the sound can be heard half a mile, a mile or such distance as may be illustrative of the use under description. When further away, the tone of the alarm is more musical, but of sufficient volume and penetration to attract the notice, in spite of other noises and general air vibrations. . . . In so far as this result is a noise or signal, it is impossible to patent the noise itself, but if that noise be produced by a patentable method, there would seem to be no reason why a valid method claim should not be included with the claim for the combination of parts shown in the device. [114]

While Chatfield agreed with Newtone that "the production of a similar noise by another method or unequivalent devices would not be infringement," in the end, he sided with Lovell-McConnell because "the result produced"—the sound—was "evidence of the occurrence of similar physical phenomena. If the instruments producing those phenomena are the same, it is a necessary conclusion that the methods of production are similar."[115] The decision essentially granted legal status to Lovell's long-standing quest for generic brand association with the technology: if the sound produced was the same, the technology infringed on the patent.

The case sent shock waves through the sound technology market. Essentially, as an *Automobile Topics* editor described it, Chatfield's decision declared that "any instrument designed to emit a sound strongly resembling the peculiar harsh noise of the Klaxon horn, might be considered an infringement of the Klaxon patents."[116] Lovell-McConnell's chief litigator, George Cooper Dean, was confident and emboldened, crowing to the trade press, "The decision is sweepingly in favor of the Klaxon patent and sustains us on all points. It holds that all claims in suit are valid and that they cover not only the defendants' Newtone horn, but also the other commercially useful and valuable forms of this kind of signaling apparatus."[117]

Judge Chatfield's decision did not stand long. In their appeal brief, Newtone's attorneys brought the question of design back to the foreground, effectively showing how different technologies might create similar sounds. This time, Lovell-McConnell's lawyers found themselves before a much less sympathetic judge, one who hated their patented sound. He dismissed an interlocutory decree obtained by Lovell-McConnell against Automobile Supply Manufacturing. Citing the language of the Sane Warning Signal campaign, Appeals Court judge Alfred Coxe called for a newer horn that would be effective as a signaling device without frightening the pedestrian. "An ideal horn has certainly not yet been invented."[118] Certainly, Coxe wrote, the klaxon was not it: "The peculiar merit of the Klaxon horn seems to be that it is capable of making a more strident, insistent and insolent noise than any which has preceded it. The sound has been described in this, and previous litigation, as . . . 'villainous.'"[119]

Not that the Newtone product was any less of a blemish on automobiling. The horns of the plaintiff and the defendant, wrote Coxe, were "equal offenders in this regard." But he declared that this equivalence in unwanted sound no longer indicated a patent infringement: "A noise is not patentable. . . . The broad claims in controversy of the Hutchison patent are invalid and . . . the claims which cover specific details, if valid, are not infringed." The appeals court issued a mandate to the district court, reversing Chatfield's decision and ordering Klaxon to pay the legal bill of $3,346.13, though Klaxon was able to get the latter requirement waived.[120] The company filed for an appeal, asking to extend the time of the injunction until that trial, but the request was denied.[121] Klaxon was losing its legal monopoly.

Other companies seized their opportunity. The H. W. Johns-Manville Company, for example, began running ads headlined "Long Horn Not Involved in Any Patent Litigation."[122] It then used Klaxon's legal strategy against Klaxon, suing a Brooklyn dealer for selling Klaxon's hand-operated mechanical horn, which, it claimed, infringed on a Johns-Manville patent.[123] Even as Miller Reese Hutchison, the inventor of the klaxon, patented a new model, redesigned to "improve the tone quality" and "render the sound less harsh," other manufacturers competing with Klaxon turned up their own volume, using the kinds of aggressive tactics in court that Klaxon had perfected against them.[124]

In November 1914, fourteen suits Klaxon had filed against New York dealers for selling Newtone horns were dismissed, and Klaxon was directed to pay the legal costs, including the cost of the appeal.[125] From this point on, Lovell-McConnell's legal control over the signal technology market slipped quickly. The company did score an occasional victory, such as when it successfully sued to have the motor-operated horn exhibited by Heinze Electric Company removed from the New York National Automobile Show of 1915.[126] But these instances were outliers.

In February 1915, as World War I raged in Europe, the legal war between Sparton and Klaxon came to a close. "Sparton Defeats Klaxon in US District Court of Appeals of New York," read a full-page ad for Sparton in *Motor Age*. "Loser must pay costs."[127] Klaxon's legal hold over the market—and the basis for its communications strategy emphasizing the klaxon as the only legal technology—was effectively over. Now when the company appeared in court, it was mostly as a defendant. In 1917 the Federal Trade Commission launched an antitrust investigation and filed a complaint against Lovell-McConnell for violating the Clayton Act. But Klaxon's marketing strategy by this time had long pivoted to something new. Its innovative campaign to command the attention of the signal technology market after the downfall of its legal monopoly is the subject of the next chapter.

5
DANGER SOUND KLAXON!
Localizing the International Brand of the Future

As Lovell-McConnell lost its legal hold on the market for sound signaling and competitors began emulating the company's communication technology, offering similar-sounding devices at cut-rate prices, Klaxon Ltd.—the incorporated marketing company for promoting the brand—was forced to shift its communications strategy. In many ways, the separation of Klaxon's legal campaigns from its advertising campaigns is an organizational artifice of this book, as both were part of an integrated business strategy designed to get Klaxon on as many cars as possible and stifle the competition. Yet with the company's legal control over the production and sale of the now omnipresent technology fading after 1913, competitors like Sparton, Stewart, Monoplex, Newtone, and the Long Horn began to cut into Klaxon's market share. Klaxon had to give consumers a new reason to use its product. It had to reinvigorate the brand, to make it stand for something more than just a piece of technology that produced an annoying sound, if it wanted to command brand loyalty by manufacturers and consumers.

Building on its past success, Klaxon turned to innovative advertising and corporate communications strategies to gain fresh advantage over the competition. This chapter focuses on how Klaxon expanded and reinvigorated its brand as the company pushed for it to become a global generic term for the technology it had innovated, despite having lost its legal monopoly. Klaxon's international strategic communications campaigns in the years leading up to World War I helped the company monopolize the brand associations of its technology in markets around the world. Again, Klaxon heralded the emergence of a new mode of commercial communications, a strategy that business writers since the late 1980s have been calling "glocalization." The company's successful campaign tied its multinational franchises to local concerns, constructing a corporate personality that it connected with local automobile clubs, dealers, and newspapers as it expanded Klaxon's market. Through a number of local campaigns, from infusing its ads with local flavor to the international strategy of hanging cross-promotional Danger! Sound Klaxon signs on dangerous sections of the road, the company linked its imaginary corporate ethos to a "safety first" sense of social responsibility that embraced an automobile-centered future, a message amplified by thousands of loyal consumers sounding their horns.

Blurring the lines between governmental discourse conveyed by road signs and advertising, Klaxon further extended its generic linguistic colonization of the signaling technology market and anchored the brand name as a linguistic icon, used both as a noun and as the root of a verb. Even if the actual sound heard was produced by Newtone's or Long Horn's version of the technology, the public was meant to, and increasingly did, hear "klaxon." Each growl of the horn reminded drivers, passengers, and pedestrians of either the company's commitment to safety and the common good or, as time went on, the ubiquity of the Klaxon sound as a feature of everyday life.

Klaxon and the Creation of the Corporate Soul

Of course, Klaxon was never "global" or heard "round the world" in the literal sense. As with World War I, the transnational event that this chapter builds toward, these terms describe developments that happened primarily in America and Europe yet had an international impact. However, as an ad from 1920 shows—an ad that built on the prewar campaign to internationalize the brand that this chapter chronicles—the company certainly wanted the public to per-

KLAXON
is heard round
the world

The Klaxon speaks a universal language. The Hindoo on the banks of the Sacred Ganges—the mujik on the Russian Steppes— the silk-hatted Britisher on crowded Piccadilly—the hustling New Yorker on little, old Broadway—all recognize and obey its vibrant, clear command.

Figure 26. Illustration of Klaxon's sound heard round the world. From *Automobile Topics*, November 6, 1920. (HathiTrust)

ceive the reach of the brand as global. In late 1912, Klaxon ran a serial ad campaign associating the company with various hypostatized nouns, concepts that people regarded favorably. One of these, titled "Reputation," in support of the company's new Klaxet horn, dramatized Klaxon's international aspirations. "Just what is the reputation behind the Klaxet? Who are its makers—its sponsors?," the ad asked rhetorically.

> In France, in Russian, in China, in Brazil, in New Zealand, in Egypt, in Cape Town, in Hawaii—*everywhere* where the automobile is known—mention of the word "Klaxon" immediately brings to mind a sharp, loud, danger-expressing note of warning. . . . Throughout the world, "KLAXON" is the generally accepted word for automobile warning signal. Just as "KODAK" means "camera," and "GILLETTE" means "razor."[1]

While this generic status was still an aspiration, this speech act declared the strategy that would drive the company forward as it blurred the line between its identity as an international producer of signaling technology and as an innovative communications company, one of the first of its kind, a vanguard in a new era of corporate communications. In other words, in addition to producing its technology, Klaxon began communicating and marketing what Roland Marchand has called the idea of a "corporate soul,"[2] a cluster of personality traits and behaviors inviting consumer identification with the company. F. Hallett Lovell announced that it was time to "start making 'Klaxon' *mean* automobile signal in the same way that 'Kodak' means camera," and for the brand name to connote a company with deep commitments to society and safety.[3]

To achieve this long-desired result, Lovell-McConnell shifted its strategy and looked to expand its market and market share. The company announced that it was increasing its capital stock to $2 million ($1 million preferred at 7 percent and $1 million common) to "provide for necessary expansion."[4] Most important to this push, Klaxon would become a communications company. After having consulted and worked with "nearly every first-class agent in the East," F. Hallett Lovell decided that the company should control and produce its own messaging. "Agency copy," Lovell said, "tends to conform to certain styles of illustration, headlining, display, etc. You can go through the pages of any magazine and name ad after ad as the product of certain agencies just from the general appearance." Because his aim was to "make Klaxon copy so distinctive that it cannot possibly denote anything *but* Klaxon to the man who glances at it from a distance," Lovell started doing all strategic communications in-house and set up a new division of the company, the Klaxon Press.[5]

Though Lovell had been approving all copy for years, and slowly moving all of Klaxon's advertising department in-house, the creation of the Klaxon Press marked a turning point. From 1913 on, the creative design, art, copywriting, and printing would be carried out entirely in the Klaxon factory as part of the production process.[6] It was a tacit acknowledgment of something that has become explicit today: in the world of consumer technology, advertising is as important as the product itself.

The look of Klaxon's new ads was as innovative as the technique. Klaxon Press announced it would use a "new exclusive type face, especially designed for use in Klaxon advertisements."[7] The type, designed by Frederic William Goudy and patented by the company, would be "artistic in appearance." And indeed, as Klaxon pushed to differentiate its devices from those of its competitors, who were producing effectively indistinguishable horns, this synesthetic sensorial strategy was crucial for the associations it created with the brand. With this new look, the Klaxon Press produced regionally specific ads for distribution, ads that would be standardized in terms of aesthetic design yet would speak to local context, an early example of "glocalizing" the international technology trade. Foundational to Klaxon's strategic communications strategy was the company's use of recombinant media:[8] tested copy and graphic content that was tailored and repurposed to appeal to the concerns of local markets. For example, at a time when antinoise legislation in Massachusetts was being considered, the Klaxon Press created an ad for the *Boston Sunday Post* in 1913 that recycled language about the proper way to sound the klaxon—using the short, effective "tiger growl"—that it had first used in 1911 and again in 1912 in national ad campaigns. The message, printed by the Klaxon Press in Klaxon's proprietary font, mentioned both the *Post* and Lester Company, a company that distributed the devices in Boston. It warned klaxon users, "Don't sound your Klaxon needlessly! It is a danger signal—not a toy nor a plaything. It should be used as a warning—not as a noisemaker. . . . In the city—don't blow a long blast where a 'Tiger' is all that is necessary. . . . it will indicate consideration for the safety and comfort of others; it will do much to overcome any prejudice that may exist in the minds of the public."[9] Klaxon had tested all the ideas in this ad before: the toy versus signal debate, and the "tiger growl" from the "Do's & Don'ts" campaign that had run in America and England. The company revived these bits, conveying the ideas of the company's commitment to safety and society and associating them to the local context, using cross-promotion both with the local newspaper that carried its ads and with the local company that distributed its franchised technology.

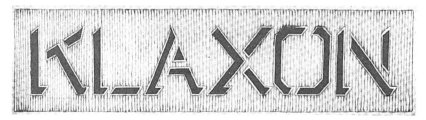

Figure 27. Klaxon type, designed by Goudy and produced in-house by the Klaxon Press. From *Motor World*, September 23, 1914. (Pennsylvania State University Library)

When local demands required messages more connected to specific circumstances, a need that the recombinant media from Klaxon's national print campaigns often could not meet, the Klaxon Press included local flavor or context in the graphic design. In one exemplary ad in the *Indianapolis Star*, rendered completely in the Klaxon font with its signature woodblock icon of the horn in the lower corner, the copy included a street-view photograph of a road curve in Meridian Heights with the caption, "One of many bad curves where you need a good signal."[10] Not only would local readers recognize the bad curve, they also would register that it was a *Star* photographer who had taken the picture, a cross-promotion allowing trust in the local newspaper to rub off on the Klaxon brand.

The company's shift to innovative in-house brand reinvigoration, drawing from and building on its previous success in strategic communications, was especially important now that its technology was no longer one of a kind. Now that consumers could no longer *hear* the difference between the klaxons produced by different companies, they needed to be taught that the idea of the company, more than the technology, was what made Klaxon horns better than the rest.

Selling Branded Sound in America and Europe

In America, Klaxon's biggest challenge was to give consumers and automobile makers who installed signaling technology in the factory a reason to buy its technology instead of like-sounding cheaper horns from rivals such as Newtone and Long Horn. One Klaxon press campaign—an extension of the ongoing "Klaxonized" campaign that listed the manufacturers and published their testimony about why they chose Klaxon—helped enlist consumers to create business-to-business pressure on manufactures by instructing potential buyers of quality cars to look under the hood and check for the Klaxon nameplate, complete with the Klaxon font: "When the car agent says the car is equipped with a Klaxon—be sure it IS a Klaxon." Since the campaign to make the name generic was working, it also meant that even if the dealer *said* the car had a Klaxon, it might not be one. "The car maker who Klaxonizes his cars pays from three to eight times as much for the Klaxon as he would have to pay for an unknown 'electric horn.' He never conceals the Klaxon or the fact that the car is Klaxonized."[11] The logic of distinction, as sociologist Pierre Bourdieu points out, is one of the features of bourgeois identity and economies of linguistic exchange. Klaxon cultivated its expensive brand, pulling its users into a mind-set where their consumption and utilization of technology said something about their refined sensibility. Klaxon wanted consumers to believe that equipping any car with another similar-sounding signal device meant that a carmaker was skimping on safety and quality.

Klaxon cultivated its brand distinction with an "artistic" synesthetic look that allowed it to associate the company with quality and refinement. As company officials continued to associate the proper use of Klaxon technology with behavior that filled the soundspace, they graphically rendered its sound in the illustration space of magazines. In this way, they linked Klaxon's corporate identity with forward-looking pro-safety automobiling. One of the first ads that used this look simply depicted the company brand as a sound following the road above copy reaffirming how the brand name was linguistically identical with "warning signal." By visually depicting a sound with a graphic look that spoke to the refined identity of the brand, Klaxon's ads were both atmospheric and abstractly situational. Indeed, in E. H. Kastor's book *Advertising*, written during World War I, Kastor noted that Klaxon's innovative synesthetic appeal to the senses had previewed the future of advertising. Citing the ad that exemplified this refined Klaxon look, Kastor wrote, "Even the more-subtle appeal to our senses can be represented graphically by the illustrator who can combine a deep knowledge of the psychology for the different senses with a strong constructive imagination. Take, for example, the sense of sound. How can the idea of sound be conveyed to the mind graphically? The simple line illustration . . . indicates how a skillful artist represented the sound of the Klaxon Horn. Could words tell the story more vividly?"[12] The ad mixes a vivid appeal to the senses with a strategic campaign that drew from years of copy used to sell Klaxon's technology and reinforced the perceptual frames associated with it. Having successfully linked its technology and corporate identity to safety and sociality through years of advertising, Klaxon now had merely to allude to these ideas while conveying a soundscape filled with richly designed sound.

Of course, the company had long been associating its branded technology with quality in its commercial copy. What made this new communications strategy significant was the way in which Klaxon refined and recombined ele-

Figure 28. Klaxon urging the generic use of its device's name to mean "warning signal" in a classy-appearing ad. From *Motor World*, September 9, 1914. (Pennsylvania State University Library)

THE WORD FOR WARNING SIGNAL

Figure 29. Standardized ad for the French market. From *Nos Élégances*, October 1911. (Bibliothèque nationale de France)

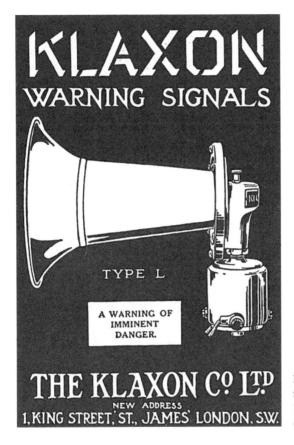

KLAXON

WARNING SIGNALS

TYPE L

A WARNING OF IMMINENT DANGER.

THE KLAXON C.º LT.D
NEW ADDRESS
1, KING STREET, ST. JAMES' LONDON, S.W.

Figure 30. Standardized look for the British market. From *The Autocar*, June 27, 1914. (HathiTrust)

ments it recycled from marketing campaigns in America and "internationalized" its communications strategy by trying to use the same tested ideas and formats abroad. Klaxon had been an international player in the technology market since 1909, yet its ads often showed a great deal of variety in graphics, slogans, and presentation. Not so after 1913, as is apparent in the ads from 1913 to 1914 in the French, British, German, Austrian, and Italian media markets. The company was "Klaxonizing" its look as part of its renewed international push. The standardized brand logo and representation of the horn for ads published in the European media markets were supplemented with slogans like "The Cry of the Auto"—*Le Cri* in French or *Il Grido* in Italian—that had been tested in American media. Though Klaxon allowed some local linguistic variation in the slogan translations, the look of these ads was as similar as the sounds produced by the horns. As Klaxon expanded its international brand into different markets and entered new soundspaces, it took this standardized look along.

Not only were these more basic ads standardized, but more complicated

KLAXON

Klaxonet L

Figure 31. Standardized ad for Berlin Consumers. From *Allgemeine Automobil-Zeitung,* August 8, 1914. (Österreichische Nationalbibliothek)

Jeder vorsichtige Automobilist
benutzt zu seiner und
anderer Sicherheit das

KLAXON

Frankfurt a. M. **The Klaxon** Filiale:
Mainzerlandstr. 175 Berlin SW. 68
Charlottenstr. 7/8

situational advertising also recombined and deployed ideas that Klaxon had developed in the United States. For example, both French and British ads pushed the idea that klaxon technology "clears the road." In both contexts, the ads conveyed similar ideas, but with local details to draw local appeal. In the British version, the picture of a road rendered clear by the user sounding the klaxon—with emphasis on a small child running to the safety of the curb—carried the impact of a thousand words. The figure of a British bobby helped convey the notion of sanctioned public safety practices to the British consumer, associating the utilitarian applications of klaxon technology with the "wand of the magician." The French version featured a variation on the "Cry of the Auto" catchphrase with the new slogan, "Protect the Pedestrian, Clear the Road." Rather than showing the empirical effect, Klaxon employed a perspectival graphic representation of the branded sound kinetically projecting the logo out in advance of the car into visual space. While the British ad represented the empirical effect, the French ad used abstract symbolism to persuade the consumer. Both ads drew on and conveyed the same tested idea—that klaxon sound technology warned the pedestrian and cleared the

KLAXON

Elektrische Huppe

Das wirksamste aller Warnungssignale

„Klaxon"
mit seinem
kräftigen,
katego-
rischen und
momentanen
W a r n r u f
entspricht in
allen Punkten
den Anfor-
derungen auf
der Route.

Unentbehrlich

für jeden Automobilisten, der sich selbst und
die Anderen schützen will.

General-Vertretung:

Brüder Barber

Wien, I. Biberstraße 9.   19

Figure 32. Standardized look for Austrians. From *Allgemeine Automobil-Zeitung,* April 26, 1914. (Österreichische Nationalbibliothek)

KLAXON

IL GRIDO DELL' AUTOMOBILE

Apparecchi dimostrativi funzionano
presso i Rappresentanti Esclusivi :   **BIELLA & C.**
Cataloghi e Preventivi a richiesta   **- MILANO -**   Via Monforte, 19 - Telefono 95-90

Figure 33. Variation on a standard theme for the Italian consumer. From *Rivista mensile del touring club ciclistico* 20:1, 1914. (Archive.org)

road, allowing for safety without a reduction in speed—but deployed pragmatic variations tailored to the local linguistic and cultural context.

The company likewise employed this localized communications strategy in its marketing of the hand klaxon, a version of the sound device that allowed the klaxon to be used on any car, truck, or motorcycle, no matter the electrical

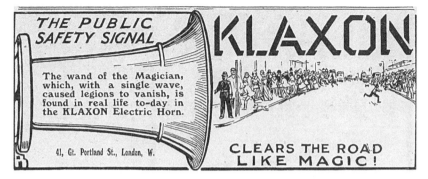

Figure 34. Klaxon's "Public Safety Signal" campaign ad created for a local context and emphasizing pedestrian safety. From *The Motor*, July 29, 1913. (Pennsylvania State University Library)

Figure 35. Another Klaxon ad created for a local context and emphasizing pedestrian safety. From *La Publicité*, April 1911. (Bibliothèque nationale de France)

system or lack thereof. Wherever the horn was introduced, the product was always accompanied by advertorials and native advertisements in the local trade and automobile lifestyle periodicals. For example, the company pushed the hand klaxon as *le klaxon mécanique* in the French market to integrate the brand into the French collective sense of perception or *sensis communis*. As part of its effort to associate the branded sound with known marks of distinction, and to push sales of *le klaxon mécanique* for cars without alternators and batteries, Klaxon-Blériot applied Klaxon's standard formula for sonic branding.

Just as the company had even been able to associate its sound in America with the Indianapolis 500, it provided all cars in the 1911 French Light Car Race with a klaxon and offered additional prizes to winners who used them.[13] Klaxon continued to sponsor racing events, associating the technology with winning French drivers and providing its *avertisseur* technology to celebrities and dignitaries. Each time racers or celebrities sounded their horns, the technology and the brand were linked to these local figures and events in the *sensis communis*.

Indeed, Klaxon had already effectively localized its sonic brand in 1910 by associating the technology in France with Blériot, the company founded by a celebrated hero of modern aviation and engineering, Louis Blériot. In 1913, Klaxon pulled off another advertising coup by getting its horn on Raymond Poincairé's presidential vehicle. The company flooded the media with stories about it, like the one in *Le Temps:* "The car with which he makes the voyage to Limousine, earning him the title of 'first tourist of France,' contains the Klaxon mécanique Blériot. The chief of state knows exactly how to work the Klaxon: 'One turn of the crank and there you go!'" (*Un tour de manivelle . . . et l'on passe!*)[14] Putting this slogan—a phrase that appeared in promotional articles for the device in *Le Petit Parisian, Le Temps, La Presse, Le Figaro,* the socialist weekly *L'Attaque,* and dozens of other newspapers—into the president's mouth showed how effectively Klaxon was able to simultaneously standardize its message and associate it with important local issues or figures.

Along with linking its technology with the head of government, Klaxon-Blériot also reached deals with the organizers of France's most prestigious bicycling race, the Tour de France. As a paid native advertisement placed in *Le Temps* indicated, under the title "The only truly practical automobile warning device [*avertisseur*]," drivers of Tour cars would all be using the Klaxon because it effectively cleared the road. Consumers looking for a gift for themselves and others to enjoy in the spring should take note. "Easter is coming," read the copy. "Drive your cars quickly and joyfully on nice days without worrying about accidents, for the Blériot *klaxon mécanique* always saves time." Echoing American ad copy, the ad for French media markets boasted "It sweeps the road clear [*balayé*]."[15] As there was less graphic advertising in French newspapers than in America, Klaxon paid to run virtually identical ad copy, inserted as what advertising scholars would call an "advertorial"—an advertisement that is designed to be mistaken for an editorial from the reader's trusted paper—in *Le Temps, Figaro, Le Galois, Le Petit Parisien, L'Attaque, Le Matin, Le Vie Automobile, Le Sport Universal Illustré,* and other outlets to push the "*petit hand klaxon.*"

As it had in France, Klaxon also pushed the hand klaxon in England using similar localized communication strategies. One editorialist in *The Autocar* plugged the horn in his column "Light Car Talk": "We all agree in denouncing the use of reverberant and strident alarms on the public roads. But in practice, we realize that there are such road dangers as blind corners . . . so we feel the need of a really penetrating alarm. I plead guilty to being a Klaxon enthusiast—a super-efficient *road clearer*." While his "aesthetic soul," as he put it to connect with his faithful readers, preferred "the melody of the nightingale whistle," such technology was not as effective and often broke down. Yet the electrical system needed to run a klaxon, with an "accumulator the size of a small suitcase," made it ineffective for many British cars. "I have just made the acquaintance of the Blériot hand Klaxon, and I can see we are going to be bosom friends." While unable to "give a prolonged blast with it as you can with its electrical cousins; it is reliable and has the true Klaxon shriek."[16] Klaxon in London, as it did with Blériot in France, assembled the signaling devices in England with diaphragms manufactured in Lovell-McConnell's home factory in Newark, New Jersey. Both French- and British-made models were promoted with ads that adopted the same Klaxon look and language. As the advertisement placed in *The Autocar* in December 1914 showed, Klaxon London offered both the Blériot Klaxon hand crank manufactured in England and the push-lever mechanism manufactured in America—along with the electric horn—so that drivers of any kind of car could fit it on their vehicle.[17]

Though Klaxon had already successfully pushed to have klaxons installed at the factory of many major car manufacturers in America, launching and promoting the hand klaxon also allowed the company to increase its US market share. Though this version of the technology lacked the push-button immediacy, the mechanical horn opened up a new market for klaxons for users whose cars, trucks, and motorcycles lacked the proper electrical setup. Most important, the availability of the hand klaxon made it possible for Ford owners to use it. No matter what country, this was a coup, as Ford, previously absent from the list of Klaxonized car manufacturers that equipped cars with the horn at the factory, was the largest producer of automobiles worldwide. Klaxon directed an ad to dealers in *Motor Age* titled "The Hand Klaxon for the Ford." As Fords often had bulb horns or "cheap buzzers," Klaxon reused the language of its adequate horn campaign and proposed in its business-to-business advertising that "one should be on every Ford you sell."[18] The hand klaxon, declared one cleverly constructed full-page ad in *Motor Age* that warned consumers about using horns that claimed to be "just as good," had incomparable "warnability."[19]

Another sales technique designed to localize the commercial soundscape instructed Klaxon dealers to "Put Hand Klaxons on the Taxi-cabs in your towns on 30 days' trial."[20] Not only would this hook taxi drivers but, since taxi patrons trusted them to get where they were going safely, it would help solidify the

YOU have a right to demand that automobiles carry *adequate* warning signals

The KLAXON
"The Public Safety Signal"

YOU want to know when an automobile is coming. You want to know in time to get out of the way.

When a motorist doesn't warn you of his approach, he has failed to do his duty to you and to public safety.

THE Klaxon is the safety signal. You always hear it. You always hear it in time. No matter how preoccupied you may be you always hear it. And its sound conveys to you an expression of danger. It is a true warning, abrupt, penetrating, purposely unpleasant.

No mother need worry
—if the motorist uses a Klaxon

CHILDREN hear the Klaxon's sharp blast—no matter how absorbed they are in their play. They can't mistake its sound for any other sound in the street. Instinctively they run to safety.

STOCKED in Australia by the following—Sydney: Bennett & Wood Ltd. Melbourne: Bennett, Wood Roche Pty., Ltd. Perth: Armstrong Cycle & Motor Agency Melbourne: Duncan & Co. Pty., Ltd. Launceston: Sim King. Adelaide: Murray Aunger. Brisbane: E. G. Eager & Son, Ltd.

KLAXON
"The Public Safety Signal"

Manufactured by
LOVELL-McCONNELL
MFG. COMPANY
Export Office : 47 Broadway,
New York, U.S.A.
Factory: Newark, N. J.

Figure 36. Klaxon's "Public Safety Signal" campaign ad combining elements from past successful ads. Such ads helped open up foreign markets, in this case Australia. From *The Bulletin*, January 8, 1914. (Pennsylvania State University Library)

brand associations each time a taxi sounded its horn. No matter where, hand klaxons could always be used, and local users could help them promote it.

The campaign to promote its hand-operated horns using the same recombinant strategic language, graphic style, and color in domestic and international markets, all localized to ring true, was a smashing success. The company was now advertising in Australia, recycling elements of its American media campaigns for a 1914 ad in *The Bulletin;* copy and graphic elements from the "No Mother Need Worry" ad and language from the "Adequate Signal" and "Public Safety Signal" campaigns were recombined in the same ad to help command the attention of an expanding market.[21] Back in America, Lovell-McConnell factories were operating twenty-four hours a day in May 1914 to keep up with orders accumulating from around the globe for the company's growing line of products, including more than 26,000 of its hand-operated horns.[22]

Thanks to the international success of Klaxon's marketing campaigns, there were over a million klaxons on the road worldwide. The sound of klaxon technology was becoming a constant feature of everyday life wherever the automobile was used, a social fact that, though profitable, presented a challenge for the company. For despite the constant barrage of ads associating its sound with safety, efficacy, and speed, the company could control neither how drivers used the technology nor how those who heard it made sense of it. Cultural critics from editorialists to poets heard abuse of the increasingly ubiquitous klaxon sound as a sign that something was askew with the social contract, as if people in the streets were rudely screaming at one another. "The Horn of Impatience," a poem by Edward A. Guest that first appeared in the *Detroit Free Press* in September 1913 before being reprinted nationally, framed the klaxon's communicative act as a kind of swearing, a sign of the impatient and intemperate comportment of those who used it.

> For blocks, around the neighbors know
>   when Pa and Ma are going out,
> An' just how long Ma takes to dress
>   they know each time beyond a doubt:
> An' how impatient Pa can be they
>   know, every night an' morn
> He goes an' gets the car an' then he
>   calls her on the Klaxon horn.
>
> At first he signals "Here I am," an
>   sits a while in peace, an' then
> He presses that old buzzer down an'
>   signals "Here I am" again.
> An' then Ma yells to one of us "For
>   goodness sake, he'll wake the town,
> Go tell him, please, to stop that noise
>   for in "a minute I'll be down."
>
> Pa sits a little longer there in silence,
>   then his fingers slip
> To where the Klaxon button is, an'
>   gives the horn an awful zip;
> There never was a "Hurry up" said
>   plainer in the world than that,
> An' Ma says: "Listen to that man!
>   Here, one of you, hand me my hat!"

By this time Pa is mad all through, as
  even passers-by can tell,
An' now the horn goes "Grr! Grr!
  Grr!" a sign of Pa's impatient spell,
An' things he'd never say in speech an'
  words that he has never sworn
He hurls at Ma when he gets sore, by
  tooting on that Klaxon horn.

Pa couldn't rile Ma quite so much the
  times these short delays occur
If he should come right out an' say the
  things she knows he toots at her.
She says she's sure that it would rile
  the sweetest woman ever born
To have a man outside the door
  A-swearing at her through a horn.[23]

If the klaxon, like other media technology, extended and amplified the senses and sensibilities, klaxon push-button technology afforded easy communication by way of impatient and demanding imperatives. As the klaxon became more generic, by the company's design, this was increasingly not a laughing matter; antiklaxon sentiment continued to grow. "From the moment you are bitten by the great Klaxon horned Gasoline Bug," wrote humorist Otis F. Wood, "the motor-car takes precedence of everything else—home ties, duty, the hope of a future life, all are forgotten for the time being."[24] The net result of cultural Klaxonization was ever more noise.

As antiklaxon sentiment grew, public debates about how technology changed those who used it became international as well. In Britain, complaints about noisy klaxons and their users referenced their impatience, insistence, and rudeness, a mode of comportment that aggravated unwitting auditors. The London *Times* framed the ongoing attempt by Parliament to create a "street noises bill" as a reaction to complaints about the klaxon: "The problem of the insistent motor horn presents two main aspects. In the first place, the question arises whether the type of warning apparatus should be standardized and fixed by law in order to eliminate the more blatant form of signaling. . . . There is consensus of opinion among motorists that at present the horn is too frequently used."[25] Though the klaxon was indeed effective at communicating in noisy traffic, the technology afforded aggression, a feedback-loop behavior audible throughout the soundscape. A noisy Hobbesian society of all shrieking against all without a legal Leviathan to control it made the end result almost worse than the safety problems the technology was designed to help solve.

Seeking to get out in front of and diffuse this negative media frame in its expanding international markets, the Klaxon Press went back to work, flooding print media with positive synesthetic graphics and copy. It sought to revive the idea that not only was Klaxon a brand that cared but that klaxon users, too, had a sense of social responsibility and wanted the technology to be used correctly. In the words of loyal klaxon user F. A. Sears of Rome, New York, whose essay on the proper use of the klaxon won a 1913 essay contest and was reprinted as an advertorial in *Motor Age,* attracting attention in the wrong way by abusing the technology defeated the purpose of signaling altogether. In a future dominated by the automobile, he said, "every citizen should bear in mind traffic ordinances . . . and the rights of others."[26] If Klaxon was to make its brand a sign of an automobile-centered future rendered more manageable by better sound signaling technology, it had first to convince consumers and the public that when they bought a klaxon, they were signaling their embrace of that future.

Advertising a Dynamic Technologized Future

In Klaxon's strategic communications, the company's constructed corporate identity was increasingly tied to the notion of technological progress, selling an idea of a future-oriented lifestyle associated with the brand. There is an uncanny similarity between Klaxon's techno-utopic messaging and the vision projected by the European avant-garde, which was fascinated by the speedy, soaring future it saw previewed in American urban modernity.[27] No advertisement created by the Klaxon Press exemplifies this resemblance—and the company's movement away from standard advertising techniques emphasizing technology, function, and price and toward an association with abstract ideas—as well as its marvelous print ad, "The Klaxon at Herald Square, New York." Klaxon's admen had already created a realistic situational ad featuring the space of Herald Square that ran in the *Saturday Evening Post* in 1910.[28] This time, the multimedia lithographic communiqué represented the synesthetic idea of the klaxon sound in relation to other sounds in the city via a painting by the "celebrated French Futurist François Souaie." The picture blurred the distinction between commercial graphic art and high art to convey a notion of symbolic refinement while associating the brand with the avant-garde sense of temporality tied to the Futurists. As the text that accompanied the image in

The Graphic Arts—declared the advertisement of the month—stated, "Advertisers were not slow to see in futurist and cubist art a novelty which offered a new class of commercial illustration. . . . It remained for the manufacturers of the Klaxon warning signals to see in these odd creations a possibility of serious adaptation."[29]

According to the copy, likely an advertorial to draw attention to the ad, the Klaxon Press commissioned Souaie, whom it promoted as "one of the leaders of the futurist school," to create a symbolic expression of "how the Klaxon note might 'look.' . . . His production, like those of his associates, will undoubtedly mystify and offend adherents of the accepted standards in art." Klaxon ran the image in the *Saturday Evening Post, The American Theosophist* and *The Pacific Printer* in black-and-white two-tone. It ran full-color reproductions in *Motor World Wholesale, Motor Age, Automobile Topics,* and *The Graphic Arts.* It also used Dacro, a lithographic process that it did in-house, to generate smaller poster versions that the company sent out to jobbers and dealers so they could distribute them to customers, and printed out postcard-size versions that it mailed directly to klaxon owners to display at home. Whether or not François Souaie, the "celebrated French Futurist," actually existed or was a creation of the Klaxon art department is unknown, though the latter is more likely. The name Souaie means "silkworm," so the tag is like saying "smooth as silk Frenchy." But the idea of an artful ruse tinged with the spirit of commerce would, in fact, be quite appropriate for a Futurist, in light of the history of the movement, its ethos, and its aims.

Futurism began as an Italian art movement but never quite caught on in France, where Cubism and Dadaism held sway. Yet Klaxon, through its regional managers in France, England, and Italy, would probably have been aware of Futurism. Moreover, employees at the Klaxon Press would likely have known how their mission to reframe sound perception, embracing mechanical noise in the name of utilitarian progress, was similar to that of the Futurists. Filippo Marinetti's *Manifesto of Futurism,* published in 1909, expressed open scorn of accepted aesthetic values and promoted the use of speed, electricity, and aggressive noisy expression to cut through the conventions of art and to free aesthetics from the burden of history. Klaxon's admen would have agreed with Marinetti's praise and promotion of the "beauty of speed," the "roaring car," and "the man who holds the steering wheel." These were precisely the same values expressed in their advertisements. "We shall sing," wrote Marinetti, "the great crowds tossed about by work, by pleasure, or revolt; the many-colored and polyphonic surf of revolutions in modern capitals; the nocturnal vibration of the arsenals and the yards under their violent

Figure 37. A classy, futuristic-appearing ad for Klaxon's discerning clientele. From *The Graphic Arts,* August 1913. (Library of Congress)

THE KLAXON AT HERALD SQUARE, NEW YORK
By the celebrated French Futurist, FRANCOIS SOUAIE

AMONG the heavier background lines may be found the clang of trolley-gongs, the rumble of elevated trains, the chugging of waiting motors, the grinding of taxicab brakes, the shouts of van drivers, the voices of newsboys, the gong of a passing ambulance.   CLOSER scrutiny reveals the fainter sounds—the shrill whistles of traffic police, the hum of human voices, the shuffling feet of pedestrians, the nagging, monotonous "honk" of the bulb horn. ABOVE THEM ALL, sharp and penetrating, the note of the Klaxon.

electrical moons."[30] This bears striking similarities to the multisensory world that Klaxon evoked in its copy, a soundscape that made its violent sound technology a necessity.

After releasing the 1909 manifesto, the Futurists staged a 1912 touring exhibit in Paris, London, Brussels, Berlin, and other cities of capital importance to Klaxon's international business. This exhibit very likely may have inspired the ad "The Klaxon at Herald Square." Featuring the work of painters Gino Severini, Umberto Boccioni, Carlo Carrà, and Luigi Russolo, the exhibit took on the personality of its manager, Marinetti, who has been described as "part impresario, part trickster and master of publicity."[31] The exhibit, like Klaxon's graphic ad, was conceptual art presented with an eye toward sales; just as the Klaxon Press did, Marinetti localized the show in relation to the context of each city to gain maximum exposure and commercial appeal.[32] Indeed, the exhibit made so much money in London selling tickets and catalogues filled with reproductions of the paintings that the exhibitors delayed sending it on to Berlin. Two of the artists in particular, Umberto Boccioni and Luigi Russolo, shared Marinetti's fascination with sound and made their synesthetic aesthetic central to their visual work.

The similarities between the "The Klaxon at Herald Square" and sound-centered Futurist paintings like Boccioni's *The Street Enters the House* (1911) and Russolo's *Dynamism of the Car* (1912) are striking. All three show a synesthetic rush of dynamic sound and speed, blurring and blending before the viewing subject, symbolized by swirling geometric movement and contrasting color tones. Though it is unclear how much Russolo's sound-inspired work was part of the exhibit, the similarity between the ideas expressed in his manifesto *The Art of Noise* (1913)—made manifest in the "noise machine" or "intonionum"[33] he built in Milan that year—and the text of the "Klaxon at Herald Square" ad is inescapable.

Russolo's manifesto declared, "Today noise reigns supreme over human sensibility . . . we are approaching noise-sound. . . . In the pounding atmosphere of great cities as well as in the formerly silent countryside, machines create today such a large number of varied noises that pure sound with its littleness and its monotony, now fails to arouse any emotion."[34] Just as Klaxon had long promoted the idea that bulb horns (the old sound) failed to cut through the street noise to arouse the senses of the driver or pedestrian, Russolo offered that "pure sound" (conventional music) led to boredom. Just as only the Klaxon could "clear the road," for Russolo, only "noise-sound" inspired emotion:

> This is why we get infinitely more pleasure imagining combinations of the sounds of trolleys, autos and other vehicles, and loud crowds, than listening once more, for instance, to the heroic or pastoral symphonies. . . . Let's walk together through a great modern capital, with the ear more attentive than the eye, and we will vary the pleasures of our sensibilities by distinguishing among the gurglings of water, air and gas inside metallic pipes, the rumblings and rattlings of engines breathing with obvious animal spirits, the rising and falling of pistons, the stridency of mechanical saws, the loud jumping of trolleys on their rails, the snapping of whips, the whipping of flags.[35]

The text that ran at the bottom of the "Klaxon at Herald Square" ad echoed Russolo's sonic sensibility. Klaxon's advertising department helped the readers see in the thicker lines the "clang of the trolley-gongs, the rumble of elevated trains, the chugging of waiting motors, the grinding of taxicab brakes, the shout of van drivers, the voices of newsboys, the gong of a passing ambulance." In the faint lines, floating in and out of the viewer's line of sight, readers were directed to see and imagine "the shrill whistles of traffic police, the hum of human voices, the shuffling feet of pedestrians, the nagging monotonous 'honk' of the bulb horn. ABOVE THEM ALL," the text concludes, "sharp and penetrating, is the note of the Klaxon."[36]

Klaxon was to the soundscape what Russolo's noise-sound was to culture: a loud but necessary blast that cut through the humdrum of everyday life and electrified the affective sensibility of the listener. In both cases, the form—the noise-sound—was necessary to achieve the desired function: to shock those who heard it out of their distracted state of complacency and connect them to the immediate present. Like the Futurists, Klaxon saw its technology, its noise-sound, as a necessity in a noisy technologized culture.

Not only did the Futurists and Klaxon manifest a similar future-oriented belief system, they also shared a mentality that linked aesthetics and ideas to commercialism. The spirit of the Futurist movement, its attention-grabbing embrace of commerce and publicity, was analogous to what Klaxon admen conveyed to promote their brand. While the Futurists' avant-garde aesthetics was meant to drive culture and cure it from its inattention to the ethos of the technological age, Klaxon was at the vanguard of corporate communications, seeking to generate a complicated public-facing corporate image or "corporate soul" that would help realize a better future. Moreover, by linking its brand to the high art of Futurism, Klaxon associated itself with what Pierre Bourdieu has referred to as "cultural capital."[37] In this way, Klaxon's corporate identity came to be tied to much more than the idea of safety, though this idea continued to be the central pillar of its commercial communication. Klaxon Press's artistic creation, loaded with cultural capital, connected the brand to a vanguard art world that shared hope for a better-engineered future, promising, above all, to make life better through better technology.

Signs and Safety First

Since automobiles entered the cultural sphere around the turn of the century, automobile clubs all over the world had been doing what they could to zealously promote automobile culture.[38] As the number of automobiles grew, traffic fatalities continued to mount, and automobile associations increasingly turned to work that promoted safety. One common undertaking along these lines was sign work: posting signage that either indicated dangerous road conditions or provided directions for drivers unfamiliar with local roads. In 1909, for example, the Bureau of Tours in Washington, DC, invited automobile club members to help post Danger and Blow Horn signs throughout the city. Similar work was done by local automobile associations throughout the United States. Sometimes, as was the case in Philadelphia, the Automobile Club of Delaware County put up "Blow Your Horn" signs to warn drivers as they approached traps where police were known to enforce compulsory sounding laws.[39]

By 1914, posting signs to promote driver caution and safety had become a standard activity of automobile clubs and organizations. The Cleveland Automobile Club, in one ambitious campaign, erected two thousand danger and direction signs in northern Ohio in 1914 alone. The signs featured a red circle in which the words "SAFETY" on the top and "FIRST" on the bottom sandwiched the word "DANGER".[40] The Automobile Club of Southern California also spent time posting signs that year warning drivers of upcoming "Dangerous Curve," "Caution—Steep Grade," and "Slow—Dangerous Summit," as well as signs related to sound that referenced antinoise campaigns, such as "Hospital—Quiet."[41]

Klaxon moved quickly to exploit these associational campaigns. Its "Safety First" campaign began in June 1913 and tapped into this movement with an innovative strategy that linked together all aspects of its communications factory: a localized advertising campaign that integrated public relations, sales, cross-promotional connections, and synesthetic graphic print advertisement. Most important, the company turned users and automobile associations into brand ambassadors. "Automobile clubs in a number of cities are now being supplied with special danger signs for road postings," *Automobile Topics* announced. The wooden tin-faced signs, reading "DANGER SOUND KLAXON," were printed at the Lovell-McConnell plant and distributed free of charge to any organization—commercial, civic, or state related—that was willing to enter into cross-promotional synergy. Tying the national campaign to the local context, the names of these organizations were then printed at the top of each sign, touting the civic responsibility of the local group and tacitly linking its identity to Klaxon's brand.

Klaxon chose the *Saturday Evening Post,* the most prestigious and expensive print periodical for automobile-related advertising (full-page ads in 1914 cost advertisers on average about $20,000[42]), to serve as the national platform for its localized ad campaign. Rendered in its expensive-looking font, the ad created by the Klaxon Press harked back to the company's earlier ads showing dangerous turns. However, in this ad, instead of the graphic sound wave "KLAXON" tracing the line of the curve, the only text was in the sign that would be spread all over North America as a reminder to all drivers of their duty when faced with a dangerous stretch of road. The sound was implied and understood through the now iconic and indexical generic noun describing the technology. The campaign to post these signs provided great press at

Figure 38. Danger Sound Klaxon signage as the focus of an ad used in a national campaign. From the *Saturday Evening Post*, March 8, 1913. (*Saturday Evening Post* Archive)

the national and local level for the company and for local automobile associations and newspapers that were involved.

For example, the Fort Wayne Commercial Club touted Klaxon's corporate responsibility in the *Sentinel*, running a press release type of story in May 1914 that announced the *Sentinel*'s and Klaxon's joint initiative to "cut down smash-ups" and reduce the number of wrecks in Allen County, where there had been "at least a dozen automobile wrecks" the previous summer. They would by do this by placing more than a hundred Klaxon signs "in appropriate places on approaches to dangerous points."[43] Similar reports of sixty-nine signs being posted by the Davenport Auto Club in Iowa appeared at the same time.[44]

Each time signs were posted by the groups that shared the credit, Klaxon hired photographers from local newspapers to document them. These images were then integrated into local and national publications, either as ads or in native stories with illustrations, to amplify the message and create demand for more signs. For example, such an ad, complete with the boilerplate copy and photographs of the Klaxon horn together with the name of the local organization, ran in the *Daily Kennebec Journal* on May 26, 1914. Next to the standard copy was a photograph of a "Danger Sound Klaxon" sign at a "dangerous curve turning off Western Avenue onto Mt. Vernon Road, 2 miles from Water Street in Augusta," taken by the *Journal*'s photographer.[45]

As the campaign spread, *Printers' Ink,* the trade journal for the advertising industry, once again trumpeted Klaxon's avant-garde approach to advertising. "A unique feature of the campaign is the 'localization' of the part of the copy, and the selection of the newspapers which are to carry the advertising according to their willingness to aid the company in securing local flavor in the copy." Klaxon's letter to newspapers explicitly stated, "We are planning to use but one newspaper in each town and will base our selection upon the paper's willingness to cooperate with us in the matter of service. We will need half a dozen photographs of dangerous curves in your locality at which our 'Danger Sound Klaxon' signs have been placed."[46] Each letter specified the number of newspapers being offered this opportunity (sixty-four in the New England region) and a deadline. "The object of our campaign is to bring out the connection of the Klaxon with local road conditions and danger points. We believe the novelty and effectiveness of this will be readily apparent to you."[47] Whoever provided the content received the cross-promotion and/or the ad revenue.

Supplemental to the localized advertising, the Klaxon Press printed booklets listing the clubs and organizations in thirty-five states that had worked to post Klaxon's signs, along with many photographs of these signs in place.[48] It even ran collections of photographs from different newspapers in a national *Motor* advertorial that hit all the notes in Klaxon's marketing literature. The "Safety First" campaign effectively integrated different media platforms and created incentives for all those involved to amplify the promotion.

Klaxon, a national and increasingly international company, amplified its efforts through local production that tailored its message to the local context and turned stakeholders into amplifiers. In July 1914, one month after a story in the *San Diego Union* announced that the city council had sanctioned the posting of Klaxon's signs at dangerous corners and that the gas companies, telephone companies, and San Diego Electric Railroad companies had allowed the signs to be posted on their poles,[49] a "Danger—Sound Klaxon" ad appeared in the *San Diego Union.* "When you see the Red Warning Sign— think of Auto Tire Company. . . . We put them up."[50] This type of coverage reinforced associations with the idea of social responsibility and concern for safety at the local level, right as Klaxon further solidified its generic status as an international brand.

Moreover, photographs of these signs at dangerous curves taken by local photographers became content for national advertising as well, creating a

Figure 39. National advertorial story showing the media synergies of the localized campaigns, with Klaxon-made signs posted by local clubs and photographs taken by local newspaper photographers. Photomontage from *The Motor,* March 1914. (Pennsylvania State University Library)

feedback loop that helped reinforce the connection between a now international technology brand and its concern for its local users. The company knew that loyal users were its best brand ambassadors and worked hard to integrate them into the local media campaigns. In northern Minnesota, where roads followed the curves of lakes and crisscrossed forests, the *Bemidji Daily Pioneer* announced that the Bemidji Auto Club was planning to post "Danger Sound Klaxon" road signs, and asked its readers for help. "The request is made that persons who know of dangerous corners or points in any of the roads of this vicinity call at the *Pioneer* for a sign and place it where it will be of value to drivers who are not familiar with conditions."[51] Each time they posted a sign or pushed their horn button, klaxon users would be promoting safety, the Klaxon, the *Daily Pioneer,* and the Bemidji Auto Club, whose name was printed on the signs.

In August, the Illinois State Highway Department dramatized how effectively the Lovell-McConnell sales managers had linked the company's "Safety First" campaign to the governmental concerns of the state, providing details of Klaxon's campaign in its official monthly publication. In light of the per-

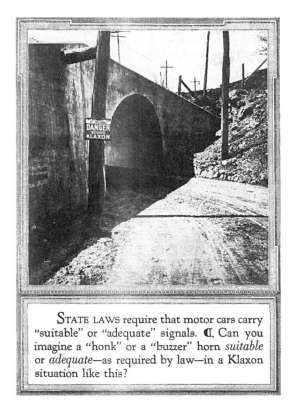

STATE LAWS require that motor cars carry "suitable" or "adequate" signals. ℂ Can you imagine a "honk" or a "buzzer" horn *suitable* or *adequate*—as required by law—in a Klaxon situation like this?

Figure 40. Ad from one of Klaxon's national print campaigns based on the localizing strategy developed for smaller, regional markets. From *Motor Age*, July 9, 1914. (Pennsylvania State University Library)

sistent problem and the efforts of road officials to warn the public of danger, local automobile clubs and associations through Illinois were officially directed to contact Lovell-McConnell since the company was "furnishing to automobile clubs, good roads associations, etc, without any charges warning signs to be erected at dangerous points along the roads. . . . The background is red, and in white letters appears the words 'DANGER-SOUND KLAXON.' Space is provided at the top for the name of the organization erecting the signs which is filled in by the Lovell-McConnell Company."[52] A similar link between Klaxon and government agencies was created when the company sent fifty tin-faced "Danger Sound Klaxon" signs to the county engineer of Fairfield, Iowa, to be placed at dangerous curves.[53]

All over the country, Klaxon's campaign effectively closed the local feedback loop of sounds, associations, and brands, erecting over 12,000 signs in thirty-five states in 1914 alone. Each time a region was blanketed with signs prompting the spread of the branded sound, local ads—like the one for W. H Young suppliers that ran in the *Oil City Derrick* in May and June of 1914—amplified the now state-sanctified imperative, helping to solidify the

Figure 41. Still extant road sign from one of Klaxon's local campaigns. (Courtesy of iCollector.com)

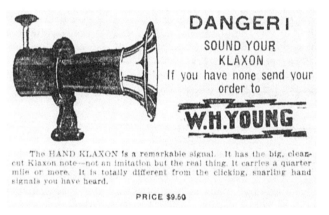

Figure 42. Local newspaper ads like this one helped reinforce the synergies of the national multimedia campaign. From *The Oil City Derrick*, May 22, 1914. (Pennsylvania State University Library)

generic term and reinvigorate the Klaxon brand. Reminding others to use their car horn in a dangerous situation, to be conscientious and safe, was quickly being recoded as the generic imperative "Sound Klaxon," which reiterated the ideas the Klaxon Press wanted to express about the corporate soul of the company.

Of course, not all media mentions of the "Safety First" campaign were laudatory. There was, in fact, significant pushback to this quasi-governmentalized corporate control of traffic signage. In Massachusetts, for example, the legislature banned the signs in May 1914 after the Massachusetts Highway Commission decided that the signs were "just plain advertising. . . . Because the word 'Klaxon' appears, instead of horn, the commission holds that the signs are in violation of the law, which says advertising matter shall not be placed on the public highway."[54] Another problem arose in Pittsburgh, where the local automobile club complained that signs there were being used by police to trap and fine drivers who failed to do so, as ordinance law gave police the right to fine drivers $500 for "failure to blow your horn."[55]

Complaints about the growing ubiquity of the "Danger Sound Klaxon" signs were not limited to the self-serving commercialism they signified. People grumbled about how they taught motorists to drive. In *The Arrow*, the newspaper of Rolfe and Pocahontas Counties in Iowa, one writer lamented that the signs fooled drivers into thinking that safety was conferred merely by sounding their horns. What drivers needed to do when approaching a dangerous curve, like the one just south of Mrs. Fae McEwan's residence, where a "Danger Sound Klaxon" sign was already posted, was to slow down and keep to the right.[56] These objections notwithstanding, with the flavor and energy that local distributors and consumers added to the "Safety First" campaign, it remained incredibly effective at amplifying the abstract corporate identity Klaxon wanted to communicate. When M. H. McCormick, an automobile mechanic in Colorado Springs, created an electric safety system that automatically sounded a klaxon mounted at the top of the entrance next to a "Sound Klaxon" sign every time a car entered or exited the garage, local and national journalists let the public know.[57]

Indeed, the regional tailoring of the message was so effective that Lovell-McConnell announced a restructuring of its organization to better serve this localized approach to integrating communications and sales. In November 1914, Klaxon's sales and advertising departments were merged into one, led by Walter P. Coghlan, the man behind the "Safety First" campaign. Each had a territorial manager who focused on cooperating with local jobbers, helping to both standardize and localize the message in the service of better sales. With the increasing importance of direct-to-factory sales, Klaxon's best manager, Charles Johnson, took the lead in the Detroit office in connecting with manufacturers.[58] The "Safety First" campaign would continue to be central to all of the company's strategic communications printed at the Klaxon Press, as evidenced by signs and examples of storefront displays being prominently displayed at the Chicago Automobile Show in January 1915. Once again, physical displays generated by the national marketing department were sent to local dealers all over the country: "Tell the motorists in your town that you are a Klaxon dealer. . . . Tell them in the newspapers, tell them through the mail, tell them in your show-window. . . . We will send window signs, window displays, stands and advertisement frames."[59]

The "Danger Sound Klaxon" campaign continued for years, helping Klaxon regional sales managers work their beats. In Wisconsin, the *Marshfield Times* ran a story when the Marshfield Auto Club put up a dozen signs around Wood Country in 1915.[60] In upstate New York, the Oneonta Automobile Club made news when it posted signs on the road from Utica, Canajoharie, and Harpursville to Oneonta in 1916.[61] The Klaxon Press was still offering free signage in Indiana later in 1916, when hiking clubs dedicated to promoting the St. Clare-Wabash Trail in Grayville erected "Danger Sound Klaxon" signs wherever the trail crossed the roads. The *Chehalis Bee-Nugget* ran the boilerplate article multiple times in July 1916 as the Chehalis Automobile Club posted signs in the name of safety.[62] As the localized campaign moved into Canada, an advertisement appeared in the *Toronto World* indicating that "Road Authorities" were placing these signs at danger points "because Klaxon is recognized as the authoritative warning signal."[63] Showing the company's ability to localize in multiple languages, when the signs appeared in Montreal, they read "Danger! Sonnez le Klaxon."[64]

Long before media fan bases were transformed into amplifiers to help promote films or causes,[65] Klaxon turned automobile associations and klaxon users into marketers who spread Klaxon's gospel of safer driving through better signaling technology across the country. They helped make sure that every time drivers took to the roads, they would be reminded at every dangerous turn and with every push of the button that "klaxon" was the word for sound signal.

Searching for New Applications and New Markets

Klaxon's ongoing campaign to localize its appeal and expand its presence in the national and international soundscape was not limited to advertising. The company was also actively and creatively thinking about new applications for the technology, which it began to promote as its advertising copy took a back seat to the sabre rattling and sounds of war in the European sound market.

"A new use for your Klaxon," read one ad from *Motor World* in September 1914. It related the story of a lawyer from Maine whose friends, after getting lost on a fishing trip and turning the wrong way, "expressed their appreciation of the merits and good work done by the Klaxon" after being signaled back to safety.[66] Klaxon had already touted its application as a factory signaling device in a 1913 ad about Crichley Machine Company of Worcester, Massachusetts, installing a klaxon as the factory whistle. Now Klaxon publicized the fact that several factories, including the Edison factories managed by Klaxon's inventor, were using the technology as fire alarms. "The Klaxons which are part of the Edison Fire Alarm System," read one ad in *National Geographic*, "are the same kind that Mr. Edison uses on his personal automobiles."[67]

Klaxon had already moved into the South American market as early as 1911, when dealers demanded that Pope Manufacturing, the local importer, start equipping their cars destined for Brazil with Klaxonet warning signals,[68] but the Klaxon Press touted another use by a farm in Peru, which used it to call workers from the fields at mealtime.[69] By 1916 the hand klaxon was being advertised in Argentina using the same global graphics the company used in Europe and North America.

In March 1916, as World War I raged in Europe and the United States was debating its options, Klaxon ran an ad in the *American Magazine* and *McClure's* boasting a perfect new venue for its technology: war. "Signal to Fire Big Guns in French Navy Given by Klaxon," the copy read.[70] In the sound-noise environment that most fascinated the Futurists, one dominated by the "very new noises of modern warfare" teased in Russolo's *The Art of Noise*,[71] Klaxon's device was the only one that could be heard through the explosions and screaming, the only means by which the directives of commanding officers could be heard. "The noise of the gun is deafening, but the Klaxons cut through it like a knife. In the French Navy, more than 600 Klaxons have been installed to thus tie together the bridge and deck. The horn that can be heard in the din of battle can be heard in the noise and rush of the street traffic." The use in warfare, the ad went on, proved that the unique klaxon tone was suited for the car of consumers driving in cities everywhere. Klaxon's utility—and its brand identity—was now, it boasted, universally known. "The use of Klaxons is so general that Klaxon has come to mean 'auto horn.'"[72] The company had succeeded wildly beyond its dreams, it seemed, in its goal of making its brand name a generic term.

As the soundscape battle shifted and soldiers from Klaxon's markets around the world set off to fight in a war where the sound of the klaxon was indeed ringing across the battlefields, a new meaning would slowly come to replace the associations Klaxon had worked so hard to establish. In 1916, Walter Coghlan, promoted to secretary of the company after his success coordinating the "Safety First" campaign, enlisted in the US Navy. Klaxon sound technology was going to war.

6
SOUNDING THE ALARM
Klaxon in the Trenches

By the end of 1914, Klaxon's ad campaigns in America were increasingly sharing the printed page with headlines and stories about the war in Europe. The noise-sound of war that so captivated the Futurists began to occupy the imagination of even the most isolationist media outlets and readers in America. Though Klaxon's "Safety First" campaign continued apace, it was clear that despite America's expressed neutrality, Lovell-McConnell was setting its sights on selling its signal for other applications in Europe, including wartime communications, as the automobile market there came to a screeching halt. Like other American international firms, Lovell-McConnell expanded its efforts in South America and Asia as European companies stopped exporting their products to these markets.

When the United States finally ended its isolation and began sending troops to the European theater, the sound of the klaxon, already a crescendoing sonic presence in the peacetime soundspace, went to war with them. The klaxon became associated with the sound of trench warfare, where sound signals and listening were exponentially more crucial for survival than they were in the urban streets. Klaxon, which had promoted its technology as a solution to the problem of communicating in noisy streets, took advantage of the military need to communicate amid the cacophonic chaos of modern war. But as the company yielded returns for its shareholders by becoming a sonic presence in the trenches and in the air, it lost control of the brand's sound association. The association of the klaxon as a representational sound and symbol of the automobile, one that the company had worked so long and so hard to promote as crucial to saving lives, melted into the shattered air. Through years of expensive ad campaigns, the company had sought to make the aggressive sound of the technology acceptable and desirable by associating it with safety; this perceptual paradigm shifted quickly with the cultural shock of war. In a short time, the klaxon sound lost its established meaning and came to be associated with the trauma of a civilization killing itself.

Klaxon Technology Goes to War

Though Klaxon was still waging aggressive advertising campaigns against its competitors in American media, it was clear that the company felt it had won the battle to make its brand name the generic word for the now global communication technology. In 1916, F. Hallett Lovell trumpeted the company's success in the *New York Sun,* claiming that Klaxon was now to the car horn what Kodak was to the camera: "The first year was hard sledding. My friends said it couldn't be done. But gradually the public began seeing the value of the Klaxon, began buying it in greater and greater numbers. One motorist in every six or seven bought it. Car makers adopted it as standard equipment. . . . The success of the Klaxon brought my dream true. I had put the word in the language—so much so that Klaxon is there with a little 'k.'"[1] Indeed, the generic nominalization indicated not only that "klaxon" had moved into the dictionary as a sound associated with the automobile but also that it had entered the popular imagination as a signifier of the particular sound the technology produced. The presence in the soundscape, and the necessity of loudness as a feature of communication, had become so normalized that the editors of *Life* wondered whether "pedestrians would get along better if they carried horns."[2]

Whether one liked it or not, the klaxon sound was now an inescapable feature of the soundscape in America and in Europe. Yet Klaxon's technology, no longer trademarked, was being copied and sold by competitors, so that even when the company was not making money, the sound association with the word *klaxon* resonated each time a horn was blown.

But despite its success and dominance of the soundscape, and even though production was booming, the Klaxon Company had to find other markets for its technology to generate revenue for its shareholders. On World War I battlefields it found a market that quickly outpaced the automobile one. The French Navy found klaxon technology necessary to communicate in the chaotic noise of a fight and used it to warn of German U-boat attacks.[3] With the sphere of war expanding, more applications for a technology that could signal through the deafening roar of modern trench warfare quickly emerged.

As the Great War moved from its first year into its second and the front became a series of deeper and deeper trenches, sound technology became ever more important. "Sonic mindedness," Yaron Jean has written—being able to hear what was going on and being able to communicate that infor-

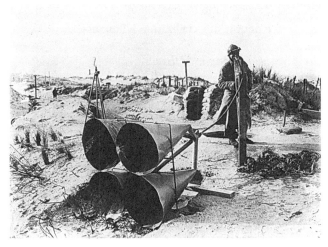

Figure 43. A French listening post on the Western Front. (Bibliothèque nationale de France)

mation to others—was crucial for success and survival.[4] Whether it was for the sound of troops moving, tanks rolling, Zeppelin motors whirring, or gas bombs hissing, listening took on paramount importance for both the Allied and the Axis powers. Interspersed among the trenches, *postes d'écoute,* or listening posts, became all important.

In many ways, World War I was a war of new technologies with new sounds. When the German army started using gas attacks on the Russian front in early 1915, all of the Allies had to respond by developing technologies to deal with the gas and to warn soldiers of gas attacks in a field of war that was largely determined by listening for and communicating with sound. The description of a 1915 gas attack by Emmanuel Bourcier, a French author who became a communications specialist for the French military, spending tense hours in listening posts, is striking:

> Suddenly a great cry rang out:
> "The Gas!!!"
> It was true. Over there, from the enemy's lines, came great greenish balls, rolling close to the earth, rolling deliberately yet swiftly, rolling straight toward us. Gas! That horrible thing, still almost unknown, which had been used for the first time only recently on the Yser. It was coming with deadly surety. . . . Orders were shouted back and forth:
> "The gas! Put on the masks!"
> We did not yet know what manner of horror it was. . . . We were swimming in an atmosphere stained a venomous color, uncanny,

"I HEARD THE KLAXON START GOING!"

Figure 44. Panicked reaction of veterans to the sound of the klaxon, captured in cartoon sketch. From *History of the American Field Service in France,* vol. 3 (Boston: Houghton Mifflin Co, 1920). (National Library of Medicine)

indescribable. The sky appeared greenish, the earth disappeared. The men staggered about for a moment, took a gasping breadth and rolled on the ground, stifled.

Some ran about like madmen, shrieking in terror, the throat choked with saliva, and fell in heaps, in contortions of agony. . . . Over all this the artillery shrieked in unchained madness. . . . It roared, it whistled, it exploded without respite, as if all the furies of hell were yelping, in a thick, metallic sky.

This first engagement is vividly present in our memory, a recollection never to be effaced.[5]

One can only begin to imagine how the trauma of a gas attack took over the minds of soldiers, and how any sound associated with an attack came to trigger a fearful response. The Allied armies needed a warning signal for gas attacks.

Just as there had been a struggle over the representational sound of the car horn during the early days of automobiling, at the beginning of the war different sounds were tried to warn soldiers of approaching gas. At first, French, British, and Portuguese troops used whatever was available, including requisitioned church bells. Eventually the British began issuing gas rattles and

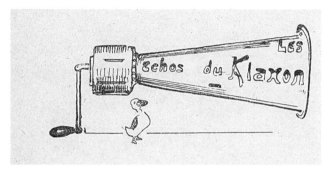

Figure 45. Masthead art from *Le Klaxon*, which gave news about the daily lives of soldiers at the front. From *Le Klaxon*, January 1, 1916. (Bibliothèque nationale de France)

a variety of gongs in different shapes that soldiers in the trenches could sound if they heard the telltale sound-signs of a gas attack.

Yet this early sound technology, clumsy and variable, proved ineffective for the same reason that early automobile horns had. The variety of sound devices added to chaos and often were not loud enough to be distinctive in the "noise-sound" of war. Something else was needed that would indicate specific threats quickly and loudly. In 1916 the French Ministry of Defense began suggesting soldiers use horns from Klaxon's French franchise, Klaxon-Blériot, which upped production of *le klaxon mécanique* and tweaked the design to meet the growing demand. Suddenly, klaxons were a growing sonic presence at the front, used to warn soldiers that poisonous gas was approaching the trenches.[6]

In France, the sound that Klaxon-Blériot had worked so hard to associate with consumer safety quickly shifted from street traffic to trench warfare as the casualties mounted into the millions. The term was becoming an iconic sound-sign defining the experience of war, as indicated by a popular wartime journal adopting the name *Le Klaxon* and featuring a running column of darkly humorous "echoes" from the front, further strengthening the association between life at the front and the sound of the klaxon.

In the United States, *Popular Science Monthly*, which had helped Americans understand the scientific implications of klaxon technology earlier in the decade, now let the public know that "a 'Honk! Honk!' in the Trenches means 'Don your gas mask!'"[7] Helping to dislodge the familiar meaning of the klaxon, the French Ministry of Defense provided an accompanying photograph to illustrate this new application, and it spread by wire across the globe, to be reproduced in dozens of news stories from New Zealand to Spain. With each iteration, the photograph sowed awareness that the meaning of the familiar aaOOgah would never be the same again.

Figure 46. French listening post sentry outfitted with gas mask and klaxon. In *The Illustrated War News*, it was captioned "The motorists' 'hoot' as a gas-alarm." From *The Illustrated War News*, January 24, 1917. (Archive.org)

Though American soldiers had not yet entered the war, news of the klaxon sound emerging as a feature of the front soundscape also began to reach American readers through the accounts of ambulance drivers, who volunteered to help the Allied powers at the front long before the United States officially entered the war. American papers reported their descriptions of the front, its sounds and its traumas, in the form of syndicated first-person accounts.[8]

Likewise, the writer John Dos Passos, who signed up with his Harvard classmate, E. E. Cummings, wrote *One Man's Initiation* based on his experience as a driver with the Notron-Harjes Ambulance Corps in 1917. He recalled the klaxon-tinged chaos:

The curtain was pulled aside and a man staggered in holding with the other hand a limp arm twisted in a mud-covered sleeve, from which blood and mud dripped on to the floor.

"Hello, old chap," said the doctor quietly. A smell of disinfectant stole through the dugout.

Faint above the incessant throbbing of explosions, the sound of a klaxon horn.

"Ha, gas," said the doctor. "Put on your masks, children." A man went along the dugout waking those who were asleep and giving out fresh masks. Someone stood in the doorway blowing a shrill whistle, then there was again the clamour of a Klaxon near at hand.[9]

As the klaxon's shriek cut through the confusion, soldiers—like the drivers before them who learned that the sound of a klaxon meant they should clear the way—came to understand that the klaxon warning signal required immediate action.

Medics doing triage on the front often described that cacophony of sound, where the klaxon's ability to cut through the noise made it a crucial warning device. As one surgeon wrote, "We went to bed as usual. At 12 midnight, we were awakened by a series of whizzing noises over our heads, a confusing roar of artillery punctuated by the blowing of a klaxon (the gas mask alert) and three shots (the gas alarm), so we sat up and put on our masks, and part of our clothes, and tin hats, and looked out. There was a tremendous drum barrage going on, the noise was terrifying, heavies and barrage all mixed up in a roar."[10]

Even before the United States entered the war, the global press was describing how the noise-sound of klaxon technology was a constant feature of the war soundscape. The English *Illustrated War News* ran photographs of listening posts and soldiers in the trenches armed with "hooter" technology. Newspapers around the world ran photographs of French and Russian soldiers with klaxons, such as the photograph of a Russian sentry in Mongolian boots that went out over the AP wire in early March 1917, annotated with an arrow pointing to the klaxon, ready to warn troops of a gas attack. The klaxon was a detail of life on both the Western and Eastern Fronts that readers everywhere could understand.

Klaxon Pivots to Wartime Applications

With the war coming to occupy more international attention, there were ominous signs that Klaxon's business might be entering into uncertain times. Not surprisingly, when Lovell-McConnell was tendered an offer to cash out in 1916, the company took it. And so, following the industry trend of consolidation and conglomeration, United Motors, one of the companies that was gobbling up the post-factory accessory market, bought Klaxon that year. United Motors' earnings surged with the addition of Klaxon to its holdings, jumping 40 percent from 1916 earnings in just nine months.[11]

The name of the company became the Klaxon Company and the capacity of its plant in New Jersey immediately doubled. With the consolidation of companies, the Willys-Overland Motors company was folded in and its version of the klaxon technology was discontinued. Klaxon retained its factory contracts with Buick, Cadillac, Oldsmobile, Oakland, Scripps-Booth, and Chevrolet.[12] With carmaker contracts already in place, and with Defense Department contracts with Allied governments growing, the United Motors plants were working at capacity round the clock, making plans to double capacity once again.[13]

Despite the shrinking automobile market in Europe, Klaxon continued to expand its production, using business-to-business advertising to persuade other industries that the klaxon sound technology could work for their fields. As Klaxon spread its technology into industry applications, it was telling that the United States Cartridge Company of Lowell, Massachusetts, now working "24 hours a day on war orders," started using a klaxon to begin and end its three daily shifts. "The din of the machines was so great under the increased activities that the gongs and whistles that were formerly used to signal the changing of shifts could not be heard. In their places klaxon automobile horns were installed." When the horns sounded, the men who had taken up their positions behind the earlier shift could step in immediately, "losing not an instant of time and making it unnecessary to stop the huge machines."[14] In the Taylorized buildup to war, the assembly line production of ear-splitting ordinance was constant. Just as only the klaxon could cut through the sound of exploding ordinance, only the klaxon could signal through the roar of wartime industrial production.

In 1917, after the United States declared war on the Axis powers, the US Department of Defense released official designations of the different sound signals that were to be used at the front. "[For] the purpose of giving the alarm the Strombo horn, which is audible for very long distances, is the most important appliance."[15] This compressed-air siren issued to each communication station, also manufactured by the Klaxon Company, was deemed the only signaling device loud enough to cut through the sound of warfare over long distances.[16]

Because of the Klaxon's affordances and reliability, the Army War College in Pennsylvania indicated a preference for klaxon technology over the Strombo horns at the beginning of 1918: the Strombo required compressed-air canisters connected to a tube, which had to be replaced. Yet there were insufficient numbers of klaxons available at that time. "Klaxon horns are generally unobtainable in sufficient quantity," the Army War College noted.[17] Soldiers lacking proper supplies often had to improvise with gongs, police rattles, or pans to pass the signal from trench to trench.

Yet increasingly, the first initial signal from command along the Western Front was sounded with a klaxon. One report from April 23, 1917, of a German assault on the French line described an attack involving a series of clouds, each with the "odor of bleaching powder." "The first attack by way of a Mortar Gas shell, at 4:15, a second and a third at 5:25 and 6:20, and each time a warning was issued by sounding a klaxon."[18] By the time the Americans entered the war, as Francis Field observed in *The Battery Book,* the Strombo sirens were associated with general alerts, whereas klaxons were "signals for local attacks," a warning that the gas had arrived.[19] Very quickly, British, Italian, French, Australian, New Zealand, German, and American troops—all from countries with established Klaxon franchises and whose automobile soundscapes were dominated by variations of the technology—adopted the horn and applied it to the problems of trench warfare communication.

The noise chaos of war seemed to require that noisy technology be immediately heard as a warning. One account of battle by the American Verne Chaney, who served with Battery D of the 129th Field Artillery in France, gives a sense of the deafening tension:

> Every night of our stay here the Huns were shelling the French position to our rear and also the fort on our right. They seldom failed to open up about eight o-clock every night with H.E. shrapnel and gas. We were annoyed a few nights with gas but no harm done.
>
> There was constant efforts by the Boche planes, to get information on those French positions but all the shots went over us with their usual whine. That didn't worry us as much as the klaxon that sounded the gas warning.
>
> There is an awful feeling when one is awakened in the early morning hours by the gas alarm.[20]

Just as immediately as the klaxon was sounded, soldiers recognized and responded to its shriek, a fact of the soundscape that became more entrenched as the war raged on. Indeed, as a sonic feature, the fear association with the klaxon was reinforced by a kind of echo effect as each trench passed the alarm down the line. This symphony of klaxons usually happened at night, when the Germans preferred to deploy their chemical weapons. As one observer embedded with American troops described it, "Every platoon had a Klaxon

Figure 47. Listening post equipped with a periscope to see no-man's-land and a klaxon warning signal. From *The Illustrated War News*, November 22, 1916. (Archive.org)

horn for sounding the alarm."[21] When they heard it, along with sounding their own horn the platoon signalers would also put up a green flare to reinforce the message and help rouse slumbering soldiers to readiness. Its immediacy made the klaxon a feature, often unwanted, of the nighttime soundscape.

Yet with the affordances of the technology, the klaxon was used not only to warn of gas alerts but also for communication with airplanes, a major new force in warfare, both ground-to-air and air-to-ground. Nothing else had the ability to penetrate the noise and to carry far enough. As early as 1915, reports of Royal Flying Corps aircraft using klaxons to signal were coming out of Australia. "Sound signals are usually made by a Klaxon horn, worked from an eight-volt battery in an aeroplane, and at a height of 2000ft., and at a distance of one mile such signals can be distantly heard on the ground above the noise of the engine."[22]

Sentry stations and lookouts employing a listening device that resembled a long tube attached to one or several gramophone horns would try to anticipate blimps or "buzzards" (enemy aircraft), which could bomb the trenches from above.[23] If the sentries heard incoming aircraft, soldiers in the trenches heard the klaxon's warning. One flight lieutenant recalled hearing the sound of the klaxon on March 21, 1916. "Woke at 1 a.m. to hear the klaxon sounding the 'Hostile aircraft' warning. . . . After a while there came to our ears a low droning sound and the klaxon went again."[24]

Yet the sentry had to listen not only for the drone of engines but also for a klaxon from an incoming aircraft, as pilots were ordered to identify themselves as friendly so as not to set off the chain reaction of klaxon warnings and anti-aircraft fire. As the Army War College ordered for American troops, "Aeroplanes for this work . . . will carry Klaxon horns and Very lights for the purposes of making themselves known and answering signals from the ground."[25] The planes would sound the klaxon, and the infantry on the advance line would signal back by way of flares, which would indicate to the planes their location within the trenches without their being seen by the enemy. British protocol was similar. "What is required," wrote one British Air Ministry observer, "is some signal from the aeroplane to the ground signifying 'where are you' on receipt of which flares would be lit. During the last few days klaxon horns have been tried with considerable success, a prolonged hoot signifying 'where are you.' The Klaxon horn can also be used to answer signals from the ground."[26] One account in the Brisbane *Telegraph* echoed this statement, showing the importance of air-to-ground sound communication by klaxon:

> Suddenly out from a dense cloud, an aeroplane appeared. It was distinguished from other similar craft by two long coloured streamers that flew from its wings. It hovered over the foremost wave of infantry, and then, from it came a series of ear-splitting shrieks, sounding high above the din of battle.
>
> "Klaxon horn calling for lights, sir," said a sergeant to his platoon commander.
>
> "Light up lads!" Shouted the officer.
>
> Almost instantly half a dozen flares burst into flame.[27]

Once the observer in the plane gathered information about the enemy's position on the map, it was conveyed back and forth between the "flapper" signaler—who used a ground-to-air semaphore system—and the horn. "The observer wrote down the message, answering each word as he read it, with a blast of his Klaxon horn. 'VE,' said the flapper. 'BD' replied the horn. 'T' added the flapper. This concluded the conversation."[28] In another case, recounted by a pilot after the war, a plane was trailing and periodically dropping bombs on a column of retreating German troops. When the pilot's observer spotted Germans "erecting something," which proved to be a nest of machine guns to ambush the advancing British troops, the klaxon allowed the pilot to warn the troops on the ground.

There was no time for the pilot to bomb the Boche positions or shoot down the German gunners. He pushed down the nose of his machine and raced for the approaching battery. Flying low over their heads he pressed the button of his Klaxon, and the raucous note sounded in the air. The battery commander looked up and paused. Then, letter by letter, the Klaxon hooted out its message of warning, and the guns halted and got into position.

The Huns saw that their ambush had failed and opened fire from long range. They were, however, too late. Directed by the airmen, the guns got to work and a few minutes later the battery galloped on past some ruined machine guns and a pile of dead and shattered Huns.[29]

The klaxon's immediacy and ability to be heard over long distances saved the British battery from disaster. The French infantry, too, found the klaxon saved lives, and the official manual described how French planes should use "a special acoustic signal: klaxons and eventually its machine gun [*mitrailleuse*] to attract the attention of those with which they desired to communicate."[30]

Yet as "Pat Crowe, Aviator" described it, Allied *and* Axis planes used klaxon technology, which created signal confusion. "The next day, while we were at teach, a big bumblebee sort of plan[e] came over and began making circles and figure eights around the chateau towers, all the while keeping up a frightful chatter with his detestable klaxon."[31] Another chronicle from a flyboy described witnessing a dogfight in which a "Boche" plane was being chased by three Allied biplanes. When the German pilot started coming under fire, the trio dived after him. The Allied pilots sent out a "signal rocket" to the gunners on the ground and "dived almost vertically, honking the while on Klaxon horns."[32] One letter written by an Australian pilot to his sister back home described the klaxon being used to call the pilots to action from the listening post near the front line:

We are warned by a Klaxon horn sounding the flight letter (in Morse code) what is wanted for the job. We will take it we are standing from 10 am to 2pm. Well time passes, twelve o'clock and no Klaxon horn sounds; half past twelve, lunch hour. We commence lunch and about half-way through when out screams the Klaxon. We listen intently. Yes it's "B" flight; my flight. Huns are about the lines. We rush off to get our flying kit. . . . It's just fifteen minutes since the Klaxon sounded, and all machines have left the ground.[33]

Once a plane was in the air, the pilot would sound the klaxon again, cutting through the noisy soundscape to communicate what he had found. Klaxon even created a special aluminum horn "of good aerodynamic quality and lightweight for airplane use."[34] Yet even with planes using klaxons to communicate from air to ground, it was hard to tell who was signaling whom since American, French, British, and German planes all used them. This confusion between air and ground was part of a larger confusion created by the ubiquity of klaxon technology as a feature of war communication in general. The spread of the technology before the war, not only with Klaxon franchising in Italy, France, England, and Germany but with rivals in each country, meant that each army was equipped with similar sound signaling technology. B. Atkins Jenkins, writing from an Allied trench opposing the German Hindenburg line on the Western Front, felt that the sound of the klaxon had the same emotional impact as the sound of an approaching shell or aircraft bomb. "It is altogether devilish, goose-fleshy, jumpy and makes one feel as one does when a Klaxon sounds suddenly. . . . You want to jump and then turn around and glare at and 'cuss' somebody."[35] He wrote of his attempt to make sense of the klaxon cacophony: "Our Klaxon was going all the time, and so were other Klaxons; nor were they like any others you have ever heard outside of Italy. They were like Brobdignagian canary birds, with a shrill and insistent chirp that splits your ears as well [as] the wind. They were not less impudent than the dog bark of the American Klaxons, but far more penetrating and weird."[36] The same kind of variation in klaxon sounds that American and European drivers and pedestrians experienced during peacetime made knowing who was warning or signaling whom all the more uncertain at the front. The sonic paradigm was shifting.

The Sound of War Trauma

The shift in perception, the re-association of the klaxon's sound with an incoming attack, was not only being created in the minds of readers far from the front as it filtered through the accounts of those in the trenches. In some of the countries with Klaxon franchises, the Klaxon's sound was also being repurposed to warn civilians of attacks. In England, Klaxon lobbied to get its technology used as "an official system for giving public warning" to civilians of Zeppelin attacks. "The instrument emits a wild and ear-piercing screech, intensely far-carrying, and its note has the additional advantage of being easily distinguishable from other sounds, and to be heard above the whirr of the loudest factory machinery."[37] Ever mindful of potential markets for its technol-

Figure 48. German plane equipped with klaxon technology to signal to the ground. From Kurt Bennewitz, *Flugzeuginstrument* (Berlin: Richard Carl Schmidt, 1922). (Pennsylvania State University Library)

ogy, Klaxon took out business-to-business ads to convince factory owners and schools to deploy Klaxon horns to "warn your workers against aircraft raids."[38] Once the source of a warning signal for an oncoming car, the representational sound of the automobile in the street, a klaxon could now also mean that Zeppelins were about to drop bombs. Wrote one columnist in the *Ballymena Observer* of the klaxon warning system in Sheffield, "The danger signal given by these instruments is said to be enough to rouse the deaf and raise the dead. . . . No Sheffield man or woman will henceforth be without audible and sufficient warning of the Hun's approach."[39] Slowly but surely, both for those who experienced war and those who read it about it in the papers, the klaxon sound became associated with the experience of war.

In the Oak Park, Illinois, newspaper *Oak Leaves,* one eyewitness, Sergeant Chester Johnson, described this shift in perception and association at the front, where soldiers lived in fear of being "awakened by the hideous sound of a klaxon horn":

> I spoke of a Klaxon horn in the preceding paragraph. Now a Klaxon horn means nothing more in Chicago than to clear the road, but here one turn of said Klaxon will cause half a million men to go through, without any hesitation, the same motions regardless of the hour it happens. For a radius of ten miles everything will ring with the ghostly scream of Mr. Klaxon. It is known by everyone connected with the war that Klaxon and

Gas Mask are always together, especially at night; one is useless without the other. The actions I speak of are men donning their gas masks, a case of act first and find out later.[40]

Just as the klaxon sound, per the marketing copy several years earlier, led people to clear the road as an almost involuntary reflex, now soldiers at and away from the front reached immediately for their gas masks in fear.

Sonic associations often lingered as a result of war trauma and made hearing particular sounds especially problematic for those trying to recover from its effects. Dr. James Robb Church, whose book *The Doctor's Part: What Happens to the Wounded in War* was one among many chronicles of life on the front, described how these terrifying associations were repeated through continued sonic conditioning. "At one end of the trench an automobile horn of the Klaxon type, I think, was fastened, and when that squawked it was better to put on your mask, for it meant that the deadly gray-green gas was coming."[41] Those whose "ego" was wounded in war, whether they be soldier or doctors, now feared what the sound might mean. As Church described it, "With the angry crash of shells, the noise of their oncoming, the illusion of quiet passes and the interest quickly centers again in the ego and what is to happen to it."[42] Once a sound, especially a loud sound, was associated with the experience of trauma, it remained a trigger for a flight response. For returning soldiers, instead of hearing the klaxon as a warning of an oncoming automobile, the klaxon sound now precipitated fear of what was to happen to them, an expectation of oncoming ordinance and potential death.[43]

The power of media reports of soldiers' experience at the front meant that the shift in sonic association passed on to the reading public. US Defense Department pictures of the klaxon being used by men in gas masks under siege in the trenches were distributed to the press, running in journals like the *London Illustrated News.* In the *Deseret Evening News,* Salt Lake City readers were told of a new gas that rolled down hills like water, and of how the klaxon alerted American troops to the "imminent danger of death" amid the din of battle: "The noise was hideous, for we were so near a battery position that the blare of guns broke into the long roll of artillery around the circle. . . . Then the Klaxon horns began to roar, and every man jerked his gas mask out of the bag that was tied to his breast in the 'alert' position and began to hurry into it."[44] One of the many chronicles of war experience, *The Cannoneers Have Hairy Ears,* told tales of the klaxon echoing through the trenches and associating the sound of the technology with mortal fear:

Figure 49. Government photograph of US soldiers using klaxons in the trenches. (Courtesy of the National Archives, Identifier: 55173164)

Suddenly one man started, his tin cup half way to his mouth. Unconsciously every soldier under the net came instantly to the alert. Somewhere out beyond the barbed wire of the trench system toward Raulecourt a Klaxon had sounded.

"Gas!" The Klaxon screamed again. Another town picked up the alarm and then another.

"Gas!" The shrieking message was passed all along the front—Raulecourt, Rambucourt, Xivray, Beaumont—and out beyond where the crescent of the sector swung on toward Metz. Back again it came to Bouconville.

The Doughboys at the crossroads had heard the call and the wild warning echoed among the ruins in a panic-stricken accelerando.

"Gas!"

Coffee was forgotten. It spilled in cascades over the ammunition boxes as unskilled hands flew to the once despised gas masks. An intangible, stealthy death was abroad in the mists—a death that no mere bravery could hope to combat.[45]

Away from the front, the sound association established by years of Klaxon's advertising campaigns was slipping; prewar sound associations with safe driving were being displaced by tales of deadly experiences that echoed in the minds of soldiers and those who cared for and about them.

In the magazine *No. 5*, published by the patients and staff at the No. 5 Australian General Hospital in Melbourne, a rewrite of a popular song gives a sense of the way in which the klaxon sound was seared into the memories that haunted soldiers back from the front:

> Somewhere a voice is calling
>   O'er land and sea;
> Mary her message bawling,
>   Quite clear enough for me.
> Where are my blankety field boots
>   (It's too ruddy dark to see)?
> Somewhere a large bomb's falling
>   (Sure of it) straight for me.
> Night, and a lot of grumping,
>   And beaucoup de ghastly bangs;
> As fast as I can I'm bumping
>   To where that Klaxon hangs.
> My poor, soft feet are grating
>   On stones that I cannot see,
> But somewhere a dug-out's waiting
>   (Thank Heaven) for me.[46]

This nightmarish description was all too familiar to soldiers suffering from the shock of war. Already at the front, these perceptual shifts were leading to different communication practices. One British officer, describing the roads to and from the front in France, noted that normal driving behavior on those roads, in cars equipped with klaxons, was different from back home. Away from the front, "men with nerves frayed by a long bombardment have been known to swear bitterly at a sudden and unexpected blast from a Klaxon horn."[47] Aware of this dynamic, people did not sound their klaxons for fear of startling the soldiers. The French humor weekly *Le Rire* published a telling anecdote about a group of nerve-weary French *poilus* (soldiers) away from the front on leave. After being triggered by the sound of a klaxon, they mistakenly threw their grenades at several workers. Their reflex action was set off by "the klaxon of a passing auto. We will see," the writer predicted, "many more of this type after the war."[48] In France, civilians living close to the front or in cities vulnerable to air attack already associated the sound with mortal danger.

The US Army knew how this sonic confusion affected troops at the front and started to change the rules of communication on the road. In 1918 army drivers were ordered to use visual signals instead of communicating by horn. "Do not make unnecessary noise with horns or klaxons," the new regulations stated.[49] In the account of the 113th Field Artillery, 30th Division, Arthur Fletcher described how this change in automobile behavior led to a situation in which "ambulances plunged along without a light and with horns silent. At the front the sound of the automobile horn meant one thing and one thing only, 'gas.' Any sounding of a Klaxon horn might result anywhere in a gas scare and much confusion, so the drivers carried small whistles to warn pedestrians and slower vehicle traffic."[50] This was absolutely imperative given the effect of sounding the horn. Safety required discipline. "If a truck driver or an ambulance driver forgot and sounded his klaxon horn on the road, the chances were real that a gas alarm would start. . . . Real gas alarms sounded in the front line trenches[,] were taken up by klaxon, and spread rapidly over the back areas sometimes to a depth of ten miles or more, in an incredibly short time."[51] Leonard Nason, in one of his many syndicated serial stories about life at the front, described this reflexive reaction or echo of warnings as "the caw of klaxons, as though it were in the next block, and then many more would answer it, like a flock of crows."[52]

Soldiers were trained before they got to the front that if they heard a klaxon, they should sound their own, to pass the warning on to the next trench. Experience reinforced the reflex. One description of a gas attack poignantly depicts how "the klaxons of the platoons on the right and left would sound, then those of the next two companies, and so on down the line. As far as one could know that alarm may have spread to Switzerland on the right and Flanders on the left. When this happened six times in one night, and that without any gas ever appearing, we all became irritable."[53] This irritability and confusion did not stop once soldiers returned from the front with their behavioral reflexes intact.

Edward Streeter's tale of a soldier writing to his sweetheart back home, *Same Old Bill, Eh Mable,* shows that the men in the trenches knew their sense perception and sound association would never be quite the same again when they heard the "old klaxon squawk": "In a half an hour, I got to go on gas guard. That means I stand in front of the dug out an when I smell something I blow a klaxon. If any old Ford ever sneaks up behind me when I get home an blows a klaxon they'll probably see me clap my derby over my face an dive in a coal hole. . . . Chained lightening. That's me all over, Mable."[54] Letters from the front, a regular feature in American periodicals of all kinds, conveyed similar painful stories and associations to the public back home, help-ing to raise awareness about what the troops at the front needed. One story from 1918 reported that the cost of preparing for chemical warfare was likely to be $250 million, covering things like gas masks for American and French soldiers, "sag paste" (used to protect soldiers' skin from poison gas), and the 15,000 Klaxon horns sent to the front in October 1918 alone.[55]

Along with raising funds, the thousands of letters printed in local and na-tional journals were reconfiguring the imaginary ideas around the klaxon. As Junius Wood wrote in the *Stars and Stripes*, "Each platoon has a sentry who hourly, night and day, reports the direction of the wind and patrols the trenches, carrying a klaxon under his arm ready to sound an instant alarm."[56] One letter, printed in *Life* magazine, described how easy it was to trick new soldiers, trained to respond immediately to the klaxon, to put the masks on and keep them on until they heard the second klaxon all-clear sound, despite the discomfort:

> After we got the masks and put them on, they told us not to take them off until we heard the Klaxon. They had a Klaxon outside of the barn for that purpose that they had taken off a machine earlier in the evening. . . . I guess we had them on fully thirty minutes before we heard the Klaxon sound, and if properly but on they are air-tight, and the chemical used in them is rather sickening the first few times worn, before getting used to it, and I was mighty glad to remove it . . . We are now waiting to pull it on the next new men.[57]

Since there was never much time to act, one could not delay. As another doughboy's account put it, "We kept our masks at alert all the time. After the slightest warning of the gas guard we would all be masked in six seconds. A Klaxon horn which could be heard for miles was the gas alarm most pop-ular with us."[58]

Another letter, written to "Mother" on paper and envelopes furnished by the American Red Cross and published in *Outlook*, described learning to live "day to day" with few amenities and fewer comforts. Everything about everyday life was different.

> We have a lot of fun talking about how the habits we have formed over here will act on us when we get home. For instance, gas alarm is always spread by the honking of klaxons. There are thousands of klaxons along the front, and when gas shells come over or it drifts back from the front

line, it sounds like Tremont Street in Boston on its busiest day. So we figure that when we get home every time we hear a klaxon on an automobile we'll jumble around for our ever-ready gas masks, at the same time hollering "Gas!" at the top of our lungs. You can expect all kinds of strange actions from me when I get home. [59]

Indeed, this account was prescient, and in many of the retrospective accounts that were published after the war, former soldiers talked of the behavioral response unavoidably triggered by the sound associations from the front:

There is also a gas guard whose duty it is to be continually on the watch, day and night, for any sign of gas. The alarm is usually given by sounding a Klaxon horn. This reminds me of an amusing incident which occurred in New York after my return. We had just stepped ashore when a huge truck came rapidly around the corner and sounded its Klaxon. I saw at least five boys, myself included, reach for their gas-masks which were hanging at their sides, and one lad had his half on before he realized where he was. Good gas discipline means getting on your mask when the Klaxon sounds and asking questions afterwards. [60]

"Gas discipline" at the front, conditioned by training and hardened by trauma, meant reflexive panic in the returning soldier who heard the klaxon's cry. Wave after wave of published letters from the front described soldiers' anxiety about this new reflex. "Speaking of noises," wrote Harry Henderson in the *Wyoming State Tribune,* "none of us will ever hear a Klaxon auto horn again without grabbing for a gas mask . . . and whenever a tire blows up on Capitol Avenue I'll probably dive under a culvert." [61] Jesse L. Petefish, from Battery A of the 124th Field Artillery Regiment, had a similar worry about the sonic stress of returning home. "I know it will make me nervous to see an automobile run with headlights and to see a house illuminated. I expect I will start yelling, 'Put out that light' or I will shoot it out, and if I hear our auto klaxon I suppose I will grab for my gas mask." [62]

One article opined "Good-bye whistles, fireworks and horns when the boys come home!" After the experience of battle, everything changed. "I am quite certain that when the boys get back to God's country such noises as whistles, Klaxon horns, fireworks, etc., will have to be eliminated because they have a peculiar effect upon those who have seen service with the American Expeditionary forces." [63] Such opinions would continue to be amplified. With stories like these resounding through the media, the new sound association with the klaxon horn crept steadily across the European and American soundscapes.

Of course, this new sonic association was not brand conscious. Indeed, the antitrust suits against Klaxon by the US government, along with intense lobbying, made sure that the Defense Department bought from other klaxon-type horn producers as the army struggled to keep up with demand from the front lines. Though Newtone horns went bankrupt in 1917, all the other klaxon-type horns were being used by Allied *and* Axis army and navy forces whose civilian automobile industries had embraced the klaxon years earlier.

The congressional accounts of war expenditures on sonic signaling devices for the first year of US involvement provide a sense of it. The alarm signals requisitioned by the US military that year included sixty-five Strombo horns, 5,739 Klaxon horns, 9,036 Stewart horns, and 10,555 Sparton horns.[64] The next year, 45,906 horns of the "klaxon type" were shipped to the front.[65] Though the Klaxon Company's competitors, especially Sparks-Withington, cashed in on war production, in the multilingual generic vernacular of the soldiers, all these signaling devices were referred to as klaxons. And with so little visibility, especially at night, the numbers of klaxon-type horns distributed to soldiers grew and grew.[66]

In the noise-sound of war, klaxons had become as essential as the gas mask and inexorably linked to the experience of war. Just as repetition had been used to associate the Klaxon brand with the ideas conveyed through advertising campaigns, now repetition reset the associations at the front and at home.

In many ways, these perceptions of the klaxon as unwanted noise rang true for many back home who, even before the war, had felt that less klaxon noise on the roadways would be a welcome relief. One syndicated article that ran in many papers across America in June 1918 traced the history of the "lawless tyrant" that invaded "peaceful retreats":

> Do what we will to dodge it, we are rarely if ever free from it. It reaches us as we wake, it startles us as we walk. All day long and well into the night it keeps up its hideous cacophony, its raucous demand, its threat and counter threat, its expostulation and blame, its roar and blatancy. . . . A day came, a *dies irae*, when everything changed. The Klaxon and the whatnot seemed to have sprung into existence overnight and to have combined in one fiendish contest of autocratic malevolence. . . . Before we knew it, we had, instead of motor signals, a roaring fauna of the street. . . . Some day we shall pluck up courage to take the unruly fellow in hand.[67]

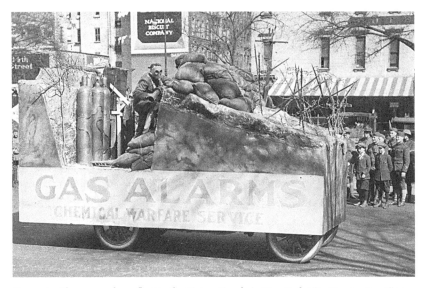

Figure 50. Klaxon gas alarm float in the Victory Parade in New York City, May 3, 1919. (Courtesy of the National Archives, Identifier: 48021 #A)

With troops returning home, this antiklaxon sentiment was now tied to caring for veterans, a structure of feeling that helped tip the debate about the place of klaxon technology in everyday life.

Confusing the perceptual frames even more, when the Armistice that ended World War I was announced in November 1918 and the roar of the guns subsided, klaxons became part of the sound of celebration. One soldier wrote of the "hundreds of thousand delirious" Frenchmen, celebrating in "spasmodic fashion":

> Personally, I feel as if I have been in a train wreck, or have been steamrollered or something such brutal. . . . The shrieking, cheering stamping mob, soldiers of all nations. . . . No human system could have stood the strain. Church bells rang, cannons boomed, horns shrieked, bugles blared, any noise making instrument was welcome. By the third day, the American brigade armed with Klaxon horns all helped to aid the French. . . . I only hope my constitution can stand up under this strain, for it is sure a dizzy existence nowadays.[68]

Even as the stories from the front moved from the chaos of battle to the cacophony of celebration after the Armistice, the confusion in sound representation became a problem for the postwar world, one to be solved through better policy and more conscious design. The soundscape that had roiled Western culture needed to be healed.

Veterans Need Quiet to Heal

Nowhere was this awareness of sound sensitivity among traumatized soldiers more prevalent than in the medical community, where healing through deliberate silence was often prescribed. "There is a legitimate nervousness, named 'shell shock,'" wrote one army doctor in 1918. "The real cases of this condition, when they are extreme, are sad to see. An officer or Tommy, who has previously been an excellent soldier, suddenly develops 'nerves' to such an extent as to be uncontrollable . . . the slightest noise makes him jump and even occasionally run at top speed to a supposed place of safety."[69]

The noise-sound of battle was a common cause of shell shock, and sensitivity to it was one of the most common symptoms. Sometimes men would experience auditory hallucinations, such as the hissing of gas mortars or whistles blowing. One British doctor who treated traumatized soldiers found that "hyperacousis, or extreme sensibility to sound, is a common and very troublesome symptom, making the patient miserable and apprehensive."[70] Loud sounds in the street would sometimes cause physical symptoms, such as dizziness or headaches. Many physicians recommended "mental quiet" for those with such sensitivity to noise.[71] They thought that the best remedy for this type of sound-triggered neurosis was months of quiet living. Hospitals— many already in "quiet zones" within cities—began to set up quiet wards; one hospital in London created "light airy wards with plenty of single rooms for the isolation of cases that are troubled with noises."[72]

Veterans in search of restorative quiet found no repose on urban streets. "When we hear the klaxon peace horn," speculated Chester Inskeep of the 124th Regiment, "we will perhaps put on our gas masks and wait for results."[73] After the war, stories and accounts like this surfaced frequently, repeating what earlier veterans had recounted, sensitizing families back home to what these sounds now meant to soldiers. It made them think twice about the reflexive mode of signaling through the soundscape that had been promoted and normalized before the war. One story, about a "shell-shocked" Indianapolis veteran who had spent twenty months in France, revealed the sonic trouble:

This young man boarded the Illinois Central at Indianapolis for a visit to Sullivan. All that went well until after the train left Dugger. Then suddenly the brakemen called out "Cass!" Passengers were alarmed to see the soldier grow suddenly most excited. They did not understand that "Cass" sounds a great deal like "Gas!" and that the word meant to the soldier that there was a deluge of Hun gas on hand. The Klaxon horn on the automobiles affected him the same way, as Klaxons were used at the front to give the gas alarm.[74]

Such stories were common in the postwar medical literature.

A seismic shift was under way in the cultural perceptual architectonics: the shock effect of war was altering the community sensibility about the meaning of the klaxon sound. There had always been dissenting opinions about whether or not the klaxon technology was the right way to solve the cultural problem of communication caused by the emergence of automobile technology in the twentieth century. But the Great War was the tipping point. As the troops returned home, the discourse against klaxon technology, led by calls for moderation and socially conscious sonic temperance, all began to crescendo.

In 1921, the *Creston Advertiser-Gazette and Plain Dealer* ran a telling editorial about the American public's growing reluctance to sound the klaxon after the war. This new behavior clashed with the normative prewar expectations of sounding the horn in the name of public safety. "Automobile drivers of the city and community, practically to a man, have received a stroke of paralysis in the hand which pushes the button that sounds the horn. Drivers do not sound their horn when approaching intersections." Now that people were mindful of how triggering the sound could be, they were failing to use their horns when they should. "Sound your horn," the editorialist urged. "It will prevent accident. Horns were placed on automobiles for a purpose."[75] People were risking their own safety, he worried, to stay silent.

The Klaxon Company, nonetheless, was at peak production. Though under new United Motors ownership, Klaxon factories had been retooled to meet Defense Department demand. Indeed, the company claimed factory output during the war "was diverted practically 100% to Government Use."[76] Now that same production was diverted back to private industry. In an increasingly conglomerating industry, Klaxon had secured contracts in the postwar period with the largest automobile makers to provide horns to be installed at the factory. Walter Coghlan, Klaxon's famous sales manager and originator of the "Safety First" campaign, who had served briefly in the navy listening to the klaxon warn of submarine attacks, returned from the war as secretary of the Klaxon Company.[77] He landed the industry-coveted factory contract with Ford, the largest automobile manufacturer in the world. Describing in *The Ford Owner* what having a klaxon meant, he boasted that it would "clear the way and permit driving along without slowing down or stopping." These words drew on prewar language. "Frequent slowdowns and stops," he wrote, "not only shorten the life of the car" but "put wear and tear on parts and 'nerves.'"[78] Yet the argument was stale, and the klaxon now troubled nerves more than it eased them. Coghlan's evangelical zeal was gone. By 1919, he resigned from the company, which had dramatically lowered its prices to stay competitive in an industry where plentiful horns were no longer sold as expensive accessories to consumers but for cheap and in bulk to manufacturers. Klaxon made up the difference with volume, increasing the number of klaxon units produced each year. In 1920, the plant moved from Newark to a much larger factory in Bloomfield.

Klaxon still had tremendous market leverage through brand recognition, which the company capitalized on with its "look under the hood and check the metal plate" ad campaign to pressure manufacturers to retain factory contracts. In 1923, Klaxon's production totaled 1,317,547 horns. A year later, General Motors saw the advantage of the brand strength and added Klaxon to its growing stable of companies. Advertising, sales, and production, which had been joined at the Newark factory, were further separated. The manufacturing of horns was now done by Remy Electric Company (later known as Delco-Remy), which moved machinery and equipment production to Anderson, Indiana. Klaxon's operations were moved to Detroit, closer to the industry's center. The klaxon, both as a sound technology and as a company, had been untethered from its origins.

During the Great War, nearly a decade of work lobbying, advertising, and persuading the public to associate the sound produced by klaxon technology with safe automobile use and social responsibility was shattered by the traumatic experience of millions across the globe. With the sense of perception and sound associations conditioned anew, klaxon technology entered a postwar cultural world more uncertain than ever about how the public would respond to the sound. Paradoxically, though retaining its dominance in the global soundscape, the now standard sound signaling technology was beginning its long decline.

7

SIDEWALK BLUES
The Klaxon in Diminuendo

By the time the Jazz Age took hold of postwar global culture, the klaxon was a ubiquitous part of the global soundscape, identified as a sound object, with *klaxon* used as both a generic noun and the root of a verb. Like jazz, the sound of the klaxon was everywhere. As the technocentered automobile culture rapidly expanded in the 1920s, debate over how to manage the place of the car in culture spread rapidly, and wherever it was discussed, the klaxon was part of the conversation.

It is hard to overstate the impact the rapidly expanding automobile culture had on postwar society and its internationalizing soundscape. With assembly line production, automobiles got much cheaper.[1] In 1908 a Model T took twelve and a half hours to assemble and cost $950; by the mid-1920s, Ford was producing a car every twenty-four seconds and the price had dropped to $290. In 1921, 1.5 million cars were sold in the United States; by 1929, the annual number topped five million. The number of automobiles on American roads roughly tripled over the course of a decade, and their sound was amplified with every purchase. Gijs Mom describes a similar growth in the European market, where car saturation and density grew exponentially in Europe—though more slowly in postwar Germany—during the 1920s.[2] The klaxon horn, as the dominant mode of communication linked to that increased traffic, was heard everywhere and all the time, a fact that Klaxon's marketing department touted endlessly.

Yet despite its omnipresence in the postwar soundscape, things had changed for the company and for the technology. Klaxon was now only one of several producers creating "klaxon-style" technology and competing for manufacturers' contracts in a quickly consolidating automobile industry. Klaxon's business approach was retooled as well, as it was forced to pivot from a post-factory accessory model based on a high price supported by a cultivated brand distinction to a low-price, volume-based production business model. Even before World War I, Klaxon had sold most of its inventory directly to carmakers to be installed at the factory. This trend accelerated as the auto industry consolidated and the speed of production dramatically increased. Klaxon's manufacturing company, once in Newark, had moved to a bigger factory in Anderson, Indiana, where it could lower the cost per unit by speeding up production and more easily distribute this increased volume to carmakers in Detroit. Yet for a world that had just endured a bloody war and an international pestilence, and in which "9 out of 10 owners and drivers know or use the Klaxon,"[3] the everyday sense of perception had shifted. After the war, the cultural perception of the klaxon, molded by years of carefully crafted advertising and media framing, no longer rang true; more often than not, use of the technology provoked a distinctly negative reaction.

Klaxon's marketing strategy, as attested by its ongoing campaigns in various international markets, did not adapt to changing cultural sensibilities but rather tried once again to mold them by returning to ready-made marketing language. As is evident from one postwar British ad, a throwback to the international prewar "Safety First" ad campaigns that embraced noise as a positive technological feature,[4] the company still tried to convince consumers by pointing to "power" and "reliability" and linking those ideas to its brand. Yet all over the world, the dominance of klaxon technology meant consumers had less choice about the sound they could project from the automobile they drove. There was a growing awareness that carmakers, not consumers, were determining the sound that "said something" about the driver and his or her relationship to the world. Exactly what it said, however, was contested as the chorus of voices articulating complaints about the klaxon grew louder and more frequent. This change in the conversations about the klaxon became a feature of everyday life. In all forms of cultural communication, the structure of feelings about the klaxon shifted, signaling the end of the klaxon's reign as a dominant communication technology that people believed could solve the problems of an automobile-centered culture.

Prewar Marketing in a Postwar Soundscape

The twenties did not come in roaring. The economic downturn, exacerbated by the 1919 influenza pandemic, caused things to stutter and restart several times as "flu bans" spread across the United States. Yet eventually, and with the help of Wall Street financing and the extension of consumer credit, the automobile market was off and running. Most of the literature on the automobile marks the 1920s as the true beginning of America's car-crazed cul-

Figure 51. Postwar reboot of Klaxon advertising for the British Victory Car in 1919. (*Grace's Guide to British Industrial History*)

ture. Europe's car craze followed in its wake. Klaxon's fortunes were tied to the explosion of the industry.

More cars meant more klaxons and, after being taught that sounding them would keep them safe, drivers did not want to stop. "Why do they do it?" asked one columnist for the British magazine *The Auto* after test driving a new car with a factory-installed klaxon he did not choose. "Armed with only the mechanical Klaxon, every time I wanted to overtake anybody I had to make a noise like a beast, because this particular horn knew nothing between silence and a 'Get out of my royal road, Heaven bless your silly soul!' blare, which made everybody turn around and say 'Who is this filthy creature, honking his way through life in such arrogance.'"[5] His interpretation of what sounding the klaxon signified was not an outlier. An increasing number of British authors now believed that the loud and instantaneous mode of "hooting" that the technology demanded was abusive and corrosive of the social fabric. When one used a klaxon, one was *screaming* at people to get out of the way. The claim that the safety benefits of enduring this technologically conditioned behavior offset the noisy annoyance no longer seemed to hold sway. Society, warned another author, needed to curb its rampant abuse: "Abuse of a horn—especially of a klaxon—is to be severely condemned at any time." Such behavior, made possible and amplified by technology, was "indicative of a nervous or overbearing nature in a driver."[6] Much had changed since the war, especially among veterans with echoes of klaxons in the trenches still ringing in their heads. A new signaling technology with better affordances that engendered better behavior was necessary.

While the postwar sense of sonic perception had changed, legal and governmental regimes dictating automobile use had not. Drivers were still required by prewar laws to use their horns constantly, which led people to interpret using a loud klaxon as rude and aggressive. In the United States, state and local laws required sounding the horn in all kinds of situations. Alabama, for example, still required drivers to sound their horn at every turn.[7] The residual form of response to the question of safety—more horn sounding—continued to lead national organizations, such as the National Automobile Chamber of Commerce, to suggest that car owners honk three times when backing up, a suggestion that echoed a Klaxon strategic campaign.[8] Yet whereas the brand promotion had once been aided by consumers' every honk, now sound signaling had become a lose-lose proposition in an America weary of the klaxon sound. Whatever safety advantages were gained by signaling were lost to annoyance and sound nuisance. "To toot or not to toot? That's a current motoring problem," wrote Carl M. Saunders in a 1920 syndicated column that ran in newspapers across America. The ongoing conflict between the need for safety and the inevitable sonic assault on your neighbor made it "impossible to lay down a rule for the horn." Neither compulsory signaling nor complete silencing of the technology by law solved the conundrum. "The din of horns is nerve-racking, we'll admit. But between a nervous breakdown and sorrowing pallbearers, we'll take the former every time."[9]

This horn-weary ambivalence about sound signaling in an automobile-centered world was echoed in all markets that carried Klaxon Company products. Though signs of a seismic shift in the culture's sonic perception were obvious during the interregnum period chronicled at the end of the last chapter, Klaxon had never been bigger in America. With the market for cars exploding in the postwar period, Klaxon was moving so much product that the company petitioned the Interstate Commerce Commission for a reduction in the rate it was charged for railroad freight.[10] Klaxon was not the only company supplying the market as competitors producing their own version of klaxon technology were growing fast. By May 1923, when Klaxon announced a 600 percent increase in production from May 1922, the company was producing 200,000 horns a month.[11] Klaxons were everywhere, and the company responded to the growing backlash against klaxon technology as it always had: bigger and louder marketing that touted its success as a social ratification of the technology.

In the spring of 1922, Klaxon ran a series of ads in the trade journal *Automobile Topics* to reassure dealers and manufacturers that its market share was firm. April, the company trumpeted, was "the biggest month in the history of the Klaxon company," in which "orders received so far promise new records for May."[12] Klaxon, another throwback ad campaign boasted, was now on "70.8 % of cars" and was "Nationally-Serviced" by way of the Remy franchises linked to the brand.[13] The marketing department wanted American consumers to know that the company had contracts with 162 car manufacturers, which installed the horns at the factory. One ad, directed to manufacturers, suggested that the Klaxon brand was a crucial factor that "makes them choose your car."[14]

The return to the rhetoric and style of the marketing campaigns of the prewar period, however, showed a certain blindness to the realities of the postwar soundscape; Klaxon's surge in advertising also displayed the anxiety about overproduction rippling throughout the automobile industry. Production was outpacing demand, which was leading to prices dropping dramatically as companies tried to unload their inventory. Klaxon was like many players in the automobile sector that turned to marketing to solve the overproduction problem. *Printers' Ink,* reporting on Klaxon's latest attempt to reinvigorate its brand, gushed about how effective Klaxon's "Ask 'em to buy" business-to-business campaign had been. In addition to ads in the trade journals, Klaxon also "made a big noise" by printing and mailing thousands of posters and postcards as part of a direct-to-consumer marketing strategy.[15] Klaxon even revived its "Danger Sound Klaxon" campaign, sending out free red tin signs to any local organizations willing to post them.[16]

Klaxon rebooted its expensive graphic campaigns in the popular press as well, where automobile advertising had quickly become a massive source of revenue for newspapers, trade journals, and magazines. As it had before the war, Klaxon took out expensive, color-saturated half- and full-page ads in the *Saturday Evening Post* and *Automotive Industries,* where it used the cross-promotional brand association of such companies as Chevrolet and Ford to tout its now "low-priced but genuine Klaxons." "Why run risks any longer . . .

weaker horns tempt danger. A Good horn is Safety Insurance. Only Klaxon quality is good enough!"[17] Recycling its prewar media, Klaxon crafted together bits and pieces from over a decade of advertisements: the graphic representation of the "sawtooth" sound wave cutting through the competing noises of the street, the "Clear the Way!" mnemonic and its association of volume and distance of sounding, and the situational representation of dangerous scenarios that the consumer might face. There was no better visualization of nostalgic associations of the Klaxon campaigns than the ads that ran in the *Saturday Evening Post,* recalling and repurposing advertising images and slogans from before the war. Yet these ads were also tone deaf, insofar as they were touting the very qualities of the sonic technology that now irritated people in the new perceptual paradigm. The sound of the klaxon might clear the way, but it also often triggered posttraumatic stress and fear among war veterans and created road rage and anger in off-road auditors exposed to the sound. Nonetheless, Klaxon went big in its advertising, starting a campaign that reproduced its print ads as large posters and distributing them to accessory stores and garages.[18] Klaxon seemed to miss a lesson from its adventures in localizing its messaging: advertising works best when it resonates with local concerns and structures of feeling. In a klaxon-saturated postwar soundscape, the reboot of prewar advertising created a dissonance that could not be remedied through repetition. This tone deafness to shifting consumer sensibilities repeated itself across the Atlantic in countries where klaxon technology was also well established.

Jazz Age Sound Saturation

During World War I, French companies had mass produced the klaxon horn for use in the trenches. The ancillary effect of this overproduction after the war was cheap and ubiquitous klaxon technology. In an era of intense inflation for consumer products, the klaxon was one of the few whose price dropped. "Before the war," opined an editorial in the staid mainstream *Le Figaro,* "one paid between 150 and 200 francs for a mechanical or button-model klaxon. Now, one can have a horn [*avertisseur mécanique*] for 45 francs. Is it the vulgarization of jazz-bands driving this low price? In any case, so much the worse for us."[19] This availability flipped the sociology of distinction: before the war, having an expensive horn was a sign that one had the means to afford the safety that the klaxon provided; after the war, it was common. And as the link to jazz indicates, the klaxon was quickly being associated with a postwar popular culture whose sounds many characterized as noise.[20]

As the company did in the United States and around the world, Klaxon in

Figure 52. One of the throwback situational ads used by Klaxon to reinvigorate the brand. From the *Saturday Evening Post,* May 5, 1923. (*Saturday Evening Post* Archive)

France returned to the same media messaging that had worked before the war, hoping to restore prewar brand association. One typical ad from 1920 in the glossy bourgeois mainstay *L'Illustration* focused on the strength of the sound and its impact on the soundscape, riffing on the standard tropes. Reminiscent of ads before the war, the graphic depicted a car rushing through town, pushing before it the klaxon sound waves that cleared the way. All heads were turned to see the bourgeois couple displaying its technological *savoir faire* and distinction; the copy boasted of the "most practical, most powerful, most sure" signaling device with "extra sound." Though this spoke to the mentality that had animated advertising before the war, the sensibility conveyed by the ad was out of place in a postwar world yearning for silence after years of eardrum-shattering explosions.

Figure 53. Blériot Klaxon ad from 1920, recycling imagery and ideas from the old formulas. From *L'Illustration*, April 17, 1920. (Scan by author)

Indeed, the cultural reaction in France against noise and the normalization of such noisy things as jazz and the klaxon was building. Journals and newspapers from across the political spectrum published screed after screed against the klaxon's noise, and legislatures started to act accordingly. By 1922, Article 26 of the revised French Highway Code stated that "devices [*appareils*] with multiple tones, because they create confusion, and devices with strident sounds, such as the klaxon, because they might provoke frightened movements and thus danger," were forbidden in populated areas.[21] The klaxon was, argued Henri Petit in the journal *La Vie Automobile,* one of the chief causes of the growing "*autophobie*" manifested in postwar daily life. "Several years ago, the klaxons of military cars brought happy hearts to the streets of the capital. But these sonic incongruities have been calmed and are now considered a thing of the past."[22] Along with exhaust smoke and the cut-out muffler, he wrote, the "usage of the klaxon in the city," for which the police were now fining drivers, was a public nuisance that only added to the bad perception of the automobile.

The Klaxon Company, the name of whose eponymous horn had become, by design, the generic word for horn—with *klaxoner* used in popular and parliamentary discourse as a verb—knew from the growing chorus of anti-noise voices that it was losing the battle for public opinion. It lobbied hard for the Klaxonet, the less "strident" of its horns, to be made legal in urban areas. Indeed, there were so many discussions of horn abuse in *La Revue du Touring Club de France* that Klaxon's lawyers contacted the organization, enjoining it from using the word "klaxon," which Klaxon had trademarked, as a generic term in its editorials. "The Klaxon Co Ltd wants us to know that the word is its property," wrote the editors. "From now on, we should abstain from employing it to designate *un appareil avertisseur*."[23] It was a toothless threat that revealed Klaxon's awareness that it was suffering from a branding backlash, a linguistic problem created through years of aggressive marketing, legal leveraging, and market dominance.

Indeed, one sign that the company was worried about the associations weighing on the brand was that it diversified its products in 1922, announcing a "new two-tone horn" that, though it looked the same and was branded Klaxon, was based on different technology and, the company said, had a different sound. The company was trying to show its sensitivity by responding to consumers and offering a softer tone for everyday use to be used first, before drivers sounded the older tone. Yet this did little to placate the antinoise critics, who were now focused on silencing the technology. Two terms, jazz band and klaxon, would soon come to stand for the noise confusion of the postwar era for many culture critics. Even in a city like Paris that forbade the klaxon, when people raged against noisy urban soundscapes, they used the word "Klaxon" as shorthand. Indeed, in the play *Poudre d'Or,* the French playwrights René Trintzius and Amédée Valentin repeatedly used the klaxon sound offstage as a dramatic device to symbolize an intrusion of unwanted sound from the outside world on the quiet repose associated with the private sphere.[24]

As in France, Germany's klaxon vendors tried to return to prewar strategic advertising methods after the war, even though the automotive sector, which had been hollowed out by the war, was slow to revive. Though the Klaxon franchise revved up its marketing department and moved the factory from Berlin to Frankfurt in 1922,[25] automotive sales were slow to bounce back in the postwar period owing to the decimation of the German middle class and the pressure on the German economy caused by the terms of the Versailles Treaty. Consumers who had the capital to buy new cars were likely to buy American cars despite the heavy tax on imports. In 1923, Ford opened an assembly line factory in Köln to skirt the massive import tax on automobiles.[26] Of the existing automobile makers, only Opel embraced the Fordist assembly line method. Even at the end of the decade, more than 40 percent of all cars sold in Germany were foreign. Yet tone-deaf German Klaxon vendors still tried to generate demand for the product using the same localized ads encouraging motorists to check under the hood to make sure the factory-installed horn was a Klaxon, as confirmed by the Klaxon metal nameplate. And as in other European countries, the klaxon sound now drew the ire of Germans who could not afford to buy a car, and of critics who believed that the postwar soundscape needed more quietness. There was good reason to be concerned about the latter. Of the six million veterans, 2.7 million were severely wounded, many suffering from shell shock caused by the trauma they had endured at the front. They had a pathological fear of loud noises that lingered long after the war.[27]

Some of this antinoise sentiment in Germany was a mark of cultural continuity. Around the time the klaxon was invented, *Antilärmverein* (Anti-Noise Society) founder Theodor Lessing had already opined that selfish noisemakers used technology like the automobile to satisfy a primal will to power, forcing themselves on others by making themselves heard.[28] By 1926, his feelings had not changed. "I hate the cries of the street merchants and newspaper vendors," he wrote. "I hate the ringing of the church bells, I hate the senseless noise of the factory sirens, but what I hate most are the stinking autos." He fantasized stealing a pocket watch so that he could be taken to prison, where he would finally have peace away from the gramophones, telephones, and car horns.[29] Though some of the noisemakers who drew his ire continued to be from the working class, such as street vendors and laborers, for most of the 1920s the automobiles he loathed were associated with the well-to-do.

Some of the shift in sonic sensibility was also a response to the new times. In the culture of the newly founded Weimar Republic, the street and its impact on the human sensorium became the source of an aesthetic and a *Zeitgeist*, tapped into by artists in the "Novembergruppe" like Otto Möller, whose 1920 painting "Street Noise" recalls the Futurists' dynamic representation of urban sound, and by the "asphalt literature" movement, writers, poets, and filmmakers whose work described the dark, teeming world of the postwar streets. "Car horns dominate the orchestra of great cities," wrote flâneur and culture critic Walter Benjamin.[30] Along with being places where people dealt with the impact of new technologies, streets themselves were often occupied by people protesting the cultural disturbance caused by an increasingly automobile-centric world. In 1924–25, even after the 1923 hyperinflation crisis was contained, the average price of a car was beyond the means of 90 percent of German families.[31] There were huge spikes in protests all over Germany demanding the government do something about automobiles and the way that they—and the wealthy people who used them, while regular *Volk* were packed into buses— forced people out of the streets.[32] The German motorcycle industry benefited from the formidable price tag on automobiles and fuel. Yet noisy horns were on both, and they still posed a fright problem for the more than 55 percent of vehicles in Germany that were horse-drawn.[33] Klaxons were no longer associated with greater safety but rather had become symbols of the postwar cultural unrest that people who wanted things to be as they were before the war resented. In 1928, as the automobile industry was finally picking up, young Joseph Goebbels plugged in to that animus, strategically railing against the dizzying soundscape of Berlin, where "bells on streetcars ring, buses clatter by honking their horns, stuffed full of people and more people, taxis and fancy private automobiles hum over the glassy asphalt. . . . Squeals and squeaks so assault the ear that the novices run the constant risk of losing their calm disposition."[34] To his ears, trained to listen for things that people loathed so that he could exploit them in his propaganda for the emerging Nazi Party, city noise was one of the many things wrong with Germany, a useful object to provoke the smoldering resentment of the "Real Berlin waiting to pounce." Just how Germans would deal with automobiles and noise was unclear.

Though other "Klaxonized" countries in Europe had benefited much more from the economic and cultural exuberance often associated with the turbulent Jazz Age, they did share an ambivalence about, and a certain weariness with, many of the sounds that seemed to accompany the changes in modernity. Negotiating and contesting those noises took on increasing importance in the politics of everyday life.

Blasting Horns and the Politics of Everyday Noise

In cities all over the world, the debate over the automobile horn and its place in postwar life took on increasing political importance. In many ways the 1920s were the decade when cities as spaces were transformed by automobiles and became "automobile cities." The vigorous debates over the role of sound signaling as a mechanism for negotiating traffic within urban spaces played an important role in that reorganization. Like the marketing literature promoting the klaxon, the antinoise discourse that lashed out against the klaxon as a symbol of a noisy modernity drew from many sources, often reproducing the metaphors and arguments in circulation before the war. As a Frank Hanley cartoon from a December 1927 *Life* magazine shows, with the nostalgic sounds of old-fashioned church chimes set in opposition to the klaxon noise that causes people to jump and grab their heads, these symbolic associations were coalescing as a kind of shorthand, fixed in the public imagination.

In most cities, the noisy sound of the automobile horn continued to be a social, political, governmental, and commercial problem. Unwanted sound is, by definition, noise, and the war on noise was a dominant theme in debates about the future of the city. In 1922 the New York Merchants' Association launched a campaign "against the fiendish contraptions" used by trucks and automobiles "to warn of their approach":

Figure 54. Satirical Frank Hanley cartoon in *Life* showing a common reaction to the klaxon's noise. From *Life,* December 8, 1927. (Pennsylvania State University Library)

The Church that felt it had to compete with Modern Conditions has a set of Klaxons put up, to take the place of the Old-Fashioned Chimes.

Who has not had ten years clipped off his life by the sudden raucous blast of a truck driver. . . . Who, walking carefully on the sidewalk, apparently out of harm's way and following some priceless train of thought, has not had momentary panic drive out all consecutive consciousness by the shrieking crackle of an automobile wending its way down an uncongested street? And, worse still, who has not known all the sensations of a maniac, when twenty impatient drivers at a street crossing commence a klaxon chorus in the useless effort to hurry the traffic policemen? . . . If the merchants' association can do anything to quiet them it will earn the gratitude of all New Yorkers.[35]

New York was one of many cities engaged in antinoise politics that was yielding results, rolling back the pro-Klaxon ordinance law from before the war. Based on a similar outcry from residents, Tokyo altered its rules of the road as well in 1922, asking drivers to wave to the pedestrian first before startling him or her with the horn.[36]

In 1923, French antinoise editorialists turned up the volume of their own complaints about the way horns disturbed the public in need of repose. They reported how Britain's interior minister had instructed police in cities across Britain to crack down on motorists and taxis that made "unnecessary noise during the night with horns or klaxons."[37] Following the British lead, the French minister of hygiene and the minister of transportation joined forces to examine "other things that could be done to preserve as much as possible the sleep of those living in big cities." Where automobile associations had once posted signs asking motorists to sound their horns, by the end of the decade it was the *Societé pour la suppression du bruit* in Paris that was posting signage directing drivers to think twice before honking: "Listen! Reflect for a second when your nervous hand wants to blare it: is it really necessary?"[38]

With reactions against the noise of automobile culture getting louder, the industry took note and tried to respond. The American automobile industry—producing over four million cars a year by the mid-1920s[39]—was the first to act. In 1924 George Graham, vice president of Chandler Motor Car Company and chairman of the National Automobile Chamber of Commerce, presented the results of an automobile industry study on how better to protect the safety and solitude of the pedestrian: "We have the pedestrian's viewpoint when we furiously resent the boisterous horn discharged directly at our ear."[40] It was neither the driver's nor the pedestrian's fault, he said, but rather an inevitable result of the "demand for swifter and better transportation, subject to the control of the individual operator."[41] This demand accounted for the explosion of registered automobiles from 13,000 in 1900 to more than 15 million in 1923. Quite simply, he pointed out, "the automobile has changed the daily life of our people." That change was discussed at the Conference on Street and Highway Safety, one of many national and international assemblies dealing with the explosion of global car culture. Among the many recommendations made at the conference was a suggestion that states adopt standard signs and signals, as well as visual cues instead of sonic communication technology, which might better direct traffic while reducing noise. Traffic lights and visual signaling from one car to another—either by hand or by using new devices—were recommended instead of acoustic signaling,[42] which had lost its utility owing to the many competing noises in the chaotic urban soundscape.

This chaotic development posed a growing problem stemming from the way klaxon technology had been sold: the impetus to use more noise to combat the problem of noise was no longer persuasive. As a *New York Times* writer observed, sounding a horn proved helplessly behind the times: "Some motorists seem to consider a horn as a medium of amusement which makes it possible to frighten innocent travelers or to make night and even day in the suburbs and along the countryside hideous by an endless series of blasts. These thoughtless folks blow their horns on every possible occasion. They are a nuisance in the neighborhoods they frequent."[43] French writers similarly argued that using klaxon technology to "clear the road," as Klaxon advertising promised drivers the ability to do, reflected a problem of sociality. Before the automobile, "there used to be a road politeness [*politesse de la route*] . . . where members of the community were fraternally united by common interest."[44] Now the "new unhinged drivers have taken possession of the road by right of conquest."[45] The "menacing aggressiveness of these drivers on town and country roads" was reflected in the "language of horns." More politeness was needed: "Do you know anything more insolent than the inescapably harsh menace of the klaxon operated by an impatient and authoritarian hand? Nothing is more humiliating than the pre-emptive order of that barbarous cry, which scorches the ears and resembles the caw of a monstrous crow with a cold mixed with the whinny of an enraged pig. It screams its odious 'Get out of there, I am coming! Move pedestrian, dive on the ground! Faster than that, or I will crash into you.'"[46] Klaxon horns' seemingly imperative orders enraged others and degraded the social contract. A softer approach was suggested. "Soften, o' automobilists, the accents of your horn; ask politely to pass." Less aggressive signaling would help remedy postwar aggression. "We need, urgently, to institute a politeness of the road."[47] Such sentiment rippled across Europe as municipality after municipality in France, Belgium, and Switzerland banned klaxons and sirens to protect the nerves of their citizens.[48]

In Europe, the growth in factory-made cars with factory-installed horns accelerated the conversation about the utility of sound signals. At scale, the klaxon was increasingly heard as a problem in older, denser cities whose soundscapes were now saturated with the sound of ever more automobiles. Whereas every klaxon signal used to help spread the brand and its technological gospel, now each aaOOgah added affirmation to the voices who decried its presence in the soundscape.

The Sound of the Klaxon in Musical Culture

With the overwhelming sound of millions of cars being added to city soundscapes worldwide each year, it was inevitable that the klaxon, already a generic brand icon used as a noun and as the root of a verb, became a ready-made linguistic sign of the noisy cultural shifts disrupting everyday life. As writers, artists, and musicians tried to make sense of the changing postwar soundscape, their work came to terms with the klaxon sound. Nowhere was the structure of feeling associated with the klaxon more striking than in music. The way that musicians used the klaxon sound relative to other sounds in their compositions suggests how to recognize what the sound meant to them.

In symphonic music, the klaxon sound was often used provocatively by avant-garde composers precisely *because* it shocked the bourgeois sensibilities of audiences and music critics. For example, composers in Berlin's Dadaist scene incorporated sounds produced by horns and machines, seeking to flip how audiences perceived them. The more they ruffled the starched sensibilities of the bourgeoisie, the better. Jefim Golyscheff's 1919 *Anti-Symphony,* for example, recast all kinds of industrial noises—the very sounds driving antinoise politics—as beautiful musical sounds.

In Paris, Jean Cocteau and other artists at the Boeuf sur le Toit embraced the klaxon just as they embraced jazz, as a noisy alternative to stifling prewar aesthetics. In fact, composer Francis Poulenc wielded a klaxon horn as part of the ensemble's "jazz band" drum kit, creating a sound that Cocteau described as a "domesticated catastrophe [*catastrophe apprivoisée*]."[49] This cocktail of analogous sounds mixed by the *barman des bruits,* wrote Cocteau, was perfectly suited for "the fatigue of our ears." Jazz, the "music of American machines," was the antidote "against a useless beauty that encourages superfluousness." Like the klaxon in the street, jazz music had the "spirit of shock" that so intrigued the avant-garde.[50]

When Erik Satie wrote the score to the ballet *Parade,* he also incorporated klaxons, sirens, and airplane and train sounds to capture the modern spirit. These realistic noises, thrown "into relief," were "of the same character as the bits of newspapers and other everyday objects that the Cubist painters employ frequently in their pictures."[51] It seems only appropriate that Picasso's costume for the American manager in *Parade* was a Cubist caricature of the French view of America, a pastiche that included cowboy chaps, skyscrapers, and a klaxon horn.

Similarly, George Antheil, an American living and working in Paris with these Dadaist and Surrealist artists, wrote *Ballet Mécanique* as a comment on modern urban life. He utilized innovative instrumentation and nontraditional electrical devices to create a dissonant, rhythmically driving piece for sixteen mechanical pianos played from a single master roll controlled by a switchboard. Along with eight xylophones and four bass drums, he supplemented the sound of his composition with two electric motors with buzzing attachments, two large pieces of steel, one siren, and one klaxon.

Some composers tried to layer the klaxon sound into more traditional symphonic music, as the American composer Frederick Shepherd Converse did when he wrote "Flivver Ten Million," to help Ford celebrate producing its ten-millionth car. Set in Detroit, the piece incorporates the industrial rhythms of factories, along with the percussive use of klaxon horns to paint a sound portrait of an automobile-centered way of life. While one *Times* critic had no problems with Converse's "humorous use of klaxon horns,"[52] critic Robert H. Hull decried Converse's musical realism as "noise without music."[53] No matter how it was used, the klaxon sound upset most ears in the concert hall.

The klaxon also became a loaded sonic symbol in recorded popular music. With the American economy booming, more people were buying record players. Blues and jazz record sales exploded in the postwar period. Natural sound and novelty sound effects were becoming easier to record with better microphone technology and, just as the early recorded bulb horns sounds had done, these sound effects helped get the listener's attention. Klaxon sound increasingly found its way into popular jazz recordings.

That jazz artists used their recorded music to say something about automobile culture and the klaxon was unsurprising. Many Black jazz musicians embraced automobiles and car culture, which gave them a mobility they felt excluded from in Jim Crow America. Duke Ellington, who proudly drove his Chandler through Harlem, once said that "jazz is like the automobile and airplane. It is modern and it is American."[54] His song "Trumpet in Spades" merges the two ideas and was meant to reflect "changes in crowd and car traffic" by changes in tempo and tone.[55] Fellow Harlemite Fletcher Henderson also embraced the sound of the automobile. In the recorded version of "Forsaken Blues," for example, he explicitly linked jazz and the klaxon as features of the modern soundscape. He used the hand klaxon as a musical instrument at a mid-chorus drum break to call the listener's attention to a change in voicing, and again at the end of the song to punctuate a break before a new horn player took over the melody.

When the self-proclaimed inventor of jazz, Jelly Roll Morton, used the klaxon's recognizable sound on his record single "Sidewalk Blues," he did so to comment on the stresses of urban life. Morton himself famously drove a klaxon-equipped Cadillac, a brand now folded into General Motors. He was well aware of the advantages of mobility that automobile culture had brought to travelling jazz musicians, especially African Americans. Yet he was equally aware of the antipathy to the noise of automobiles, which triggered a new kind of "blues" that weighed on the minds of many jazz fans. With "Sidewalk Blues," Morton used the recorded klaxon to paint a musical vignette, capturing a story of cause and effect that new urban listeners—like the millions of African Americans migrating to the automobile-saturated cities up north for jobs—could understand.

The recording begins with the sound of a man whistling and a general ruckus of voices and sounds over which a loud push-button electric klaxon sounds, as if the auditors were acoustic witnesses to a near accident. Morton's voice screams out at an imagined pedestrian, a victim of the modern urban soundscape: "Hey, Get out of the way! What are you trying to do, knock a streetcar off the track? You're so dumb, you should be president of the deaf-and-dumb society!" In response, the absent-minded and traumatized object of this tirade replies, "I'm sorry, boss, but I got the Sidewalk Blues." Morton then leads his band into a ten-bar introduction before announcing the melody in the first twelve-bar theme, followed by a second twelve-bar melody. But just as the klaxon pushed the soundscape and introduced a new kind of blues for the city dweller, Morton pushed the twelve-bar song form, melding it with the thirty-two-bar Tin Pan Alley standard form. As with Henderson's "Forsaken Blues," the klaxon is re-sounded in the middle of the C theme as a percussive break and returns again at the end to bookend the recording. The song seems to articulate a variation on a salutary theme that was widespread across the jazz cannon: the cure for the "sidewalk blues," a pedestrian condition caused by the constant assault of urban sound, was to sing the blues away.

Klaxon's marketing department was also interested in the power of popular music and radio advertising as a means to manage the public's affective associations. In 1924 the company commissioned the song "Danger Sound Klaxon" as a musical number for performance on the radio or at trade shows. The song's words, by J. K. Gould, were a pastiche of old copy, echoing taglines from "Klaxon Gets Action" and other earlier campaigns. The lyrics were not entirely recycled; they responded to the pedestrian criticism that was mounting in the public debate about car horns:

There are buzzers and chimes
And whistles sometimes
    That screech in a traffic jam

In the midst of your cares
And all unawares
    They frighten you weak as a lamb

But Klaxon's polite
They warn you just right
    They call it a pedestrian's delight

Again, Klaxon's musical media strategy was nostalgic and a pastiche of ear-lier advertising efforts, stuck in the culture of the first decade of the compa-ny's marketing campaigns. There were not really any chimes competing for attention anymore, and the only whistles that one heard in the street were from traffic cops. Klaxon acknowledged the variety within the soundscape but—as it had always done—promoted the idea that safety and utility should count more than agreeability or musicality. Aggressive sound that shocked the pedestrian and driver alike was preferable to an aesthetically pleasing sig-nal. Nonetheless, knowing the growing perception that the shriek produced by klaxon technology was aggressive and rude, the company sought to asso-ciate it with the exact opposite, politeness. The song musically characterized the sound as giving just the right warning to pedestrians. The chorus—as did the waltzlike feel of the song—echoed the slogans of yesteryear, lining them up one nostalgic stanza after another:

> Put a Klaxon horn up on your car to warn
> The absent kind of minded folks
> For it chases the chicks
> And it hurries the hicks
> And rouses the old slow pokes
> If you use a Klaxon
> You can get quick action
> It's a signal none can scorn.
> So buy, beg or steal
> For your automobile
> A Klack, Klack Klaxon horn.

The second verse repeated more of Klaxon's greatest advertising slogans, but the song was as stale as the ad copy. Before returning to the chorus, it fin-ished with a nod to the law, evoking a traffic accident and echoing the idea that judges and insurance adjusters preferred the "safety" of the klaxon tone: "But each owner pays / Or gets thirty days / And then the judge repeats this little phrase" (Chorus). Yet having a song allude to institutions of risk man-agement, law, and the threat of punishment did little to appeal to the joy that automobile culture often sought. The sentiment and the structure of feel-ing in the song were both strikingly behind the times and discordant with the speedy excitement associated with the roaring automobile culture of the 1920s. More than anything, Klaxon's commercial tune revealed the company's marketing dilemma: Klaxon was trying to occupy the middle ground between promoting automobiling and recognizing it as a dangerously transformative trend. It was a decidedly unfun place to be.

An American in Paris and the Turn against the Klaxon

There was a reason that Klaxon's musical marketers found themselves in a tough spot. Indeed, cities everywhere were studying noise and working on solutions to the problems it caused in everyday culture, often turning to engineers for fixes. In New York City, E. E. Free, the science editor of *The Forum*, began a systematic, scientific study of city noise in 1926 using a Western Electric "audiometer" like the one developed a year earlier by Bell Telephone Laboratories to measure and record sound levels in what Bell Labs called "sensation units."[56] "No city need put up with its present clamor if the citizens really want a change. . . . Just as soon as enough people demand quiet they can have it."[57] Free singled out "private automobiles and their too-easily-tooted horns" as something that could be addressed through regulation.[58] The study called for a reappraisal of laws compelling motorists to sound their horn as a warning. "No automobile horn or other warning signal shall be blown on streets equipped with traffic lights or provided with traffic officers (horn signals being then totally unnecessary) and horn signals in other locations shall be limited to a single sound lasting not over one second."[59] Wrote one *New York Times* columnist, "With the restriction of Klaxon horns and the tendency to use them unnecessarily I am in hearty accord."[60]

Across America and Europe, as Karin Bijsterveld has meticulously chronicled,[61] similar political urges and antinoise initiatives emerged, many of them singling out the klaxon and recommending traffic lights. In Britain, the urgency of remediating the impact of unwanted sound had coalesced into a growing political movement, now led by scientists. The British Medical Association (BMA) offered recommendations for dealing with the sonic scourge plaguing the postwar recovery. "The present increase in unnecessary noise is a factor in creating neurosis," it declared, "and may be regarded as analogous to the shell shock that followed deafening bombardments during the war."[62] The klaxon was one of the worst offenders: "The public suffered from noise because it was unorganized and had no way to voice its opposition to the worst causes of unnecessary noise. Each new addition has been accepted with astonishing complacency. The unsilenced motor cycle, the klaxon, the heavy lorry, the aeroplane, the steam tractor and the pneumatic drill, have been tolerated in turn."[63] Though the *British Medical Journal* (*BMJ*) editorialists noted that scientific studies had proved that people's perception of sound changed and that there was "no limit to man's capacity for adapting himself to noxious influences once he regards them as inevitable," they did believe it possible and prudent to silence the more bothersome "noise that has worked its way into the texture of life."[64]

The BMA worried about the long-term impact of noise and what the pleasure in making noise said about people. "They discover for themselves that noise is a symbol of power. . . . It is permissible to speculate whether it is a sense of frustrated power, a teasing inferiority complex, that drives the motorist to substitute the klaxon horn for the drum." Over time, noise degraded the health and moral fiber of the public. If traffic safety was the issue, the *BMJ* suggested regulating the speed of traffic; klaxons were not the answer. "The association is of the opinion that klaxons and electric hooters should be rigidly suppressed, certainly in towns and villages; but if, in the interests of the public, it is found that some warning instruments must be used, a low toned bulb horn should be substituted."[65] Politicians used the scientific recommendations to strengthen the force of their legislative push. In 1927, Conservative Lord Montagu, writing from his quiet country estate in Beaulieu, spoke out against the noisy impact of automobile ownership becoming commonplace: "Noise in our streets and roads has so much increased that it is becoming a real curse of modern life."[66] Even drivers who preferred the musical bulb horn were often "compelled to abandon it in favour of something louder, on account of the greater danger both to themselves and to others."[67] It was time, he argued, for the government to finally tackle the problem. Shortly thereafter, Wilfrid Ashley, minister of transport, ordered the government to consider "whether the use of klaxon and similar horns should not be prohibited in urban areas and motorists made to rely on bulb horns, which do not make such a strident noise."[68]

In the House of Commons, political parties found common ground in the idea that "the use of any piercing electric motor-horn at any hour of the night" was "an offence." MP Philip Morrell stated plainly that "the root of the evil lies in the motor-horn. It is the perpetual hooting of horns that makes life in many places almost intolerable, and if the evil of noise is to be diminished, the first thing to do is to regulate the use of the horn." All "speculative" and "unnecessary hooting" should be "made an offence punishable by fine and imprisonment."[69] In 1928 the Royal Automobile Club, following robust debate within the association, proposed banning the "klaxon and similar autohorns." Not only were they noisy, they were "rather an encouragement of bad driving than a means to safety." If horns were to be used, there was a need for better technology, horns that might approximate the "pleasant" sound of the old bulb horns yet signal as immediately as the "mechanical hooters."[70]

As a model for how government could silence unwanted sound, many

British writers and legislators pointed to France, where municipal statutes across the country were prohibiting klaxon technology. "France has already taken action against unpleasant hooters, forbidding the klaxon and the siren in urban districts and enforcing the comparatively melodious bulb horn."[71] The préfet de police in Paris went one step further, making it illegal to use any horn between 1 and 6 a.m. Yet writers commenting on the Parisian laws pointed out how, despite thousands of fines being issued in a more rigorous enforcement campaign, it was difficult to get taxicabs to stop honking their horns.[72] Indeed, one municipal councilor of Paris likened the use of the klaxon to "legal charivari," which "continually over-excited the nerves."[73]

In a sense, the French driving public had adopted communicative behavior conditioned by a feedback loop of decades of compulsory signaling combined with a powerful consumer discourse that equated sounding the horn loudly and repeatedly with safety. Paris was singled out by travelers from all over the world, who marveled at the amount of honking that went on in the French capital. But now by law, and even though the generic name associated with the brand had been modified into the common verb for honking, *klaxoner*, it was often not the motor-driven klaxon sound that Parisians were hearing but rather a wide variety of bulb-driven horns, some of them with sound produced by a reed, and other newer horns, such as the Ciccaphone,[74] which used a vibrating membrane or diaphragm. Nowhere was the polyphonic pluralism of car horns in the post-klaxon era better sonically represented than in George Gershwin's famous ode to Jazz Age Paris, *An American in Paris*, written during and after Gershwin's trip to the city in 1928.

Gershwin had gone to Paris to learn more about composition, finding affinity with many avant-garde musicians who incorporated the sounds of the streets into their music as a kind of sonic realism. In *An American in Paris*, Gershwin sought to convey the feel of the urban soundscape, its rhythms and musical dissonances and its impact on the modern subject, through his own version of musical realism. What comes across when one listens to the piece is the musicality of the horns that so fascinated Gershwin, so different from the ubiquitous klaxons that dominated New York's soundscape. It seems to confirm a claim made in the *Chicago Daily Tribune* in 1924 that "Parisians want all auto horns to be musical."[75]

Much of the first part of the piece evokes traffic noise, the "sound of the *place de la Concorde* during rush hour,"[76] the honking of taxis heard by an American—connoted by melismatic blues notes on the clarinet—walking down Parisian streets. Though for years musicologists thought that the score indicated horns that were musically pitched, in fact the pitches of the bulb horns in a 1929 recording sounds a good deal like the horns that were regaining market share in Paris, a city that had made it illegal to sound the klaxon.[77] Indeed, in the same year as Gershwin's sonic ode to Parisian horn polyphony was performed, Klaxon unveiled its own version of the compressed-air horns that were starting to gain popularity in a world that, while wanting the push-button affordance of klaxon technology, yearned for the more melodic horns of the early days of the automobile.

All over the world, the mechanical tone of the ubiquitous klaxon was increasingly associated with a kind of noisy selfish behavior scorned by politicians, doctors, and moralists. Faced with such moral opprobrium, consumers and the *sensis communis* started to turn away from the klaxon and toward something less abrasive. Klaxon, once a sound associated with safety and the promise of technology to solve the problems caused by technology in the age of the automobile, was now associated with mass-produced rudeness. Over time, the new compressed-air horns, a technology that responded to the call for melodic horns while retaining the technological affordances of electric push-button devices, prevailed. Having a horn like this now said that the user was concerned with the sound experience of others while still being at the vanguard of technological innovation in an automobile-centered world.

Of all the literary representations of Jazz Age culture and its aspirational automobility, F. Scott Fitzgerald's rendering of Jay Gatsby's car, "a rich cream color, bright with nickel, swollen here and there in its monstrous length," stands out as one of the most iconic, especially in relation to the logic of class envy and the social distinction the auto conspicuously conferred.[78] For the narrator, Daisy's voice was not the only sound object in Gatsby's world that sounded like it was "full of money." Personifying the conspicuous tastes of the postwar nouveau riche, Gatsby did not use a klaxon but instead was an early adopter of a new, more musical push-button horn that sounded more expensive and conveyed his effortless class distinction. "At nine o'clock, one morning late in July, Gatsby's gorgeous car lurched up the rocky drive to my door and gave out a burst of melody from its three noted horn."[79] The sound that so fascinated the narrator, a multitone compressed-air horn, was a throwback to the exhaust-driven trumpets of the prewar period, like the Gabriel horn or the horns used by the German kaiser; it let others know that someone as stylish as Gatsby was coming down the road. Though Gatsby nonetheless hit and killed Myrtle Wilson with his car, his horn was indeed the kind of signaling technology that quickly emerged to compete with the klaxon for dominance within the symbolic economy of the bourgeois consumer trying to say something through his choice of technologies. As the klaxon achieved the status of industry standard, it became less distinct, its once prized technological newness fading from the public imagination. To have one's horn stand out in crowded streets as distinctive, one needed something new.

This sentiment was echoed by one of the most famous American pop sign-ers of the late twenties, Eddie Cantor. His "Automobile Horn Song," recorded in 1929, featured a three-tone horn similar to Gatsby's. Cantor sings that more than anything else in the world, he wants to "get myself an automobile with a horn that goes"—a three-tone air horn with four notes (C-E-G-E)—a sound included in the recording. In the middle of the second verse, right after the line "With a horn on my little coupé, things will be coming my way," the singer's joy and the song's rhythm are interrupted by the harsh sound of a klaxon. The latter belongs to a distinctly Irish-sounding police officer who tells him to "Pull over, there . . . what's a matter with you?" He scolds Cantor for speeding and driving on the wrong side of the street. So while the new, more musical three-tone compressed-air horn is associated with the happy-go-lucky Cantor and the joy of driving, the klaxon was associated with being a Prohibition-era killjoy. Being an early adopter of the latest communication technology paid off in the social recognition it conferred on the consumer. Klaxon, however, no longer offered anything new.

Science Tips the Scale

At the same time that the klaxon was losing its appeal and social distinction in automobile-centered popular culture, scientists around the world were study-ing the impact of horn sound on the soundscape and on the people who lived in soundscapes, using audiometer technology. A new measurement unit, the decibel, became the standard all over the world. In 1929 the British govern-ment directed the National Physical Laboratory in London to systematically study horn sounds to ascertain their physiological impact on pedestrians, to come up with objective measurements for "stridency," and to suggest better technology.[80] The request reproduced the language of reports by the Ministry of Transport, which insisted that "complaints against excessive and nerve-racking noises from motor horns constitute a legitimate grievance."[81] The National Physical Laboratory measured the sound level produced by differ-ent tones of horns with the idea of recommending a horn that would be safe and yet not have as negative an impact on public health. Its scientific find-ings were trumpeted by British moralists, who used them to bolster their case against the klaxon as a symbol of all that was wrong in postwar culture. Wrote G. Sterling Taylor in his 1929 essay "The Car Mind":

It is now considered polite behavior for a driver to make the most amaz-
ing noises with his horn if any foot passenger or any other car should
dare to use the highway. . . . If the individual is allowed to hoot (or, in
other words yell) at any fellow being who dares to use the road when he,
the hooter, wishes to use it, then it will not be long before he begins to
believe that the rest of existence can be conducted on the principle, that
the highway of life is for the man who can push the most people out of
the way.[82]

Sound mattered to society, and the way that it was used produced more than
noise. The affordances of sound technology, the ease and volume, also produced social subjects conditioned to communicate with one another and to
negotiate space.

At around the same time in France, a special laboratory of Arts et Métier
Paris Tech, together with the Paris prefect of police, undertook a similar sur-
vey. They measured the sound level produced by different horns in decibels
to determine which horns should be considered a public nuisance. Like their
British counterparts, they condemned the harsh "cacophony" of klaxons and
suggested using horns with more musical sounds.[83]

In America, Shirley Wynne, the health commissioner of New York City,
turned to the engineers at Bell Telephone Laboratories to measure city noise.
Bell set up roving measurement trucks in thousands of places and tested
thirty-four different horns, presenting its findings to the New York City Noise
Abatement Commission.[84] Bell found that the objectionable nature of some
horns (the klaxon was measured at 100 decibels by Bell's J. C. Steinberg in
1930)[85] went beyond its raw decibel measurement. Most of the available horns
were objectionable, especially the Klaxon and klaxon-type horns such as the
Sparton and Long Horn. The commission called for engineers to create "an
auto horn that will combine the maximum warning effect with the least
amount of objectionable noise."[86]

Scientific findings seemed to move automobile manufacturers, which
responded by redesigning the signaling devices they put on their cars. A fol-
low-up study a year later indicated that only 7 percent of the new horns disturbed the senses.[87] By the early 1930s the sound technology market was shifting, trying to resonate with the preferred sensibilities of the buying public.

Faced with a public that in all aspects of cultural communication increasingly had a negative association with the klaxon sound, klaxon signaling technology entered a new phase of diminuendo in the soundscape. As an auditory
topos, a brand, concept, and symbol that stimulated an ongoing conversa-

tion about the place of the automobile in society and the struggle over the soundscape, the klaxon would remain a potent though residual technological form. Nonetheless, the sound technology and its acoustic production—a harsh sound so powerful it could cut through the noise of the streets—had lost its appeal as a consumer product that could solve the problems of the automobile-centered world.

Conclusion
QUIETING THE KLAXON

The story of the klaxon's diminuendo, fading as quickly as it had arisen as an answer to the safety problems of automobile technology, turned on more than its association with war and its status as an iconic aural symbol of a noisy modern life. It also slipped out of favor in the cultural sensorium as part of a general trend away from using sound technology to navigate through traffic. This desire for quiet technology was already present when automobile technology emerged and became dominant in everyday life. But as the klaxon's sound faded from the soundscape, the technology associated with quietness started its ascent. Residual technologies and behaviors conditioned by signaling technology lingered on in automobile culture, but as the political movement against noise gained power in cities and countries everywhere, engineers turned their attention to other solutions to the social problems created by the automobile.

First and foremost, with the increasing noise associated with cars, the eye—rather than the ear—became the sense organ that signaling technology engineers tried to make primary to achieve better communication among drivers. Engineers looking to solve the problems of traffic safety that sound signaling had failed to fix began to tinker with visual signaling through signs, semaphore, and traffic lights in the 1920s. Since the utility of sound signaling decreased as the cacophony of competing horns grew, slowly but surely visual signaling technology became more widespread. Most US cities had red octagonal stop signs by 1920, and Europe began adopting them in the 1930s. In 1931 the League of Nations adopted a uniform system of street signs, something that the tourism industry favored to avoid traveler confusion.[1]

On heavily traveled roads, electrically engineered visual signals utilizing the automatic timer technology developed during the Great War made traffic lights possible in American cities by the late 1920s. The number of traffic lights

Figure 55. A new automated traffic light for managing traffic in Washington, DC, 1925. Visual signaling began to replace the noisy horns and whistles. (Library of Congress)

increased in cities throughout the twenties. New York had ninety-eight auto-matic lights in 1926, and by 1928 it had more than 260. London first began installing timed signal lights in 1931, and city after city began adopting scien-tific management theories to better design streets for the automobile-centered world. Gradually, through education campaigns and social practice, automo-bilists and pedestrians alike came to rely more on looking and waiting rather than listening as they negotiated traffic.[2]

It was not only at crossroads that visual signaling began gaining traction. Citing the rise in traffic fatalities, the State of New York suggested that driv-ers use arm signals with the left arm—straight out with the hand pointing to turn left, straight out with the palm directed toward the rear to stop, and moving the arm in a circular manner to turn right—to indicate their inten-tion to other drivers.[3] Consumers could buy special gloves to make sure their hand signals were seen. Around the world, car companies and government agencies began educational initiatives to try to teach people conditioned by decades of sound signaling a new way to manage their mobility.

As the number of cars grew on global streets, traffic management authori-ties continued to focus on reducing sound signaling. In Japan, by 1932, there were more than 100,000 automobiles on Tokyo's narrow roads. Laws required all cars to have both a bulb horn, to be used courteously first, and a klaxon horn, which was to be used only in an emergency. Though such cultural con-ditioning tied to social obligations of politeness and quietness allowed the Japanese to avoid the noisy road rage that characterized the American streets, it did little to alleviate congestion.[4] So, in 1931, Tokyo began installing a staggered light system, and continued to improve the engineering of its streets.

Though traffic circulation in cities was better regulated through this global trend, the noise caused by people blowing their horns continued to be a problem. Drivers were conditioned to do so. And so, as the klaxon faded as a presence from the soundscape, cultures turned to a variety of solutions—political, legal, and technological—to quiet the impact of automobiles and the new horn technology that replaced the klaxon.

Changing Noisy Behavior

All over the world, as antinoise leagues formed to diminish the din, they appropriated established tropes tied to the politics of noise and called for quieting the klaxon. As Karin Bijsterveld has shown in *Mechanical Sound*, engineers, producers of consumer technology, citizen groups, and politicians engaged in a complex transnational push in the interwar years to identify and abate noises created by machines and people.[5] In French-speaking countries, *la lutte contre le bruit* took front and center in political discourse, with mayors and police chiefs stressing the need for better legislation. Increasingly, noise was cast as a question of social hygiene. The private associations that became part of this fight also tried to reeducate drivers conditioned by a quarter century of noisy sound signaling.

In an era of political factionalism, noise politics became a powerful mechanism quilting together diverse coalitions yearning for quiet. Conservative writers such as Georges Duhamel rode the wave, railing against the technology he tied to "Americanization"—a long-running conversation aided by the framing of klaxons as an American technology—and calling for a *Parc National du Silence*.[6] The hotel and tourism syndicates, promoting social and scientific solutions to noise, posted signs across France stressing that "*Le silence de chacun / Assure le repos de tous*"—"The silence of each / Assures the repose of all." Speaking from the National Congress of Mayors, Aix-les Bains mayor Henri Clerc pushed for "legislation on noise to halt the abusive usage of upsetting sound devices." Automobile horns, he argued, were the worst offenders. "There should be a suppression pure and simple of the klaxon."[7]

Though French cities banned them, drivers conditioned by decades of commercial persuasion and sound signaling regulations continued blasting their horns. In 1933, noise expert André Le Troquer called for Paris's police chief, Jean Chiappé, to do more to "quiet noises which trouble the work and repose of the residents of Paris."[8] Despite a "special force of the préfecture de police" that existed to enforce laws on the books, "road klaxons [*klaxons de*

route] are employed freely in Paris where they are an instrument of torture."
Parisians needed to learn from big cities in Germany and England, which
banned klaxons and arrested drivers who used them. Préfet Chiappé, who
also made anxiety about Americanization a feature of his politics, responded
that the policing problem was "complex and delicate." "Klaxon horns with
strident or multiple sounds" were already banned, and neither raising fines
nor periodic crackdowns had done much to change behavior. In 1933, Chiappé
launched a "noise brigade" to educate the public and suggest creative counter-
measures against klaxon users.[9]

All across France, a governmental response to *le klaxon* was afoot. Called
before the Assemblée Nationale to address the problem in 1933, Le Troquer
denounced drivers who worked through "busy crossroads" by sounding
their horns, resulting in "infernal ear ringing from the screaming cacophony produced by the klaxon." After a while, "the ear can only hear noise."[10]
He implored the Assembly to go beyond just banning the klaxon at night.
"I denounce the klaxon like any technology that has become dangerous . . .
because it gives drivers the illusion of security. . . . We now use the word
klaxon as a verb."[11] Two years later, Chiappé was still answering questions
about klaxons before the legislature: "I have done my best. I have banned the
use of klaxons after 10 p.m. and before 7 a.m. I hesitate to go further at the
moment."[12]

In Switzerland, *la lutte contre le bruit* was particularly pronounced, partly
because of the importance of the tourism and hospitality industry, which
had made quiet repose part of its appeal. Municipalities everywhere passed
strict legislation banning technologies that created unwanted noise. In 1926,
Geneva banned the klaxon and "horns with a high or strident sound"; by
1933, federal laws had followed suit.[13] When local politicians called for it, cities would strictly enforce these measures, as did the resort town Evian, across
lac Léman (Lake Geneva) from Lausanne, whose newspaper published a glow-
ing account of how the town punished the "shrieks of klaxons" with exacting
fines.[14] Different regions of Switzerland experimented with a special *semaine
du silence* during which useless noises troubling the public tranquility were
prohibited and noisemakers were fined. At the top of the list were "point-
less klaxons, too strong or too prolonged."[15] But if the behavior conditioned
by the signaling technology feedback loop was set, then perhaps what was
needed was better technology. Even if the sounds heard in traffic were about
to change, the modern ideological construct—faith in technology as the driver
of progress—had been completely integrated into emerging subjectivities.

English noise politics had a similar register and created similar responses.

In his essay "Reflections on the Age of Noise," the British writer Adam Gowans Whyte emphasized the difficulty of quieting the "rushing, banging, grinding, shrieking, hooting, rattling, and general thundering" that characterized everyday life in a technologized society.[16] Yet try they must; noise was political, he argued, because people had an "animal sensitiveness" to it. Wired to flee from loud noises, humans "experience the same effect from the blast of a raucous motor horn, which often defeats its purpose by arresting the movements of the pedestrian."[17] More attention needed to be paid, he wrote, to the "aesthetic factor" of sound from a scientific standpoint. Engineers could create automobile technologies that would mitigate the noise problem that turned populations against cars. Already some automobiles were "not as noisy as they used to be" and "expensive ones are reasonably quiet." Better technology meant quieter technology, and if carmakers spent as much attention to creating quiet cars as they did to "cheapness in production," they could solve the problem.

Carmakers were indeed seeking solutions through engineering and changes in design. As Stefan Krebs has shown, the industry in America, Germany, and France quickly shifted from open- to closed-body car design in the mid-1920s and started emphasizing "silent comfort," or the protection of those inside the car from outside noise, in its advertising.[18] Gijs Mom evocatively calls this redesign of the automobile a "part of a general process of 'cocooning,' a redefinition of travelers' relation to the environment."[19] In the coconstructed sensory world of driving, consumers were being trained to hear outside noises as a problem.

In many ways, the commercial interests driving automobile culture and the antinoise movement shared a similar desire: to allow people to enjoy cars without the annoyance of noise. It was as if both wanted to capture the promise automobile technology had once inspired in the cultural imaginary without any of the residual casualties that characterized its growth. Essayist Wayne Gard said it best when he wrote in 1932, "What the anti-noise movement promises is a return to the quiet of the horse-and-buggy age without sacrificing any of the gains of modern manufacturing, construction or transit."[20] They wanted all the convenience of automobile technology without any of the unwanted sound.

If it was difficult to get people to change their noisy, conditioned behavior through laws and rhetorical calls to action, then perhaps engineers could do something to achieve more quietness. In addition to designing quieter cars and more pleasing horns, places where people lived and worked could be designed to keep out the noise. The "Crusade of Quietness," as it was sometimes called in England, slowly became as much about selling commodities designed to dampen unwanted sound as it was about instituting and enforcing governmental regimes against noisy technologies. For example, after leaders of the British Anti-Noise League visited the Motor-Cycle Show of 1933, they suggested manufacturers should engineer quieter features, such as quieter car doors, for automobiles. Then they took to the floor of Parliament to lobby for laws requiring motorists to use visual signaling, to flash "light beams" instead of using "hooters or klaxons at night." From their perspective, "noisy warnings are clearly favored by those in a great hurry who wish to signal their approach hundreds of yards ahead." Calling such behavior "pure hoggishness," they argued that drivers sent the message with their horn that "anybody within a mile get out of my way or there'll be trouble." Flickering the lights or using hand signals, on the other hand, was the "gentlemanly way of making progress."[21]

The Anti-Noise League came prepared, presenting Parliament with a "noise map" of London, along with the results of polls they had undertaken throughout England. They added to that data the results of yet another field test of horns by the National Physical Laboratory, confirming that klaxons constituted "excessive, unreasonable or unnecessary noise."[22] The *British Medical Journal,* which had also reported on the tests, added persuasive weight from another deliberative body, arguing that "motor horns, the obvious purpose of which is to make the pedestrian jump, should be sternly suppressed, for by confusing him they are apt to defeat their own ends."[23] Klaxon technology had, indeed, been designed (and promoted) to make people jump out of the way; and now men of science, from physicists to physicians, were adding their weight to a wave of public opinion against it. Based on the overwhelming evidence of scientific and public opinion, the league suggested, all "irritating and offensive" horns should be prohibited. Moreover, horn technology should be reengineered and standardized so that horns would "cause no annoyance to others."[24] The City of London responded with new laws banning the use of motor horns between 11:30 p.m. and 7 a.m. Roving traffic cops were instructed to "crack down on any driver who touches his klaxon button."[25] The minister of transport extended this disciplinary regime into all "built-up" areas throughout the country.[26] By 1934 the minister of transport was pushing to ban klaxons during the daytime as well as at night.[27]

Antinoise politics gained ground in Italy as well. In 1932 an antiklaxon campaign began in Milan, once the site of a Klaxon franchise, with city officials calling for a "week of silence." The Milan Automobile Club joined the crusade, organizing a competition among its members to see who could

ANOTHER LABOUR FOR HERCULES.

SIGNOR MUSSOLINI. "GOOD! AND NOW TO END THIS TYRANNY OF NOISE AND MAKE
ROME AS PEACEFUL AS SHE IS GREAT."

[According to a recent article in *The Times* on "Noise in Rome," the din of motor-traffic among the Seven Hills
is intolerable and calls for drastic regulation.]

Figure 56. A 1933 cartoon from *Punch* praising strongman Mussolini for doing what democracies seemed unable to do: quieting the klaxon. From *Punch*, August 23, 1933. (*Punch* Archive)

"make the least use of the horn or klaxon."[28] By 1934, laws in Milan compelled motorists to flash their headlights at crossroads instead of sounding their horns. Rome also set out to limit the way in which "drivers try to drive too fast and to force their way through the traffic, however dense, by continuous sounding of the Klaxon."[29] In 1933 the governor responded to a campaign against warning signals in the Roman press by instituting "silence zones" at night. Later that year, Italy's fascist strongman, Benito Mussolini, banned klaxons completely. Il Duce's fiat was praised by *Punch* in London and by other politicians around the world frustrated by democratic delays in the war on noise.[30] Yet the war on noise was no laughing matter, and officials, voters, and populations all over the world were noticing and reacting. Madrid and Barcelona both introduced regulations forbidding horns between 1 a.m. and 7 a.m. Madrid even created a special force of motorcycle police tasked with fining klaxon users on the spot. The reaction against Madrid's police measure showed how fraught such attempts to regulate sound signaling could be; after the motorcycle police collected over three hundred fines the first night of the campaign, taxicab drivers stopped working the following day in protest.[31]

In February 1932, Berlin's police chief praised his Parisian equivalent for erecting new red traffic lights to help coordinate traffic circulation. He also commended the Parisian ordinance that forbade drivers from using their klaxons, saying he was in favor of employing "severe measures against intense noises."[32] Though German legislators worried that motorists would have to reduce their speed if not allowed to use a horn, thus threatening one of the most attractive aspects of automobiling, German traffic laws were amended in May of that year. It was now illegal for drivers to use the horn to clear the way.[33] Some cities, including Stuttgart, had a complete local ban on sounding the motorized horn at night.[34] As they rose to power, the Nazis—though they wanted everyone to be able to own a Volkswagen[35]—would also make antinoise politics a plank in their populist culture war.[36]

All over the world, nations and municipalities worked to reset everyday signaling behavior with new, quieter technologies and antinoise regulations. A 1936 report on an international push to change traffic laws to quiet the klaxon underlines the growing consensus that klaxons "rendered life annoying and often made all sound signaling less effective." Legislatures around the globe worked to reduce the frequency of sound signaling. Though automobile safety was initially in question, after a brief period the number of accidents diminished in each city as people drove more carefully.[37]

American cities lagged behind European ones in muting the klaxon, but they were moving in the same direction.[38] As in Europe, "klaxon" had become a generic term associated with noise.[39] Syndicated columnist Glen Frank took the word association a step further, naming the horn blowers "Klaxonians," and decrying them as "blusterers who overpowering our ears, think thereby to overpower our will."[40] Cities all over America tried to silence these disturbers of the peace by banning klaxons and fining Klaxonians.

By 1930, New York City mayor Fiorello La Guardia had made antinoise politics central to his administration, creating a noise abatement committee to study the problems and suggest solutions. New York traffic commissioner Philip Hoyt began mailing warnings to drivers identified by a new antinoise squad. "No persons," the letter read, "shall use a horn or other device for signaling except in a reasonable manner as a danger warning, nor shall any such person produce or cause . . . a sound which shall be unnecessarily loud or harsh."[41] In 1934, Mayor La Guardia proclaimed that "every person is entitled to have a certain amount of peace and quiet. There is no reason . . . for people to toot automobile horns."[42] His "noise abatement commissioner," Major Henry Curran, began studying how other cities were handling the problem of "enforcing a curfew on motor horns." Curran decried "the unnecessary use of automobile horns" as the most annoying noise: "We know from experience that cars can be driven in this city without use of a horn."[43] Moreover, noisy horns not only disturbed the peace, they made bad drivers. Fines would now be imposed for the "tooting of motor horns . . . forbidden between 11 p.m. and 7 a.m."[44]

Chicago followed the same trend. The city council, which had already passed several rounds of legislation against types of horns and against the use of horns by private citizens, called for the police to stop "unnecessary uses of automobile horns. . . . Sometimes the motorist prefers to make a pedestrian jump out of the way rather than slow down himself. The Council's purpose is to reduce the city noises which wear on the nerves."[45] More decisively, the councilmen argued that engineers needed to develop quieter products; from cars to railroads, "quietness must be built in."[46] By 1935 the movement had spread to state government. The Illinois General Assembly updated the state's Traffic Code to prohibit "the use of automobile warning devices that emit unusual or excessively loud signals."[47] Klaxon's "road-clearing" technology was quickly becoming anathema, an unwanted holdover from a time gone by.

More important for the story of what culture was asking from technology, the deliberations of the Chicago legislature signaled that body's faith in having engineers fix the problems that legislation could not. Rather than managing unwanted sounds by prohibiting noisy technology and the behavior it gave rise to, the legislature called for innovations in quiet technology, what I have elsewhere called "commodity quietness."[48] "For complete success in reducing the city tumult, quietness must be built in. . . . Any steps which can be taken to muffle the sounds without causing the activity to lag will be of great benefit." Though the costs of new technologies were often prohibitive, as many who contributed to these enterprises noted,[49] the call to use technology to combat the problems created by technology pointed to the same faith in technology as a solution to problems that had animated the sales of the klaxon in the first place.

The Automobile Industry Responds

As the chorus against klaxon technology grew around the world, the automobile industry responded with educational initiatives promoting less noisy technologies and quiet communication strategies for managing automobile culture. Along with print advertising, carmakers turned to sound films. In England, Ford's 1934 *Safety First* film, narrated by the editor of *The Autocar,* emphasized the importance of using hand signals to communicate with other drivers, waiting for traffic lights to execute turns, and driving at slower speeds.

Sound signals are nowhere to be heard. In the 1935 Ford short, *Your Driving Test*, British viewers were reminded that the Ministry of Transport examiner was watching for proper hand signals and "road courtesy." Chevrolet's 1937 short film for the American media market, *Seeing Green*, promised that standardization of visual signals, semaphores, and lights would answer the problem of safety. Electrical engineers and better road system design would solve the problems of car traffic that the noisy horn had once promised to remedy.

Automobile makers, too, began to appeal to consumers' shifting sensibilities by engineering quieter products. In France, following the publication of another Arts et Métier study of different horn sounds, Peugeot reported that it was reengineering its horns. Concretely, the company designed an electric push-button horn intense enough to be heard through the soundscape yet producing a more pleasant sound. Peugeot hoped to create a device that would keep drivers safe while avoiding the problems and resentment caused by the "*hurlement du klaxon*."[50] Too long had pedestrians been "seized with panic after hearing the brutal call of the klaxon." If the automobilist wanted to be heard and seen as an up-to-date consumer and early adopter, he or she would need the latest "melodious" horn, one that would impress people seeking relief from the raucous klaxon sound.

Engineering a less noisy sound technology to communicate in traffic was a business problem for a sound market increasingly turning against the clear-the-way technology that shrieked at other drivers and pedestrians. In America, Klaxon itself had been selling the New Klaxon (Beep) horn since 1927, to give consumers a choice of sound. By 1933, General Motors, which still owned the Klaxon brand, was installing more melodious Air Tone horns on all its cars.[51]

Consumers demanded less noise and more silence in their automobiles. Quiet design, in terms of both the sound that cars produced and the external sounds they mitigated, was increasingly featured in automobile advertising as the industry responded to consumer demand. As the open-air design gave way to the closed-body car, automobile manufacturers built sonic comfort into their brand. This created a perception paradox: the industry-manufactured desire for quiet mobility or "acoustic cocooning" triggered a "new sensorial awareness among car owners, foregrounding small irritations they had not noticed in an open car. The insulation from the world beyond the windshield became a major task for automotive engineers."[52] Safety was, of course, paramount, but the kind of quiet repose that had long been a feature of the ideal bourgeois lifestyle was soon interpolated into the private mobility of the car. Companies touted new innovations created to manage a marketplace now conditioned to want silence. With visual signaling technologies standard in the 1930s, including the stop signs and stop lights that now helped drivers negotiate traffic, the original penetrating aaOOgah of the klaxon was no longer necessary or desirable.

Nowhere was this engineering turn away from noise-producing technology more evident than at the Klaxon Company itself, which was desperately trying to reinvigorate its sonic brand while maintaining the horn's nostalgic association with the early days of automobile technology. Though the company still recycled media tropes established over two decades of advertising, its commercial discourse became associated with a completely different sound. For example, an ad from the March 28, 1936, edition of *Collier's* offered the old Klaxon narrative emphasizing safety for families as conferred through the use of technology, an idea implied by the accompanying picture of a baby in a playpen. As it always had, the Klaxon sound "admonishes" the consciousness of the distracted pedestrian or driver and forces him or her to attend to oncoming traffic. But now the priests of technological progress, the engineers, had improved the design, changing the horn to a "new" two-tone compressed-air horn, which is shown in the ad. The brand name is deemphasized by highlighting the parent company, Delco-Remy, under which a rapidly consolidating General Motors had gathered Klaxon.[53]

Another ad from the same 1936 *Collier's* campaign echoed the many "Danger Sound Klaxon" ads, now decades old, with an image of a blind turn and the promise of safety conferred through the affordance of the famous technology. Titled "Sound Your Klaxon," it included the throwback image of a blind turn and copy that promised safety through the touch-button ease of the signaling device. Only now the two-tone compressed-air horn linked these tropes to a new sound and breathed fresh life into the brand. Klaxon wanted to keep the slogans that had worked for years while changing the sound device it was selling. The shift in sound brand can be seen in the June 6, 1936, iteration. It emphasized the "new note" with its "strikingly modern" sound while reminding readers of the visual icons of the old brand. Though still trying to tap into the nostalgia for the early days of automobiling, the company was adapting to the ever-changing world of car culture. In the new soundscape, the aaOOgah sound was no longer desirable; the technology had become regressive. In Morehead, Minnesota, the president of the state automobile association gave a speech in which he looked back nostalgically, regaling his audience with stories from the days when members of the automobile clubs in Minnesota had banded together to put up "Sound Your Klaxon" signs.[54]

But times had changed. Car manufacturers like Ford still promoted factory-installed Klaxon brand horns, but now made sure to emphasize that it was

Figure 57. Ad for the Klaxon Road Commander. After introducing more modern-sounding technology, Klaxon wanted people to know the tone had changed but the brand still commanded attention of the right kind. From the *Saturday Evening Post*, May 16, 1936. (*Saturday Evening Post* Archive)

Klaxon's new, "modern" two-tone air horn technology with its different note. Chevrolet was the last of the GM brands to hold on to the original klaxon sound signal. Yet by the mid-thirties, it was also rebranding itself with the sound of the new two-tone air horn. In its *Chevrolet Leader News* road safety film features of the 1930s, the soundtrack for the transition image into the title card for each episode was the rhythmic two-tone air horn sound, like a trumpet fanfare for the automobile with the horns turning toward the camera, before the air horn sound transitioned into John Philip Sousa's patriotic *U.S. Field Artillery March* (aka "Caissons go rolling along"). The prominence of the sound of Klaxon's new horn in effect canceled the sound of the old technology. The old aaOOgah was now marked as nostalgic only.

Listening to the sound films of the 1930s confirms this nostalgic association in the cinematic sound design. In *The Public Enemy* (1931), for example, the street sounds when James Cagney picks up Jean Harlow in his flashy gangster car are predominantly the aaOOgah of the old klaxon, intended to convey aurally the dangerous urban 1920s. Films set in the present, such as Capra's 1934 road film *It Happened One Night*, used two-tone horns in

Figure 58. Industrial use of the klaxon in France. From *La Revue Industrielle*, April 1930, no. 74. (Bibliothèque nationale de France)

their sound design. By the time of John Ford's *The Grapes of Wrath* (1939), the behind-the-times association of the original klaxon sound had become standard in Hollywood's soundscape: the broken-down jalopy of the Joads and other poor Oakies all emit the aaOOgah of the old klaxon, whereas the expensive new cars of the bank supervisors or the well-dressed labor wranglers looking to exploit the day laborers all have the two-tone compressed-air horns. The sound of the horn conveyed social distinction. To be sure, the complaints about honking horns did not abate after the klaxon sound was replaced by a new horn sound. No-honking zones and prohibitive hours continued to spread across the world. Yet the memory of the klaxon remained, a sign of a past rapidly fading away.

In Europe, though the sound has long gone, the generic noun (*"le klaxon,"* car horn) and verb (*"klaxoner,"* to honk) remain in the French language to this day. Klaxon as a company continued to make sound signaling devices, but for trains, factories, and ships. In France, Klaxon rarely advertised in automobile journals after 1930; instead, the company marketed its product's industrial application, as in the advertisement from *La Revue Industrielle,* as "the voice of the factory." The ads that did appear for the automobile promoted "*Le nouveau Klaxophone électrique,*" Klaxon's two-tone compressed-air horn with a more "agreeable" sound.[55]

In America as well, the Klaxon Company continued to rebrand itself as a maker of signaling devices for industrial and defense uses. As the old aaOOgah sound disappeared from the soundscape, so too did the fantasy that sound technology would remedy the safety concerns emerging from an automobile-centered world. Faith that newer and better technology could fix the problems caused by technology remained a potent ideology, but it attached itself to new objects. One need only consider how contemporary consumers, lured by advertising, have turned to noise-cancellation technology to achieve mobile acoustic cocooning.

To this day, car horns continue to dominate the soundscape as the biggest cause of noise complaints, a cultural fact that remains remarkably durable.[56] The periodic reaction against automobile technology as a source of noise pollution is now a constant feature of soundscape management around the globe, producing an ever-changing array of ordinance laws, government regulations, and thousands of quiet technologies, such as GM's "QuietTuning" luxury silence technology, that promise to protect the consumer from unwanted sound.[57] The cultural reaction formation witnessed in relation to the klaxon— that first great technological application that promised to solve the safety problems related to an automobile-centered world—has continued, though the sound it once made is now only a spectral signal slowly fading from memory.

The story of the klaxon's rise and fall reveals a familiar pattern that emerging technologies often follow: engineers seeking to fix a contemporary problem created by a previous technology develop a technological solution that promises to improve people's lives. Capital and psychic investment flow to it, and the advertising machine promotes it using a rhetoric that strengthens the public's belief that better technology is always the solution to our problems. For a time, it seems to work, before problems tied to its actual use or the implications of a dominant technology being applied at scale reveal themselves. At that point, another new technology emerges that promises to address these problems, and the cycle begins anew. Yet beyond these broad strokes is also a story about the dynamism of culture, as the movement toward each of these plot points is driven by communities responding to the impact of the new technology. People react to new technological forces by striving to make sense of them as they seek to communicate their hopes or concerns about the ever-changing world they inhabit. They promote, complain, organize, and act, adopting or rejecting or reaching a compromise with these technologies as a feature of their lives.

The klaxon was always an accessory technology, an epiphenomenon connected to the seemingly unstoppable rise of the automobile, itself a dominant technology that continues to alter the way we live and the worlds we share more than a hundred years after it was created. For a time, people around the globe were led to believe that this new electrical signaling device would help drivers use the automobile more safely by allowing them to communicate more easily with one another and with pedestrians in the streets. When the horn failed to achieve its promise, cultures turned to other technological solutions that their proponents promised would help manage the impact of the automobile.

The story of the klaxon's rise and fall in the soundscape also reveals how our sense apperceptions, including our way of hearing the world, are contingent on culture. Our modes of listening can be conditioned by the presence of a device and the promotional communication that accompanies it, yet can be quickly altered by an unforeseen association with a traumatic event that turns people against it. It is possible, as this story shows, for people to get used to almost anything if the wide variety of communicative forces within culture guides that acculturation. It is also possible, as this story shows, for communities to resist a dominant technology and strive to rebalance their lifeworld through an ongoing conversation. That much, it seems, is up to us.

NOTES

Introduction

1. Steven D. Thatton, "Automobile Horns," *Harper's Weekly*, January 7, 1911, 26.
2. John Dewey, *The Public and Its Problems* (New York: Henry Holt, 1927), 217.
3. George Simmel, "Sociology of the Senses," in *Simmel on Culture*, ed. David Frisby and Mike Featherstone (London: Sage, 1997), 116.
4. R. Murray Schafer, *The Soundscape: Our Sonic Environment and the Tuning of the World* (Rochester, VT: Destiny Books, 1994), 7.
5. Nick Couldry, *Listening beyond the Echoes: Media, Ethics, and Agency in an Uncertain World* (Boulder, CO: Paradigm, 2006), 6.
6. Henri Lefebvre, *Critique of Everyday Life: Foundations for a Sociology of the Everyday*, vol. 2, trans. John Moore (London: Verso, 2008), 45.
7. In this sense, on the culturally conditioned side of hearing sound, I have in mind something like what Annales historians such as Lucien Febvre, Fernand Braudel, or Roger Chartier conceived of as a historical *mentalité*. These contingent mentalities guide or frame how we perceive and make sense of physical sound; they determine how we hear and listen. I think of the social or cultural function of these structured mentalities as akin to *sonic paradigms* or *perceptual regimes*. These perceptual regimes—tied closely to powerful cultural forces— shift slowly in ways reminiscent of how Antonio Gramsci described the slow shift in the unconscious ideological frames governing culture that he called the "national popular." In what follows, as I describe the shifts in soundscape surrounding klaxon technology, I also nod to Jacques Rancière's work on conditioned sensibilities, what he called the *sensis communis* or our shared communities of sensation.
8. Emily Thompson, *The Soundscape of Modernity: Architectural Acoustics and the Culture of Listening in America, 1900–1933* (Cambridge, MA: MIT Press, 2004).
9. On the transformative idea of automobility, see John M. Packer, *Mobility without Mayhem: Safety, Cars, and Citizenship* (Durham, NC: Duke University Press, 2008); Cotton Seiler, *A Republic of Drivers: A Cultural History of Automobility in*

America (Chicago: University of Chicago Press, 2008); and Gabrielle Esperdy, *American Autopia: An Intellectual History of the American Roadside at Midcentury* (Charlottesville: University of Virginia Press, 2019). On the anxiety produced by mobility within cultures, see Brian Ladd, *Autophobia: Love and Hate in the Automotive Age* (Chicago: University of Chicago Press, 2008).

10.   Though its arrival was diffused over time and space, one might even be tempted to characterize the coming of the automobile as a "sonic event," as R. Murray Schafer described the eruption of Krakatoa, because of its explosive impact on the human sensorium.

11.   Mike Goldsmith, *Discord: The Story of Noise* (Oxford: Oxford University Press, 2012), 38.

12.   Charles Baudelaire, "Loss of a Halo," in *Paris Spleen: Petits Poemes en Prose,* trans. Louise Varèse (New York: New Directions, 1970), 94.

13.   Walt Whitman, *Leaves of Grass: A Textual Variorum of the Printed Poems,* vol. 1, ed. Sculley Bradley, Harold W. Blodgett, Arthur Golden, et al. (New York: New York University Press, 1980), 10.

14.   Charles Baudelaire, "The Bad Glazier," in *The Parisian Prowler,* trans. Edward R. Kaplan (Athens: University of Georgia Press, 1997), 14.

15.   On Carlyle's rage reaction to noise and the people and things that produced it, see John M. Picker, *Victorian Soundscapes* (Oxford: Oxford University Press, 2003).

16.   Karin Bijsterveld, Eefje Cleophas, Stefan Krebs, and Gijs Mom call this same phenomenon "diagnostic" in *Sound and Safe: A History of Listening behind the Wheel* (New York: Oxford University Press, 2014).

17.   Edwin Chadwick, "On the Sanitary Advantages of Smooth and Impermeable Street Surfaces," *Journal of the Society of Arts,* September 29, 1871, 789.

18.   James Carey, *Communication as Culture: Essays on Media and Society* (New York: Routledge, 1989).

19.   On this early moment, when the new automobile shared the streets with older vehicles, see Gary S. Cross, *Machines of Youth: America's Car Obsession* (Chicago: University of Chicago Press, 2018); James J. Flink, *America Adopts the Automobile, 1895–1910* (Cambridge, MA: MIT Press, 1970); idem, *The Automobile Age* (Cambridge, MA: MIT Press, 1993); and Clay McShane, *Down the Asphalt Path: The Automobile and the American City* (New York: Columbia University Press, 1996).

1. Sound Competition

1.   Henri Lefebvre, *Critique of Everyday Life,* vol. 2, trans. John Moore (London: Verso, 2008), 13.

2.   On the everyday change spurred by the automobile, see James J. Flink, *America Adopts the Automobile, 1895–1910* (Cambridge, MA: MIT Press, 1970).

3.   On automobility and its relation to speed of modernity, see Gijs Mom, *Atlantic Automobilism: Emergence and Persistence of the Car, 1895–1940* (New York:

Berghahn, 2015); and Stephen Kern, *The Culture of Time and Space, 1880–1918* (Cambridge, MA: Harvard University Press, 2003).

4.   Karin Bijsterveld, Eefje Cleophas, Stefan Krebs, and Gijs Mom, *Sound and Safe: A History of Listening behind the Wheel* (Oxford University Press, 2013). In the introduction to *The Oxford Handbook of Sound Studies* (Oxford University Press, 2012), editors Trevor Pinch and Karin Bijsterveld describe the diagnostic mode of listing, as distinct from other modes such as monitory and exploratory listening, this way. "Whereas *monitory* listening is used to determine *whether* something is wrong, diagnostic listening reveals *what* is wrong. *Exploratory listening* is listening to discover new phenomena" (p. 14). Kate Lacey offers an important intervention into the politics and ethical dimension of listening, arguing that beyond these modes of listening amid the noise of modernity, we should be learning and cultivating a mode of "listening out" for things beyond what we know and expect to hear. See Lacey, *Listening Publics: The Politics and Experience of Listening in the Media Age* (Cambridge: Polity, 2013).

5.   "Noise," *Harper's Weekly,* November 2, 1895, 1033.

6.   Gijs Mom, *The Electric Vehicle: Technology and Expectations in the Automobile Age* (Baltimore: Johns Hopkins University Press, 2013). Early in the debates over sound representation, it was suggested that electric automobiles, like electric trollies, be represented by bells rather than horns because of their relatively slow speeds. By 1913, after the question was settled, Klaxon would boast that six of the existing electric car companies installed klaxon horns at the factory.

7.   Harry C. Marillier, "The Automobile: A Forecast," *New Review* (October 1895): 396.

8.   Ibid., 386.

9.   Ibid., 393.

10.   Ibid., 394.

11.   Gabrielle Esperdy, *American Autopia: An Intellectual History of the American Roadside at Midcentury* (Charlottesville: University of Virginia Press, 2019).

12.   Marillier, "The Automobile," 394.

13.   Ibid., 395.

14.   Ibid,. 396.

15.   T. A. de Weese, "Progress toward the Age of the Horseless Carriage," *Cosmopolitan,* February 1896, 417.

16.   J. H. Girdner, "The Plague of City Noises," *North American Review* (September 1896): 296.

17.   Ibid., 298.

18.   Ibid.

19.   J. H. Girdner, "To Abate the Plague of City Noises," *North American Review* (October 1897): 463.

20.   Ibid., 464.

21.   Ibid., 468.

22.   Harry E. Dey, "Favors the Vibrating Bell," *Horseless Age,* January 1897, 12.

23. Pazienza, "The Dangers of the Motor Car," *Spectator,* October 21, 1899, 567.

24. Walter Coleman Parker, *Automobiling* (New York: Parker Music Co., 1905).

25. On the long story of this relationship to automobile culture, see Brian Ladd, *Autophobia: Love and Hate in the Automotive Age* (Chicago: University of Chicago Press, 2008).

26. "The 'Noise' Question," *Horseless Age,* December 1896, 1.

27. Ibid.

28. Ibid.

29. Ibid, 2.

30. "Automobile Warning Signals," *Chicago Daily Tribune,* January 28, 1900, 31.

31. "International Convention for the Regulation of Automobile Traffic," *Horseless Age,* October 27, 1909, 472.

32. John Scott Montagu, "New Forms of Locomotion and Their Result," *Fortnightly Review,* May 1902, 882.

33. Ibid., 887.

34. "Rules Governing the Use of Motor Vehicles in Paris," *Horseless Age,* November 1896, 11.

35. New Speed Rules in France," *Horseless Age,* June 26, 1901, 274. James Laux provides a definitive chronicle of these early days of negotiations between industry and culture in *In First Gear: The French Automobile Industry to 1914* (Montreal: McGill–Queen's University Press, 1976).

36. "Automobile Club de Grande Bretagne et d'Irlande: Extrait de réglement," *Le Chauffeur,* February 11, 1900, 48.

37. Harold Langford Lewis, *The Law Relating to Motor Cars: Being the Motor Car Acts, 1896 and 1903; with an Introduction and Notes, Together with the Regulations of the Local Government Board, and of the Secretary of State, under the Acts* (London: Butterworth Shaw & Sons, 1904), 12.

38. Ibid., 131.

39. Marillier, "The Automobile," 389.

40. "The Regulation of Motor-Cars," *Quarterly Review* (October 1906): 512.

41. Henry Norman, "The Public, the Motorist, and the Royal Commission," *Fortnightly Review,* April 1906, 686.

42. *Parliamentary Papers,* vol. 35, "Reports from Commissioners, Inspectors and Others; Report of the Royal Commission on Motor," vol. 1 (1906): 37.

43. Ibid.

44. Ibid., 38.

45. Ibid., 70.

46. Ibid., 73.

47. "Automobile Legislation," *Horseless Age,* September 19, 1900, 22.

48. "Royal Commission on Motor Cars," Second Day, 27, in *Parliamentary Papers,* vol. 35, 139.

49. Ibid.

50. A. Frenchman, "Motoring 'within' German Laws," *Motor Way,* July 1907, 33.

51. "Royal Commission on Motor Cars," Second Day, 27, 138.
52. Ibid.
53. Ibid., 139.
54. Ibid., 204.
55. For a good chronicle of the early days of British automobile culture, see Kenneth Richardson, *The British Motor Industry, 1890–1939: A Social and Economic History* (London: Macmillan, 1977). On the relation between motoring and the press, see Jennifer Shepherd, "The British Press and Turn-of-the-Century Developments in the Motoring Movement," *Victorian Periodicals Review* 38, no. 4 (Winter 2005): 379–91.
56. *Horseless Age*, June 19, 1901, 254.
57. *Horseless Age*, July 27, 1904, 91.
58. E. McFarland, "Automobiling in Montana," *Horseless Age*, October 5, 1904, 350.
59. "The 'French Jericho Horn,'" *Cycle and Automobile Trade Journal*, June 1, 1906, 162.
60. Dr. F. L. Bartlett, "Eighteen Months' Experience with a Light Gasoline Automobile," *Horseless Age*, January 7, 1903, 64.
61. "The Psychology of the Selfish Motorist," *Lancet* (September 8, 1906): 664.
62. *Horseless Age*, August 24, 1904, 191.
63. "Here and There," *Motor-Car Journal*, March 20, 1909, 78.
64. "Kansas Legislators," *Automobile Review*, March 18, 1905, 300.
65. "Show Section," *Motor*, December 1906, 166.
66. *The Cycle and Automobile Trade Journal*, December 1, 1905, 209.
67. "Megargel Reaches Nebraska," *Motor Age*, September 7, 1905, 18.
68. "The New York Shows," *Horseless Age*, January 17, 1906, 142.
69. *Motor-Car Journal*, October 16, 1909, 706.
70. "A Seasonable Rhapsody," *Motor-Car Journal*, January 1, 1910, 949.
71. Quoted in Clay McShane, *Down the Asphalt Path: The Automobile and the American City* (New York: Columbia University Press, 1994), 197.
72. Frederick S. Crum, "Street Traffic Accidents," *Publications of the American Statistical Association* 13, no. 103 (1913): 474.
73. David Butler and Anne Sloman, *British Political Fact, 1900–1979* (London: Macmillan, 1980), 317.
74. "Recent Decisions: Interpretation of Iowa Law," *Horseless Age*, October 6, 1909, 384.
75. 165 Ind. 465, 74 N.E. 615, 1 L.R.A.N.S. 238, 6 Am. Ann. Cas. 656; *Indiana Springs Co. v. Brown*, 165 Ind. 465, 74 N.E. 615, 617 (1905).
76. Ky. St. § 3739g, Russell's St. §§ 322–29; *Webb v. Moore*, 136 Ky. 708, 125 S.W. 152 (1910).
77. "Legislative and Legal," *Horseless Age*, June 3, 1903, 665.
78. "Verdict of High Importance," *Automobile Topics*, May 31, 1902, 305.
79. *Horseless Age*, September 8, 1909, 275.
80. "Odd Road Signs," *Motor Way*, October 1907, 92.

81. *Club Journal*, June 15, 1910, 214. On the role of the police in educating the public about how to drive within the confines of the changing laws, see Sarah A. Seo, *Policing the Open Road: How Cars Transformed American Freedom* (Cambridge, MA: Harvard University Press, 2019).

82. On the growing pastime of automobile touring, see Peter J. Hugill, "The Rediscovery of America: Elite Automobile Touring," *Annals of Tourism Research* 12 (1985): 435–47.

83. Alfred Harmworth Northcliffe, *Motors and Motor Driving* (London: Longman, Green and Co., 1906), 447.

84. *Motor*, March 1907, 169.

85. See, for example, Peter Payer, "The Age of Noise: Early Reactions in Vienna, 1870–1914," *Journal of Urban History* 33 (2007): 733–93.

86. "Less Noise, says Bingham," *Sun*, July 19, 1908, 1.

87. Charles Lethbridge, "The Syren," *Autocar*, September 5, 1908, 382.

88. "Noise Abatement: A Lady Crusader," *Evening Post*, October 19, 1909, 6.

89. John Stowe, "Motley Motoring Manners," *Motor-Car Journal*, October 9, 1909, 685.

90. "Horns vs Whistles," *Motor-Car Journal*, May 16, 1908, 249.

91. Ibid.

2. First Encounters

1.   James J. Flink, *The Automobile Age* (Cambridge, MA: MIT Press, 1993), 30.

2.   See James Carey, *Communication as Culture: Essays on Media and Society* (New York: Routledge, 1989).

3.   "Two New Electric Carriages," *Automobile Topics*, May 16, 1903, 300.

4.   "La corne électrique," *Journal Amusant*, November 25, 1905, 14.

5.   "Autos Are in Demand, Many Buyers at Show," *New York Tribune*, January 2, 1908, 5.

6.   A. D. McFadyen, "Dr. Miller Reese Hutchison," *Journal of the Patent Office Society* 19, no. 3 (March 1937): 193.

7.   "Instrument That Enables Deaf to Hear," *Telephone Magazine* (March 1905): 167.

8.   "Interesting Origin of the Klaxon Horn," *Philadelphia Inquirer*, December 26, 1909, 8.

9.   For a description of the ongoing quest to develop better battery technology, which had applications to both electric and gasoline automobile technology, see Gijs Mom, *The Electric Vehicle: Technology and Expectations in the Automobile Age* (Baltimore: Johns Hopkins University Press, 2004), 118–23.

10. McFadyen, "Dr. Miller Reese Hutchison," 194.

11. Ibid.

12. "F. Hallett Lovell Is Dead at 94; Manufactured Klaxon Car Horn," *New York Times*, May 20, 1962, 86.

13. "Where'd You Get That Noise," *Sun*, January 3, 1916, 14.

14. It is now uncontroversial that culture gives us ways of seeing the world. Yet

many still assume that we hear sound without ideological filters. The emergence and acceptance of the klaxon helps illustrate Heidegger's phenomenological point that there is no such thing as raw sound, that we are taught the meaning of the sounds filling our lifeworld. We are taught how to listen, hear, and interpret sound by culture. This important phenomenological point, that we learn to perceive through acculturation, helps us understand the klaxon's rise and fall.

15. *The Klaxon Warning Signal* (Newark, NJ: Lovell-McConnell Manufacturing Co., 1909), 1.

16. *Les Marques Internationales*, August 31, 1909, 449.

17. *The Klaxon Warning Signal*, 4.

18. Ibid.

19. Ibid.

20. "Biggest Noise Maker: Alabama Man Invents a Horn That Can Be Heard Five Miles," *Topeka State Journal*, October 3, 1908, 7.

21. For a good description of the emergence of the automotive trade journals, such as *The Horseless Age*, see Flink, *The Automobile Age*, 29.

22. H. H. Brown, "The Best Way to See an Automobile Show," *Horseless Age*, December 29, 1909, 755.

23. Ibid., 775.

24. "A New Type of Automobile Horn," *Scientific American* 98, no. 1 (April 18, 1908), 280.

25. On the importance of racing for promoting automobile culture, see Flink, *The Automobile Age*, 30–31; and Gijs Mom, *Atlantic Automobilism: Emergence and Persistence of the Car, 1895–1940* (New York: Berghahn Books, 2015).

26. "Depalma Smashes 10 Mile Record at Fair Grounds Auto Races," *New Orleans Times-Picayune*, February 21, 1909, 14. Of note in these races was the dominance of Joan Cuneo, a pioneering woman racer, who won several races at the 1909 event. For a history of automobile racing, see "Before NASCAR: The Corporate and Civic Promotion of Automobile Racing in the American South, 1903–1927," *Journal of Southern History* 68, no. 3 (August 2002): 629–68.

27. G. E. Bird, "Honk Honk Honk," *Automobile Topics*, April 3, 1909, 1825.

28. The 1907 Columbia version of the song, including the sound of the horn, can be heard at https://www.loc.gov/item/jukebox-728728/.

29. "The Klaxon Horn," *News and Courier*, June 5, 1909, 7.

30. "Pittsburgh Show Pleases All Visitors," *Automobile Topics*, April 3, 1909, 1827.

31. "The Olympia Show," *Motor-Car Journal*, November 20, 1909, 818.

32. Ibid., 842.

33. Matthew Lavine, "'Something about X-Rays for Everyone': Emerging Technologies and Open Communities," *History and Technology* 31, no. 1 (2015): 37–54.

34. *The Automobile Blue Book*, vol. 3 (New York: Automobile Blue Blook Publishing Co., 1910), 14.

35. "Tools of the Craft," *Field and Stream*, August 1909, 389.

36. Ibid.

37. Jean-Pierre Bardou, Jean-Jacques Chanaron, Patrick Fridenson, and James M. Laux, *The Automobile Revolution: The Impact of an Industry*, trans. and ed. James M. Laux (Chapel Hill: University of North Carolina Press, 1982), 22.

38. On the important rise of "haptic" push-button technology and its link to the electrical revolution in technology, see David Parisi, *Archaeologies of Touch: Interfacing with Haptics from Electricity to Computing* (Minneapolis: University of Minnesota Press, 2018).

39. *Motor*, March 1910, 7.

40. *Motor Boat*, July 10, 1909, 53.

41. *Los Angeles Herald*, January 23, 1910, 2.

42. "The Klaxon," *Comoedia*, June 26, 1910, 2.

43. Steven D. Thatton, "Automobile Horns," *Harper's Weekly*, January 7, 1911, 26.

44. Ibid.

45. On this, see Jeremy Packer, *Mobility without Mayhem: Safety, Cars, and Citizenship* (Durham, NC: Duke University Press, 2008).

46. Michael L. Bromley, *William Howard Taft and the First Motoring Presidency, 1909–1913* (Jefferson, NC: McFarland, 2003), 135.

47. "Horse versus Automobile: A French View," *American Review of Reviews*, September 1910, 368. James Flink asserts that there were 458,000 motor vehicles (trucks, motorcycles, and automobiles) registered in the United Statess in 1910. See Flink, *The Automobile Age*, 26.

48. "Notes of the Industry and Sport," *Horseless Age*, December 22, 1909, 749.

49. Marshall McLuhan, *Understanding Media: The Extensions of Man* (Berkeley, CA: Gingko Press, 2003), 300.

50. Ibid., 301.

3. Klaxon and the Rise of Modern Advertising

1. Raymond Williams, "Advertising: The Magical System," in *Culture and Materialism* (London: Verso, 1980), 170–95.

2. Ibid., 189.

3. Ibid., 179.

4. Ibid., 180.

5. See Henri Lefebvre, *The Critique of Everyday Life*, vol. 1, trans. John Moore (London: Verso, 1991).

6. *Indianapolis Star*, March 2, 1910, 14.

7. Marshall McLuhan, *Understanding Media: The Extensions of Man* (Berkeley, CA: Gingko Press, 2003), 300.

8. *Motor Boat*, August 25, 1909, 55.

9. *Motor Boat*, September 10, 1909, 43.

10. *Life*, March 3, 1910, 351.

11. Douglas B. Ward, "The Reader as Consumer: Curtis Publishing Company and Its Audience, 1910–1930," *Journalism History* 22 (Summer 1996): 47.

12. Eric Jaffe, "The Evolution of Traffic Accidents in New York," *Bloomberg City Lab*, December 16, 2011.

13. On this notion, see Matthew Jordan, "'Tween Orwell and Rockwell: The Re-culturing of Paranoia in the *Spy Kids* Films," in *Secret Agents: Popular Icons beyond James Bond*, ed. Jeremy Packer (London: Peter Lang, 2009), 77–88.

14. *Motor*, December 1909, 7.

15. See Flink, *The Automobile Age*, 191.

16. For a description of early automobile advertising finding its mode of persuasion, see Rob Schorman, "This Astounding Car for $1,500: The Year Automobile Advertising Came of Age," *Enterprise & Society* 11, no. 3 (September 2010): 468–523; and Pamela Walker Laird, "'The Car without a Single Weakness': Early Automobile Advertising," *Technology and Culture* 37, no. 4 (October 1996): 796–812.

17. *Motor*, September 1911, C20.

18. *Motor*, June 1912, 40.

19. *The Autocar Imperial Year Book* (London: Iliffe & Sons, 1914), iii.

20. In 1912, the inventor Allan A. Pencross announced in *Automobile Topics* that he had created a product to rival the Gabriel ten-tone horn, but one that would "need no musical talent to operate." It was to use phonograph technology as a warning signal, and Pencross entered into negotiations with Henry W. Savage for the rights to use melodies from *The Merry Widow* and *Little Boy Blue*, as well as "Farewell" by Gilbert and Sullivan. The product never made it to market. *Automobile Topics*, September 14, 1912, 332.

21. *Motor*, June 1910, 11.

22. *Motor Car*, April 1911, C3.

23. *American Motorist*, December 1913, 3

24. *Motor*, October 1910, 9. Ironically, the princess, Anna de Castellane, was born Anna Gould, daughter of the notorious American robber baron Jay Gould, whose nouveau riche ruthlessness (especially in relation to telecommunications patent ownership) was the antithesis of noblesse oblige.

25. On this, see Schorman, "This Astounding Car for $1,500."

26. *Cycle and Automobile Trade Journal*, April 1, 1911, 58.

27. *Motor Car*, April 1912, 35.

28. Steven D. Thatton, "Automobile Horns," *Harper's Weekly*, January 7, 1911, 26.

29. Ibid.

30. "For Silencing Automobile Horns," *New York Times*, August 6, 1911, C4.

31. A. D., "Manufacturers' Communication: Noises That Save Life," *Motor Age*, September 14, 1911, 45.

32. *McClure's*, October 1910, 147.

33. *Cosmopolitan*, November 1910, 45.

34. William Allen Johnston, "Reaching Consumers through Non-Consumers," *Printers' Ink*, February 9, 1911, 33.

35. Ibid.

36. Ibid.
37. Johnston, *Printers' Ink*, 35.
38. Ibid., 36.
39. Ibid.
40. *Motor World*, December 29, 1910, 800.
41. *Motor World*, February 9, 1911, 656.
42. *Motor World*, February 16, 1911, 720.
43. *Motor World*, March 16, 1911, 1017.
44. *Automobile Topics*, January 6, 1912, 375.
45. *Automobile Topics*, April 6, 1912, 391.
46. *Automobile Topics*, October 12, 1912, 551.
47. *Automobile Topics*, September 7, 1912, 219.
48. See Umberto Eco, "The Multiplication of the Media," in *Travels in Hyperreality* (London: Harvest, 1986), 145–50.

4. Klaxon and the Mutable Law of the Technology Business

1. See Jürgen Habermas, *The Structural Transformation of the Public Sphere: An Inquiry into a Category of Bourgeois Society*, trans. Thomas Burger (Cambridge, MA: MIT Press, 1991).
2. "Pursing the Price Cutters," *Motor World*, June 1910, 639.
3. "Holds the Makers Responsible," *Motor World*, September 29, 1910, 826.
4. Ibid.
5. *Motor Age*, January 5, 1911, 233.
6. "Klaxon's 'Sewing up' Contract with Distributors Frowned Upon," *Printers' Ink*, January 18, 1917, 65–66.
7. Ibid.
8. "Klaxon and Jones Settle Their Suits," *Motor World*, March 16, 1911, 1.
9. "Recent Litigation in Motor Industry," *Motor Age*, January 18, 1912, 12.
10. "Ever Ready Is Enjoined," *Motor Age*, March 21, 1912, 7.
11. *Automobile Trade Journal*, March 1912, 108.
12. "Sustains Klaxon Patents," *Motor Age*, January 11, 1912, 8.
13. "Klaxon People Sue 'Newtone' Makers," *Automobile Topics*, April 8, 1911, 37.
14. "Patent Cases Keep New York Courts Busy," *Motor Age*, December 21, 1911, 9.
15. "Klaxon Makers Increase Capacity," *Motor Age*, May 30, 1912, 51.
16. *Canadian Knowles Co. v. Lovell-McConnell*, Ont: H.C.J Memo Decisions, *Dominion Law Reports*, vol. 1 (Toronto: Canada Book Co, 1912), 906–7.
17. *Le Sport Universel Illustré*, July 7, 1912, 832.
18. "Le 14e Salon de L'Automobile, *Le Figaro*, October 23, 1913, 4.
19. Lovell-McConnell Buys Klaxon Patents," *Automobile Topics*, May 24, 1913, 101.
20. On the origins of traffic law derived from older forms of managing streets and the relationship between automobile law and self-regulation, see Sarah A. Seo, *Policing the Open Road: How Cars Transformed American Freedom* (Cambridge, MA: Harvard University Press, 2019).

21. "Accessoires," *La Revue de L'Automobile*, December 25, 1910, 444.
22. Louis Rachou, "Jurisprudence municipale: La trompe des automobiles," *Revue Municipale*, 1913, 105–6.
23. "La France automobiliste," *Le Sport Universel Illustré*, January 5, 1913, 44.
24. "Tribune de simple police," *Revue de Touring Club de France*, December 15, 1920, 565.
25. Rachou, "Jurisprudence municipale."
26. L. Baudry de Saunier, "Une victoire de la Ligue Automobile de France," *Omnia: La Revue Pratique d'Automobilisme*, June 6, 1914, 335.
27. The case referred to a 1909 French law that decreed "a steam-whistle or siren must not be used . . . as a siren is likely to frighten horses." Described in Robert P. Mahaffy and Gerald Dodson, *The Law Relating to Motor Cars* (London 1910), 439.
28. "Einen Signalapparat," *Allgemeine Automobil-Zeitung*, April 5, 1913, 45.
29. "Verordnung über den Verkehr mit Kraftfahrzeugen," *Reichsgesetzblatt*, February 3, 1910, 391.
30. Mahaffy and Dodson, *The Law Relating to Motor Cars*, 459.
31. *Allgemeine Automobile-Zeitung*, April 19, 1913, 2.
32. "Motor-Horn Nuisance: Regulations in Berlin and Paris," *Times*, July 16, 1914, 7.
33. "Headlights and Motor Horns in Italy," *Motor-Car Journal*, January 22, 1910, 1023.
34. Martin Bruck, "Ueber die Abgabe von Warnungssignalen," *Allgemeine Automobile-Zeitung*, August 30, 1913, 20.
35. Ibid., 21.
36. "Widersprechende Entscheidungen über die Benutzung der Hupe," *Allgemeine Automobil-Zeitung*, May 3, 1913, 20.
37. One case in Stuttgart had led to a definition requiring tones to be between middle C on the piano and approximately one octave higher, which was deemed by the court to be more easily perceived by the ear as a warning signal.
38. "Die Zulässigkeit der Klaxonhupe," *Allgemeine Automobil-Zeitung*, March 14, 1914, 21.
39. "Rachet Horns Win Victory in German Prohibition Fight," *Automobile Topics*, April 4, 1914, 557.
40. *Automobile Topics*, March 16, 1912, 227.
41. "Motoring," *Academy*, March 30, 1912, 410.
42. Ibid.
43. E. H. Hodgkinson, *The Tyranny of Speed, or The Motor Peril and Its Remedy* (John Lane, 1911), 24–25.
44. "The Motor Vehicle in Parliament," *Auto*, August 3, 1912, 897.
45. "The Abuse of the Hooter," *Auto*, August 10, 1912, 927.
46. "The Use and Abuse of the Motor Horn," *Auto*, August 31, 1912, 1010.
47. "Motor Notes: International Road Congress," *Irish Times*, June 18, 1913, 5.
48. "Insistence of the Motor Horn: Revolt of the Public," *Times*, July 14, 1914, 14.

49. "The Use of the Klaxon: To the Editor of *The Times*," *Times*, July 16, 1914, 7.
50. Ibid.
51. "The Hooter Nuisance: Bad Language of the Road," *Times*, July 21, 1914, 21.
52. Ibid.
53. W. B., "Horn Blowing," *Autocar*, October 3, 1914, 547.
54. Owen John, "On the Road: Warning Signals and Their Necessity," *Autocar*, July 11, 1914, 56.
55. Ibid.
56. Ibid., 58.
57. "Talk Law in Bay State," *Motor Age*, April 21, 1910, 13.
58. Ibid.
59. W.H.B. Fowler, "Misuse of the Auto Signals Serious Nuisance," *San Francisco Chronicle*, June 28, 1912, 11.
60. "Klaxon Maker Has Bay State Contest for Warning Signal Regulation," *Automobile Topics*, October 18, 1913, 765.
61. "Month in the Motor Trade," *Motor*, December 1913, 172.
62. "Charles Johnson in Detroit for Klaxon, *Automobile Topics*, June 13, 1914, 362.
63. *Automobile Topics*, December 23, 1911, 267.
64. *Automobile Topics*, March 2, 1912, 107.
65. "Klaxon within the Law," *Motor Age*, September 28, 1911, 43.
66. "Stop Horn Nuisance: Father of Chicago Muffler Cut-Out Ordinance Talks on Warning Signal," *New York Times*, November 12, 1911, C10.
67. *Automobile Topics*, December 30, 1911, 319.
68. *Automobile Topics*, January 20, 1912, 611.
69. "Removes Ban on Klaxon," *Motor Age*, November 30, 1911, 36.
70. "Great Victory for Organized Motorists," *Motordom*, May 1913, 7.
71. Klaxon's ad selectively extracted from the coroner's report, omitting the dire warnings about the impact of automobiles on society. According the coroner's board, New York City "is fast becoming as perilous as a battlefield." (See William Allen Johnston, "Taking the Automobile Seriously," *Collier's*, January 11, 1913, 50.)
72. *Automobile Topics*, February 17, 1912, 3.
73. "Holds Its Class Legislation," *Motor Age*, January 25, 1912, 105.
74. *Automobile Topics*, March 9, 1912, 167.
75. *Automobile Topics*, March 23, 1912, 283.
76. *Automobile Topics*, April 13, 1912, 447.
77. *Automobile Topics*, April 27, 1912, 567.
78. *Automobile Topics*, May 11, 1912, 687.
79. "Less Noise in Newark: City Council Adopts Law to Restrain Users of Auto Horn," *New York Times*, April 22, 1912, 12.
80. *Automobile Topics*, October 5, 1912, 487.
81. Xenophon P. Huddy, "Stop, Look and Listen," *Motor*, January 1910, 136. *New York Central & H.R.R Co. v. Maidment*, 168 *Fed. Rep.* 21, made it "the duty of an

automobile driver approaching tracks where there is restricted vision to stop, look and listen."

82. "Notes from New York," *Auto*, August 3, 1912, 910.
83. "Des Moines Open to the Klaxon," *Automobile Topics*, July 13, 1912, 558.
84. "New Traffic Ordinance Permits Use of Klaxons in Seattle," *Star*, April 5, 1913, 8.
85. "Cincinnati Allows Electric Horns," *Automobile Topics*, October 5, 1912, 530.
86. "Notes from New York," *Auto*, July 6, 1912, 795.
87. *Automobile Topics*, May 24, 1913, 75.
88. *Motor Age*, April 3, 1913, 47.
89. "Motor Car Literature," *Motor Age*, February 22, 1912, 20.
90. William Allen Johnston, "Taking the Automobile Seriously," *Collier's*, January 11, 1913, 50.
91. Ibid., 52.
92. Ibid.
93. *Automobile Topics*, July 12, 1913, 631.
94. "Decides against Bulbs," *American Motorist*, February 1914, 118.
95. "Has new Warning Signal Ordinance," *Automobile Topics*, January 3, 1914, 613.
96. *Automobile Topics*, July 20, 1912, 603.
97. *Automobile Topics*, August 23, 1913, 67.
98. "59 Klaxonized Cars," *Automobile Topics*, October 25, 1913, 811.
99. *Automobile Topics*, November 22, 1913, 83.
100. "Bishop Pleads for Electrification Now," *Chicago Daily Tribune*, June 9, 1913, 10.
101. "Best Insurance against Accident," *Motordom*, September 1915, 147. On the variety of "volunteerism" safety campaigns exhorting drivers to be courteous and respectful of others, see Seo, *Policing the Open Road*, 42–45.
102. "La France automobiliste," *Le Sport Universel*, February 1911, 44.
103. "Horn Politeness Demanded in France," *Automobile Topics*, August 3, 1912, 774.
104. Prince P. D'Arenberg, "La courtoise de la route," *Bulletin Officiel de la Automobile-Club du Nord*, February 1914, 41.
105. "Circulation des automobiles," *Revue Municipale*, January 1, 1915, 1914, 8.
106. "Documents & information," *Revue Municipale*, January 1, 1915, 10.
107. "Negligence—Motor Vehicle, King's Bench Act Rule 933," *Virginia Law Register* 17 (March 1912): 889–90.
108. "Makes Injunctions Harder to Get," *Automobile Topics*, November 9, 1912, 837.
109. Ibid., 838.
110. "Klaxon Suing Car Dealers," *Automobile Topics*, January 25, 1913, 807.
111. "Sparks-Withington Takes Up Fight," *Automobile Topics*, February 8, 1913, 1003.
112. "Two New Klaxon Suits," *Automobile*, September 18, 1913, 535.
113. "Unusual Attack by Klaxon Maker," *Automobile Topics*, October 11, 1913, 667.
114. "Appeal Will Be Made in Klaxon Suit," *Automobile*, January 15, 1914, 215.
115. Ibid.
116. "Newtone Reveals Its Battle Front," *Automobile Topics*, April 25, 1914, 801.
117. "Klaxon Patents Upheld," *New York Tribune*, January 11, 1914, 5.

118. "Court Says Noise Can't Be Patented," *New York Tribune*, June 10, 1914, 18.

119. *Automobile Topics*, June 13, 1914, 371.

120. "Final Stages in Horn Controversy," *Motor Age*, November 12, 1914, 20.

121. "Horn Patent Litigation Draws to Close," *Automobile*, December 10, 1914, 1085.

122. *Motor*, February 1914, 230.

123. "Long Interests Sue Klaxon Dealer," *Automobile*, March 19, 1914, 666.

124. "Patents Assigned to Packard and Klaxon," *Automobile*, May 14, 1914, 1020. Hutchison made a fortune on his klaxon patent royalties. In 1910 alone, he made $41,921 on royalties, equivalent to well over a $1 million in today's money. Edmund Morris, *Edison* (New York: Random House, 2019), 96.

125. *Automobile Topics*, January 2, 1915, 603.

126. "Klaxon Removes Competitor's Horn from Show," *Automobile*, January 7, 1915, 44.

127. "Sparton Defeats Klaxon," *Motor Age*, February 25, 1913.

5. Danger Sound Klaxon!

1. *Automobile Topics*, September 21, 1912, 351.

2. Roland Marchand, *Creating the Corporate Soul: The Rise of Public Relations and Corporate Imagery in American Big Business* (Berkeley: University of California Press, 1998).

3. Quoted in John P. Wilder, "Selling the Goods That Nobody Wants," *Printers' Ink*, January 2, 1913, 20.

4. "Klaxon Company Increases Stock," *American Motorist*, June 1913, 539.

5. Wilder, "Selling the Goods."

6. "The Klaxon Printing Plant," *American Motorist*, November 1913, 1005.

7. "Klaxon Establishes Printing Plant," *Automobile Topics*, September 20, 1913, 412.

8. On the idea of recombinant media and its impact on global culture, see Marwan M. Kraidy, *Hybridity, or the Cultural Logic of Globalization* (Philadelphia: Temple University Press, 2005).

9. *Boston Sunday Post*, May 25, 1914, 43.

10. *Indianapolis Star*, Saturday, May 30, 1914, 7.

11. *Automobile Topics*, December 20, 1913, 403.

12. E. H. Kastor, *Advertising* (Chicago: LaSalle Extension University, 1922), 109.

13. "News and Notes," *Motor*, June 20, 1911, 833.

14. *Le Temps*, October 25, 1913, 4.

15. *Le Temps*, March 20, 1914, 4.

16. Runabout, "Light Car Talk: Penetrating Alarms," *Autocar*, August 22, 1914, 352.

17. *Autocar*, December 5, 1914, 800.

18. "The Hand Klaxon for the Ford," *Motor Age*, April 23, 1914, 45.

19. *Motor Age*, August 6, 1914, 51.

20. *Motor Age*, May 28, 1914, 55.

21. *The Bulletin*, January 8, 1914, 26.

22. "Lovell-McConnell Working Nights," *Automobile Topics*, May 30, 1914, 186.

23. Reprinted in *Arizona Sentinel* and *Yuma Weekly Examiner,* October 9, 1913.

24. Otis F. Wood, "James Montgomery Flagg in Words and Pictures," *San Francisco Chronicle,* March 28, 1915, 4.

25. "Insistence of the Motor Horn," *Times,* July 14, 1914, 14.

26. *Motor Age,* February 6, 1913, 75.

27. On this ambivalent fascination with the American future, see Jean-Phillipe Mathy, *Extrême Occident: French Intellectuals and America* (Chicago: University of Chicago Press, 1993).

28. The ad featured the tagline "You can change human nature" and depicted a bustling crowd of men, women, and children being protected by a klaxon. *Saturday Evening Post,* September 17, 1910, 48.

29. "The Klaxon at Herald Square, New York," *Graphic Arts,* August 1913, insert.

30. F. T. Marinetti, "The Manifesto of Futurism," *Le Figaro,* February 20, 1909, https://archive.compart.uni-bremen.de/2014/website/fileadmin/media/lernen /Futurist_Manifesto.pdf.

31. Milton A. Cohen, *Modernism, Manifesto, Melée: The Modernist Group, 1910–1914* (Oxford: Oxford University Press, 2004), 15.

32. Barbara Pezzini, "The 1912 Futurist Exhibition at the Sackville Gallery, London: An Avant-Garde Show within the Old-Master Trade," *Burlington Magazine,* July 2013, 471–79. On the tie between different futurisms and dangerous speedy automobiles as legacies of this moment, see Ricardo Vidal, *Death and Desire in Car Crash Culture: A Century of Romantic Futurisms* (Oxford: Peter Lang, 2013).

33. See Gavin Williams, "A Voice of the Crowd: Futurism and the Politics of Noise," *19th-Century Music* 37, no. 2 (2013): 113–29.

34. Luigi Russolo, *The Art of Noise,* trans. Robert Filliou (New York: Ubu Classics, 2004), 4.

35. Ibid., 7. For a discussion of how the Futurists "read sound," see Greg Goodale, *Sonic Persuasion: Reading Sound in the Recorded Age* (Urbana: University of Illinois Press, 2011).

36. "The Klaxon at Herald Square, New York," *Saturday Evening Post,* July 5, 1913, 43.

37. See Pierre Bourdieu, *The Field of Cultural Production: Essays on Art and Literature* (New York: Columbia University Press, 1993).

38. For a description of the importance of automobile clubs, see Gijs Mom, *Atlantic Automobilism: Emergence and Persistence of the Car, 1895–1940* (New York: Berghahn Books, 2015), 106–7; and James J. Flink, *The Automobile Age* (Cambridge, MA: MIT Press, 1993), 27–28.

39. *Club Journal: Official Bulletin of the Automobile Club of America,* June 25, 1910, 214.

40. "Cleveland Club's Sign Work," *American Motorist,* December 1914, 896.

41. "Sign Posting in California," *Club Journal: Official Bulletin of the Automobile Club of America,* May 1914, 130.

42. "Automobile Advertising," *Saturday Evening Post,* July 10, 1915, 48. Klaxon was

one of five advertisers that spent more than $100,000 advertising in the *Saturday Evening Post* in 1914.

43. "A Guard against Auto Accidents," *Fort Wayne Sentinel,* May 18, 1914, 16.
44. "Erect Danger Signs," *Rock Island Argus,* May 25, 1914, 6.
45. *Daily Kennebec Journal,* May 26, 1914, 2.
46. "Localizing Newspaper Copy," *Printers' Ink,* April 23, 1914, 69.
47. Ibid.
48. "Klaxon Danger Signs Erected on Roads in Thirty-Five States," *Automobile Topics,* May 9, 1914, 995.
49. "Klaxon Signs Mark Dangerous Corners," *San Diego Union,* June 7, 1914, 5.
50. *San Diego Union,* July 12, 1914, 5.
51. "Klaxon Signs Arrive," *Bemidji Daily Pioneer,* June 19, 1915, 1.
52. *Illinois Highways,* August 1915, 89.
53. "County Engineer Gets Road Signs," *Fairfield Daily Journal,* February 22, 1915, 4.
54. "Massachusetts Bars Klaxon Warnings," *Automobile Topics,* May 30, 1914, 190.
55. "Campaigning against 'Blow Your Horn' Signs," *Horseless Age,* September 30, 1914, 474c.
56. "Keep to the Right," *Arrow,* August 19, 1915, 1.
57. "A Unique 'Safety First' Idea," *American Motorist,* October 1914, 744.
58. "Changes in Klaxon Selling Organization," *American Motorist,* November 1914, 838.
59. *Motor World Wholesale,* July 15, 1914, 77.
60. "Putting Up Danger Signs," *Marshfield Times,* February 3, 1915, 1.
61. "Oneanta: 'Sound Your Klaxon' Signs Being Erected on All Highways," *Motordom,* August 1916, 110.
62. "New Danger Signs," *Chehalis Bee-Nugget,* Friday, July 28, 1916, 2.
63. "Danger Sound Klaxon," *Toronto World,* May 7, 1916, 3.
64. C. B. Hutchins, "City of Montreal Is Largest in Dominion," *Kossuth County Advance,* November 8, 1916, 1.
65. On the notion of fandom, see Paul Booth, ed., *A Companion to Media Fandom and Fan Studies* (Oxford: Wiley Blackwell, 2018).
66. "A New Use for Your Klaxon," *Motor World,* September 23, 1914, 61.
67. "Klaxon as Factory Signal," *Motor Age,* January 23, 1913, 52.
68. "Brazilians Want Klaxons," *Automobile Topics,* May 6, 1911, 257.
69. *Life,* April 4, 1916, 668.
70. *McClure's,* March 1916, 77.
71. Russolo, *The Art of Noise,* 7.
72. *McClure's,* March 1916, 77.

6. Sounding the Alarm

1. "Where'd You Get That Noise?," *Sun,* January 3, 1916, 14.
2. E.O.J., "The Man with the Horn," *Life,* November 18, 1915, 66.

3. "Lettre d'un marin," *Le Figaro,* January 30, 1915, 3.

4. Yaron Jean, "The Sonic Mindedness of the Great War: Viewing History through Auditory Lenses," in *Germany in the Loud Twentieth Century,* ed. Florence Feiereisen and Alexandra Merley Hill (Oxford: Oxford University Press, 2012), 51–62.

5. Emmanuel Bourcier, "The Gas Attack," *Scribner's Magazine,* June 1918, 726–28.

6. *Le 37e régiment d'infanterie coloniale dans la Grande guerre, 1914–1919* (Bordeaux, Impr. de G. Delmas, 1919).

7. "A 'Honk! Honk!' In the Trenches Means 'Don Your Gas Masks!,'" *Popular Science Monthly,* May 1917, 664.

8. "Klaxon Auto Horns on French Front Warn Trenches of Gas Attack," *University Missourian,* July 12, 1916, 4.

9. John Dos Passos, *One Man's Initiation: 1917* (New York: Library of Alexandria, 1922), 77.

10. American Expeditionary Forces, "The Experiences of Surgical Team no. 11A, "*History of Base Hospital No. 18* (Baltimore: Baltimore Base Hospital 18 Association, 1919), 83. For an interesting account of the acoustic ecology of the war from the perspective of a war nurse, see Mary Borden, *The Forbidden Zone* (New York: Doubleday, 1930). See also Nora Lambrecht, "'But If You Listen You Can Hear': War Experience, Modernist Noise, and the Soundscape of the Forbidden Zone," *Modernism /Modernity* (2017), online.

11. "United Motors Earns $9 a Share," *Automobile,* April 26, 1917, 1.

12. "United Motors Buys Klaxon," *Sun,* September 17, 1916, 10.

13. "United Motors Plants Working to Capacity," *Wall Street Journal,* October 16, 1916, 2.

14. "Klaxon Change Shifts in Big Munitions Factory," *National Geographic Magazine,* February 1916, 112.

15. US Army, American Expeditionary Forces, *Defensive Measures against Gas Attacks* (US Army, 1917), 25.

16. According to Benedict Crowell, assistant secretary of war and director of munitions, the horns were manufactured by the Klaxon Company, the cylinders by Harrisburg Pipe & Pipe Bending Company, and the air compressors by the Ingersoll-Rand Company of New York. Benedict Crowell and Robert Forrest Wilson, *How America Went to War,* vol. 5, *The Armies of Industry* (New Haven, CT: Yale University Press, 1921), 583.

17. Army War College, *Gas Warfare, Pt. 1* (US Government Printing Office, 1918), 28.

18. Army War College, *Gas Warfare,* 36.

19. Francis Field, *The Battery Book* (New York: Devine, 1921), 69.

20. Handwritten World War One Notes of Vernon Cheney, Sr., National Archives Identifier 17343227. Cheney served in a unit commanded by Captain Harry S. Truman, future president of the United States.

21. Richard A. Newhall, "With the First Division—Winter 1917–1918," *Historical Outlook,* October 1919, 360.

22. "Aircraft in the War," *Lithgow Mercury*, February 26, 1915, 6.
23. Jonathan Lighter, "The Slang of the American Expeditionary Forces in Europe, 1917–1919," *American Speech* 47, no. 1/2 (1972), 27.
24. "From the Diary of a Flight Lieutenant," A.A.C., *The Journal of the R.N. Anti-Aircraft Corps* 2, no. 3 (February 1, 1919), 97.
25. Army War College, *Notes on the Methods of Attack and Defense to Meet the Conditions of Modern Warfare* (US Government Printing Office, 1917), 24.
26. "Notes on Contact Patrol Work," August 31, 1916, AIR 1/823/204/5/43, 5.
27. "Aeroplane Contact," *Telegraph*, January 31, 1919, 7.
28. Ibid.
29. "An Airman Saves the Guns," *Western Argus*, January 21, 1919, 2.
30. Grand Quartier Général, *Manuel du Chef de Section d'Infanterie* (Paris: Edition de Janvier, 1918), 322.
31. Lieut. James Richard Crowe, *Pat Crowe, Aviator* (New York: N. L. Brown, 1919), 20.
32. Otis F. Wood, "Cavalry of the Clouds," *Pittsburgh Gazette Times*, March 12, 1918, 6.
33. "Fighting in the Air," *Echuca and Moama Advertiser and Farmer's Gazette*, February 14, 1918, 3.
34. "Klaxon Company," *Aviation and Aeronautical Engineering*, February 1, 1917, 53.
35. B. Atkins Jenkins, *Facing the Hindenburg Line: Personal Observations at the Fronts and in the Camps of the British, French, Americans and Italians during the Campaign of 1917* (New York: Revell, 1917), 208.
36. Ibid., 238.
37. "Attacking Air Raiders," *Lincolnshire Echo*, February 12, 1916, 2.
38. *Sheffield Daily Telegraph*, June 18, 1917, 3.
39. "Zeppelin Warnings," *Ballymena Observer*, February 17, 1916, 4.
40. "They Like Oak Leaves: Sergt. Chester Johnson's Letter," *Oak Leaves*, November 9, 1918, 36.
41. James Robb Church, *The Doctor's Part: What Happens to the Wounded in War* (New York: Appleton, 1918), 230.
42. Ibid., 216.
43. Ibid., 230.
44. Herbert Corey, "New Gas, That Rolls Down Hill Like Water, to Be Used in Great Drive by Allies on Western Front," *Desert Evening News*, May 25, 1918, 1.
45. Robert Casey, *The Cannoneers Have Hairy Ears* (New York: J. H. Sears, 1927), 92.
46. "Popular Song," *Tatler* 5, September 4, 1918, 78.
47. R. H., "Middle Articles: At the Front. XIV On Roads," *Saturday Review*, June 23, 1917, 569.
48. B. de Pawoloski, "Inventions nouvelles et dernières, *Le Rire*, March 17, 1917, 4.
49. US Army, *Regulations for Standard Motor Vehicle Operation, Expeditionary Forces* (US Government, October 1918), 2.

50. Arthur L. Fletcher, *History of the 113th Artillery Regiment 30th Division* (Raleigh, NC: History Committee of the 113 F.A, 1920), 61.

51. Ibid., 65.

52. Leonard Nason, "Chevrons," *Oxford Mirror*, March 1, 1928, 2.

53. Richard A. Newhall, "With the First Division—Winter 1917–1918," *Historical Outlook* (October 1919): 360.

54. Edward Streeter, *Same Old Bill, Eh Mable* (New York: Frederick A Stokes, 1919), 84.

55. Milton Bronner, "Spend Millions for Hun Hell," *Des Moines News*, October 21, 1918, 3.

56. Junius B. Wood, "Night Patrols Always Active in Toul Sector," *Stars and Stripes*, March 15, 1918, 3.

57. "Gassed," *Life*, July 4, 1918, 72.

58. Elmer H. Curtis, *Going and Coming as a Doughboy* (Palo Alto, CA: P. A. Stewart, 1920), 7.

59. "From a Soldier's Letter: A.E.F. France," *Outlook*, November 6, 1918, 377.

60. Slater Washburn, *One of the Yankee Division* (Boston: Houghton Mifflin, 1919), 45.

61. Harry Henderson, "Tells of Yankee Lads Over There," *Wyoming State Tribune*, July 6, 1918, 2.

62. "'With the Colors,' Letters of Interest from Morgan County Boys in the Country Service," *Jacksonville Daily Journal*, December 22, 1918, K1.

63. "Loud Whistles Doomed after War: Veterans Drop Flat at Sound," *Oakland Tribune*, November 17, 1918, A4.

64. United States Congress, House Select Committee on Expenditures in the War Department, *War Expenditures: Hearings Before Subcommittee No. 4 (Quartermaster Corps) . . . Sixty-sixth Congress . . . On War Expenditures . . . Serial 5* (Washington, DC: Government Printing Office, 1921), 1142.

65. Crowell and Wilson, *How America Went to War*, 536.

66. Wood, "Night Patrols Always Active," 3.

67. "Concerning Motor Horns," *Kansas City Star*, June 13, 1918, 14.

68. Jimmie Glenney, "Paris Was Wild with Joy," *Chester Times*, December 16, 1918, 7.

69. R. J. Manion, *A Surgeon in Arms* (New York: Appleton, 1918), 163.

70. Henry Viets, "Shell-Shock: A Digest of the English Literature," *Journal of the American Medical Association* 69, no. 21 (November 24, 1917): 14.

71. Ibid., 20.

72. Ibid., 19.

73. *La Crosse Tribune*, December 12, 1918, 2.

74. "Heard on the Curb," *Sullivan Daily Times*, June 6, 1919, 5.

75. "Sound Your Horn," *Creston Advertiser Gazette*, July 20, 1921, 3.

76. *Hardware Review*, October 1919, 55.

77. "Among the Makers and Dealers," *Motor Age*, March 28, 1918, 46.

78. Walter P. Coghlan, "A Sound Proposition," *Ford Owner*, June 1918, 118.

7. Sidewalk Blues

1. On the postwar boom in automobile production, see James J. Flink, *The Automobile Age* (Cambridge, MA: MIT Press, 1993); and Brian Ladd, *Autophobia: Love and Hate in the Automotive Age* (Chicago: University of Chicago Press, 2008). Postpandemic readers will hear an echo in the pandemic-induced recession in the years after the war, which sped up the process of industry contraction that was already under way. After the Spanish flu and innovation in production realized by Henry Ford in the manufacturing of cheaper automobiles, the consensus of automobile historians is that this marks the arrival of what is known as the automobile age.

2. Gijs Mom, *Atlantic Automobilism: Emergence and Persistence of the Car, 1895–1940* (New York: Berghahn, 2014).

3. *Automobile Topics*, April 24, 1920, 1359.

4. The slogan also resonated with the name and concerns of the Safety First council, formed in London in July 1919. *Auto*, August 14, 1919, 860.

5. "Why Do They Do It?," *Auto*, October 7, 1920, 1040.

6. John Phillimore, "Motoring for the Owner-Driver, Art of Driving," *Financial Times*, May 2, 1921, 5. By 1923, Phillimore would embrace the sounds of the new compressed-air horn technology.

7. "Lighting and Equipment Laws in Various States," *Automobile*, May 20, 1920, 1164.

8. "N.A.C.C. Recommends Cautions in Driving," *Automobile*, March 16, 1922, 639.

9. Carl M. Saunders, "Just Toot Your Own Horn," *Syracuse Herald*, June 13, 1920, 15.

10. "Klaxon Co. Asks Lower Freight Rates for Horns," *Automotive Industries*, May 18, 1922, 1085.

11. "Digest of Eastern Automotive Trade News," *Motor West*, July 15, 1923, 71.

12. *Automobile Topics*, May 13, 1922, 1204.

13. *Automobile Topics*, April 29, 1922, 995.

14. *Automobile Topics*, March 18, 1922, 411.

15. Roy W. Johnson, "Klaxon's Bargain Drive to Offset the Slump," *Printers' Ink*, June 15, 1922, 110.

16. "Fulton County Club Meeting," *Motordom: Official Publication of the New York State Automobile Association*, December 1921, 17.

17. *Saturday Evening Post*, June 9, 1923, 56.

18. "Klaxon Adds Giant Ads to National Campaign," *Printers' Ink*, October 19, 1923, 71.

19. "Le Masque de Fer," "Echos," *Le Figaro*, September 2, 1921, 1.

20. See Matthew F. Jordan, *Le Jazz: Jazz and French Cultural Identity* (Urbana: University of Illinois Press, 2010).

21. Décret du 31 Décembre 1922, "Code de la Route" (Paris: Charles-Lavauzelle & Cie, 1923), 44.

22. Henri Petit, "Autophobie," *La Vie Automobile*, August 10, 1922, 1.

23. "Le Mot 'Klaxon,'" *La Revue de Touring Club de France*, December 1921, 389.

24. "Chronique Théatrale," *Le Temps*, May 21, 1928, 2.

25. W. F. Bradley, "Mechanical Features of the German Cars," *Motor Age*, October 7, 1921, 14.

26. Gijs Mom, *Atlantic Automobilism: Emergence and Persistence of the Car, 1895–1940* (New York: Berghahn, 2015), 310.

27. See Philipp Blom, "Forces Unbound: Art, Bodies and Machines After 1914," in *Nothing but the Clouds Unchanged: Artists in World War I*, ed. Gordon Hughes and Philipp Blom (Los Angeles: Getty Publications, 2014), 9.

28. See John Goodyear, "Escaping the Urban Din: A Comparative Study of Theodor Lessing's *Antilärmverein* (1908) and Maximilian Newer's *Ohropax* (1908)," in *Germany in the Loud Twentieth Century*, ed. Florence Feiereisen and Alexandra Merley Hill (Oxford: Oxford University Press, 2012), 19–34.

29. Quoted by John Donald in "A Complex Kind of Training: Cities, Technologies and Sound in Jazz-Age Europe," in *Talking and Listening in the Age of Modernity: Essays on the History of Sound*, ed. Joy Damousi and Desley Deacon (Canberra: Australian National University Press, 2007), 23.

30. Walter Benjamin, *Selected Writings*, vol. 2, pt. 1, *1927–1930* (Cambridge, MA: Harvard University Press, 1999), 24. Though silent, Joe May's *Asphalt*, shot in 1928 at UFA, perfectly dramatizes the noisy urban ethos of Weimar Berlin that captivated the movement. The film follows the fall of Albert, a policeman perched on a pedastal inches away from shrieking, smoking, and swarming cars, who directs traffic from dawn till dusk. He is lured into breaking the law he is sworn to uphold by a femme fatale jewel thief who seduces him to avoid prosecution.

31. Reinhold Bauer, "A Specifically German Path to Mass Motorization? Motorcycles in Germany between the World Wars," *Journal of Transport History* 34, no. 2 (December 2013), 104.

32. See Uwe Fraunholz, *Motorphobia: Anti-Automobiler Protest in Kaiserreich und Weimarer Republik* (Göttingen: Vanderhoeck & Ruprecht, 2002).

33. R. J. Overy, "Cars, Roads, and Economic Recovery in Germany, 1932–8," *Economic History Review* (August 1, 1975): 471.

34. Joseph Goebbels, "Around the Gedächtniskirche," in *The Weimar Republic Sourcebook*, ed. Anton Kaes, Martin Jay, and Edward Dimenberg (Berkeley: University of California Press, 1994), 561.

35. "The City of Dreadful Noise," *New York Tribune*, November 28, 1922, 12.

36. "Attention Hon. Motorist!," *American Motorist*, September 1922, 18.

37. "La guerre aux bruits nocturnes," *Le Galois*, July 23, 1923, 3.

38. "Echos," *Le Figaro*, February 20, 1928, 1.

39. Overy, "Cars, Roads and Economic Recovery," 468.

40. George M. Graham, "Safeguarding Traffic—A Nation's Problem—A Nation's Duty," *Annals of the American Academy of Political Science* (November 1924): 174.

41. Ibid., 175.

42. Ibid., 185.

43. "Common Sense Big Factor in Sounding Auto Horn," *New York Times*, June 7, 1925, 13.

44. Michel Zamacoïs, "La politesse de la route," *Bulletin Officiel de l'Automobile-Club du Nord*, July–September 1924, 6.

45. Ibid., 7.

46. Ibid.

47. Ibid.

48. "La Circulation," *Journal de Genève*, October 14, 1928, 6.

49. Jean Cocteau, *Le Coq et L'Arlequin* (Paris: Stock, 1979 [1918]).

50. See Jordan, *Le Jazz*, 40–42.

51. Quoted in Jean Cocteau, "Parade: Ballet Réaliste: In Which Four Modernists Artists Had a Hand," *Vanity Fair*, September 1917, 106.

52. "London Concerts," *Musical Times*," October 1, 1929, 931.

53. Robert H. Hull, "Realism in Our Time," *Sackbut*, August 1930, 11.

54. Duke Ellington, *The Duke Ellington Reader* (Oxford: Oxford University Press, 1995), 53.

55. Ibid., 212.

56. On Free's report, see Emily Thompson, *The Soundscape of Modernity: Architectural Acoustics and the Culture of Listening in America, 1900–1933* (Cambridge, MA: MIT Press, 2004), 148–49.

57. E. E. Free, "Noise: The Forum's Second Report on City Noise," *Forum*, March 1928, 382.

58. Ibid., 388.

59. Ibid., 389.

60. James Lawlor, "Noiseless Ash Cans: A City's Great Need," *New York Times*, May 15, 1927, X12.

61. See Karin Bijsterveld, *Mechanical Sound: Technology, Culture and Public Problems of Noise in the Twentieth Century* (Cambridge, MA: MIT Press, 2008).

62. "Noise and the Public Health: Memorandum of Evidence Submitted by the British Medical Association to the Minister of Health," *British Medical Journal*, November 10, 1928, 210.

63. Ibid.

64. "The Age of Noise," *British Medical Journal*, November 10, 1928, 855.

65. "*Noise and the Public Health*," 210.

66. Lord Montagu of Beaulieu, "Road Noises: An Increasing Evil," *Times*, August 6, 1927, 11.

67. Ibid.

68. *Report of Conference on Road Traffic Noises and Priority of Traffic at Cross Roads* (London: His Majesty's Stationery Office, 1929).

69. Philip Morrell, "Speed and Noise: The Motor Horn," *Times*, August 28, 1928, 8.
70. Similar debates were taking place in Germany, where many legal scholars suggested that the bulb horn should once again be the only horn allowed by law. See Von Hauptmann Fries, "Signal-Instrumente, Beleuchtung und Nummernschilder in neuen Kraftfahrgesetzen," *Allgemeine Automobil-Zeitung*, April 1920.
71. R. E. Davidson, "About Motoring: Noise," *New Statesman*, April 23, 1927, 58.
72. Ernest Dimnet, "The Capital of Noise," *Saturday Review*, August 18, 1928, 204.
73. Fernand-Laurent, "Une Sourdine à vos trompes MM: Les Chauffeurs?," *Le Petit Parisien*, December 5, 1927, 2.
74. *L'Illustration*, May 16, 1925, Announces 21.
75. "Parisians Want All Auto Horns to Be Musical," *Chicago Daily Tribune*, May 29, 1924, 10.
76. Howard Pollock, *George Gershwin: His Life and Work* (Berkeley: University of California Press, 2007), 432.
77. "Information diverse," *Le Temps*, January 16, 1929, 4. Mark Clague has written and spoken on this discovery about Gershwin, which helps us better understand the move toward more musical horns. For a report on this find, see Michael Cooper, "Have We Been Playing Gershwin Wrong for 70 Years?," *New York Times*, March 1, 2016.
78. F. Scott Fitzgerald, *The Great Gatsby* (New York: Simon & Schuster, 2013), 64.
79. Ibid, 63.
80. See Bijsterveld, *Mechanical Sound*, 118.
81. "Traffic Noises and Dangers," *Times*, May 8, 1929, 13.
82. G. R. Stirling Taylor, "The Car Mind," *Fortnightly Review*, September 1929, 323.
83. Marcel Béreaux,"Vers un 'code sonore' automobile," *Je Sais Tout*, September 1928, 396.
84. On the politics of noise abatement campaigns, see Karin Bijsterveld, "The Diabolical Symphony of the Mechanical Age: Technology and Symbolism of Sound in European and North American Noise Abatement Campaigns, 1900–1940," *Sound Studies of Science* 31, no. 1 (February 2001): 37–70.
85. J. C. Steinberg, "Noise Measurement," *Electrical Engineering*, January 1931.
86. "Fined in First Test of Anti-Noise Law," *New York Times*, May 1, 1930, 38.
87. Wayne Gard, "The Drive against Din," *North American Review* (December 1, 1932): 541.

Conclusion

1. Clay McShane, "The Origins and Globalization of Traffic Control Signals," *Journal of Urban History* 25, no. 3 (March 1999): 379–404.
2. On the education campaigns in Belgium, see Donald Weber, "Safety or Efficiency? Strategies and Conflicting Interests in Belgian Road-Safety Policy, 1920–1940," *Technology and Culture* 56, no.2 (April 2015): 394–419.

3. "Blame Failing to Signal for 2,000 Accidents: NY Motor Body Gets up Statistics," *Chicago Daily Tribune*, April 7, 1929, A13.

4. "Japan's Roads," *Lincoln County News*, December 15, 1933, 3.

5. Karin Bijsterveld, *Mechanical Sound: Technology, Culture, and the Public Problem of Noise in the Twentieth Century* (Cambridge, MA: MIT Press, 2008).

6. Henri Lemesle, "Le Bruit et les bruiteurs," *Le Mercure de France*, September 1, 1931, 301.

7. "Le XXIe Congres des Maires de France: Lutte contre le bruit," *Revue Municipale*, February 1931, 1559.

8. "Le Troquer dénonce les bruits de Paris," *Le Populaire*, July 8, 1933, 2.

9. For more on Chiappé, see the chapter on him in Brooke Blower, *Becoming American in Paris: Transatlantic Politics and Culture between the World Wars* (Oxford: Oxford University Press, 2010).

10. *Bulletin Municipal Officiel*, July 8, 1933, 2889.

11. Ibid., 2890.

12. *Bulletin Municipal Officiel*, January 12, 1935, 230.

13. "Lettre ouvert á M. Frédéric Martin chef du Départment de Police," *Journal de Genève*, March 20, 1933, 3.

14. "Haute-Savoie: La Lutte contre le bruit," *Gazette de Lausanne*, June 16, 1933.

15. "La Semain du silence" *Journal de Genève*, June 12, 1935, 3.

16. Adam Gowans Whyte, "Reflections on the Age of Noise," *Fortnightly Review* (July 1932): 72.

17. Ibid., 74.

18. See Stefan Krebs, "The French Quest for the Silent Car Body: Technology, Comfort and Distinction in the Interwar Period," *Transfers: Interdisciplinary Journal of Mobility Studies* 1, no. 3 (2011): 64–89.

19. Gijs Mom, "Orchestrating Automobile Technology: Comfort, Mobility Culture, and the Construction of the 'Family Touring Car,' 1917–1940," *Technology and Culture* 55 (April 2014): 300.

20. Wayne Gard, "The Drive against Din," *North American Review* (December 1, 1932): 542.

21. "Awheel in the West: Light Signals Instead of Klaxons," *Western Daily Press and Bristol Mirror*, October 27, 1933, 4.

22. For more on this transcultural testing of street noise and horn technology, see chapter 4 in Bijsterveld, *Mechanical Sound*, 91–118.

23. "Measurement of Noise," *British Medical Journal*, September 19, 1931, 542.

24. "Standard Horn for Motor-Cars: Anti-Noise League's Proposals," *Times*, November 14, 1933, 11.

25. "No Night Tooting," *Chicago Daily Tribune*, September 7, 1934.

26. Clair Price, "Hootless London Plans War on Clamor," *New York Times*, October 21, 1934, SM8.

27. "Nouvelles à l'étranger, Grande-Brétagne: Lutte contre le bruit," *Le Temps*, September 1, 1934, 2.

28. "Street Noises of Rome," *Times*, September 13, 1933, 9.

29. "The Din of Rome," *Times*, April 1, 1931, 13.

30. A Leonard Raven-Hill in *Punch*, August 23, 1933, 12. Mussolini and Chiappé were later praised in *Punch* by E. V. Lucas, "Letter to an Exile," *Punch*, November 1, 1933, 494.

31. Price, "Hootless London Plans War on Clamor," SM8.

32. "Le préfet de police de Berlin loue l'action de M. Chiappe," *Le Figaro*, February 25, 1932, 2.

33. Reichsgesetzblatt, Jahrgang 1932, Teil 1, § 19, 210, https://alex.onb.ac.at/cgi -content/alex?aid=dra&datum=1932&page=284&size=45.

34. Price, "Hootless London Plans a War on Clamor."

35. See Bernard Rieger, *The People's Car: A Global History of the Volkswagen Beetle* (Cambridge, MA: Harvard University Press, 2013).

36. Carolyn Birdsall, *Nazi Soundscapes: Sound, Technology and Urban Space in Germany, 1933–1945* (Amsterdam: Amsterdam University Press, 2012).

37. "Conférence Internationale de Psychotechnique," *Le Travail Humain* 4, no. 2 (1936): 228.

38. See Karin Bijsterveld, "The Diabolical Symphony of the Mechanical Age: Technology and Symbolism of Sound in European and North American Noise Abatement Campaigns, 1900–1940," *Social Studies of Science* 31, no 1 (February 2001): 37–70.

39. H. L. Mencken attributed this trend of linguistic nominalization, the constant development of manufactured "Americanisms," to the influence of advertising in American culture. H. L. Mencken, *The American Language: An Inquiry into the Development of English in the United States* (New York: Knopf, 1921), 195.

40. Glen Frank, "Frank Opinions: Men We Do Not Like," *San Antonio Express*, December 14, 1929, 7.

41. "Our Anti-Noise War Starts Politely," *New York Times*, September 28, 1930, X14.

42. Hal Foust, "Gotham Plans Move to Tone Down Auto Horn," *Chicago Daily Tribune*, August 18, 1935, A6.

43. "Noise Drive Opens, City Taking Lead," *New York Times*, September 10, 1935, 1.

44. Ibid.

45. "City Noises," *Chicago Daily Tribune*, November 26, 1934, 10.

46. Ibid.

47. Foust, "Gotham Plans Move to Tone Down Auto Horn"

48. See Matthew F. Jordan, "Becoming Quiet: On Mediation, Noise Cancellation and Commodity Quietness," in *Conditions of Mediation: Phenomenological Perspectives on Media*, ed. Tim Markham and Scott Rodgers (London: Peter Lang, 2017), 237–47.

49. In a 1931 symposium on soundproofing, R. V. Parsons of the Johns-Manville Corporation stated, "Perhaps for a while only the rich man, the big business executive, the creative genius will possess offices and houses that are essentially sound-proof," but he held out hope that "some philanthropist of the near

future" would endow "thinking places—sound-proof buildings where people could go to think out their problems." C. Engel, "Views and Reviews," *Musical Quarterly* (January 1, 1931): 407.

50. Karbu, "Prochaine réglementation des avertisseurs," *Peugeot-Revue*, February 28, 1930, 21.

51. "Sounds to Jump By: A History of Horns," *New York Times*, April 2, 1961, A13.

52. Karin Bijsterveld, Eefje Cleophas, Stefan Krebs, and Gijs Mom, *Sound and Safe: A History of Listening Behind the Wheel* (Oxford: Oxford University Press, 2014), 51.

53. On the story of General Motors, see David Farber, *Sloan Rules: Alfred P. Sloan and the Triumph of General Motors* (Chicago: University of Chicago Press, 2002).

54. "Moorhead and Dilworth Members Are Guests at Annual Banquet," *Moorehead Daily News*, Saturday May 27, 1939, 1.

55. *Omnia*, January 1, 1933, 92.

56. See, for one of many examples, the *New York Times'* interactive archive, "New York's War on Noise," at https://archive.nytimes.com/www.nytimes.com/interactive/2013/07/13/nyregion/nyc-noise-timeline.html.

57. See Jordan, "Becoming Quiet."

SELECTED BIBLIOGRAPHY

Attali, Jacques. *Noise: The Political Economy of Music.* Trans. Brian Massumi. Minneapolis: University of Minnesota Press, 1985.

Bardou, Jean-Pierre, Jean-Jacques Chanaron, Patrick Fridenson, and James M. Laux. *The Automobile Revolution: The Impact of an Industry.* Trans. and ed. James M. Laux. Chapel Hill: University of North Carolina Press, 1982.

Bijsterveld, Karin. *Mechanical Sound: Technology, Culture and Public Problems of Noise in the Twentieth Century.* Cambridge, MA: MIT Press, 2008.

Bijsterveld, Karin, Eefje Cleophas, Stefan Krebs, and Gijs Mom. *Sound and Safe: A History of Listening behind the Wheel.* Oxford: Oxford University Press, 2013.

Bull, Michael. *Sounding Out the City: Personal Stereos and the Management of Everyday Life.* Oxford: Berg, 2000.

Bull, Michael, and Les Back, eds. *The Auditory Culture Reader,* New York: Routledge, 2015.

Carey, James. *Communication as Culture: Essays on Media and Society.* New York: Routledge, 1989.

Corbin, Alain. *Village Bells: Sound and Meaning in the 19th-Century French Countryside.* Trans. Martin Thom. New York: Columbia University Press, 1998.

Crary, Jonathan. *Suspensions of Perception: Attention, Spectacle, and Modern Culture.* Cambridge, MA: MIT Press, 1999.

Cross, Gary S. *Machines of Youth: America's Car Obsession.* Chicago: University of Chicago Press, 2018.

Esperdy, Gabrielle. *American Autopia: An Intellectual History of the American Roadside at Midcentury.* Charlottesville: University of Virginia Press, 2019.

Feiereisen, Florence, and Alexandra Merley Hill, eds. *Germany in the Loud Twentieth Century.* Oxford: Oxford University Press, 2012.

Flink, James J. *America Adopts the Automobile, 1895–1910.* Cambridge, MA: MIT Press, 1970.

———. *The Automobile Age.* Cambridge, MA: MIT Press, 1993.

Goldsmith, Mike. *Discord: The Story of Noise.* Oxford: Oxford University Press, 2012.

Goodale, Greg. *Sonic Persuasion: Reading Sound in the Recorded Age.* Urbana: University of Illinois Press, 2011.

LaBelle, Brandon. *Acoustic Territories: Sound Culture and Everyday Life.* New York: Continuum, 2010.

Lacey, Kate. *Listening Publics: The Politics and Experience of Listening in the Media Age.* Cambridge: Polity, 2013.

Ladd, Brian. *Autophobia: Love and Hate in the Automotive Age.* Chicago: University of Chicago Press, 2008.

Laux, James M. *The European Automobile Industry.* New York: Twayne, 1992.

———. *In First Gear: The French Automobile Industry to 1914.* Montreal: McGill–Queen's University Press, 1976.

Lefebvre, Henri. *Critique of Everyday Life: Foundations for a Sociology of the Everyday,* V. 2, Trans. John Moore. London: Verso, 2008.

Marchand, Rolland. *Advertising the American Dream: Making Way for Modernity, 1920–1940.* Berkeley: University of California Press, 1985.

———. *Creating the Corporate Soul: The Rise of Public Relations and Corporate Imagery in American Big Business.* Berkeley: University of California Press, 1998.

McShane, Clay. *Down the Asphalt Path: The Automobile and the American City.* New York: Columbia University Press 1996.

Mom, Gijs. *Atlantic Automobilism: Emergence and Persistence of the Car, 1895–1940.* New York: Berghahn, 2015.

———. *The Electric Vehicle: Technology and Expectations in the Automobile Age.* Baltimore: Johns Hopkins University Press, 2013.

Packer, Jeremy. *Mobility without Mayhem: Safety, Cars, and Citizenship.* Durham, NC: Duke University Press, 2008.

Picker, John M. *Victorian Soundscapes.* Oxford: Oxford University Press, 2003.

Pinch, Trevor, and Karin Bijsterveld, eds. *The Oxford Handbook of Sound Studies.* Oxford: Oxford University Press, 2012.

Rae, John B. *The Road and the Car in American Life,* Cambridge, MA: MIT Press, 1971.

Richardson, Kenneth. *The British Motor Industry, 1890–1939: A Social and Economic History.* London: Macmillan, 1977.

Schafer, R. Murray. *The Soundscape: Our Sonic Environment and the Tuning of the World.* Rochester, VT: Destiny Books, 1994.

Seiler, Cotton. *A Republic of Drivers: A Cultural History of Automobility in America.* Chicago: University of Chicago Press, 2008.

Seo, Sarah A. *Policing the Open Road: How Cars Transformed American Freedom.* Cambridge, MA: Harvard University Press, 2019.

Smith, Mark. *Listening to Nineteenth-Century America.* Chapel Hill: University of North Carolina Press, 2001.

Smith, Meritt Roe, and Leo Marx. *Does Technology Drive History? The Dilemma of Technological Determinism.* Cambridge, MA: MIT Press, 1994.

Sterne, Jonathan. *The Audible Past: Cultural Origins of Sound Reproduction*. Durham, NC: Duke University Press, 2003.

———. *MP3: The Meaning of a Format*. Durham, NC: Duke University Press, 2012.

Thompson, Emily. *The Soundscape of Modernity: Architectural Acoustics and the Culture of Listening in America, 1900–1933*. Cambridge, MA: MIT Press, 2004.

INDEX

advertising, types of: advertorial, 107–11, 128, 132, 133, 138, 139, 145, 146; atmospheric, 127; business-to-business, 126, 134, 159, 165, 181; editorial, 80–81, 85–88, 97; endorsement, 58, 84, 87–88; native, 45–48, 50, 54, 57–58, 98, 107, 132–33, 144; reason-why, 77, 81; situational, 62–83, 127, 130, 138, 182–83

ad wars, 76–81, 90

Aermore, 29

airplanes, 161–62, 164, 191–92, 195

air raid, 165

Air Tone, 212

Allied, 154, 155, 157, 159, 163, 164, 172

American Automobile Association, 52, 107

American Red Cross, 170

American Road Association, 108

Americanization, 4, 205, 206

Annales school, 219n7

Antheil, George, 191

anticompetitive business practices, 90, 114

antiklaxon sentiment, 137, 173, 208

antinoise politics 35, 57, 82, 111, 125, 143, 184–88, 191, 195, 205, 207, 208, 210

Anti-Noise League (British), 208

aristocracy, 50, 80

Armistice, 173

Army War College, 159, 162

Arts et Métier, 200, 212

Ashley, Wilfrid, 196

asphalt, 9, 16, 17, 186, 187, 106, 239n30

assembly line production, 114, 159, 177, 185

audiometer, 195, 199

Australia, 135, 160, 161, 163, 168

Autochime, 29

automobile age, 4, 19, 83, 98, 238n1

automobile accidents, 20, 22, 32, 34, 72, 73, 84, 99, 113, 210

automobile associations: American, 107; Minnesota, 213; New York, 110

automobile clubs, 21, 33, 122; Bemidji Auto Club, 146; Chehalis, 150; Cincinnati, 115; Cleveland, 143; Davenport, 144; Delaware County, PA, 143; Marshfield Auto Club, 150; Milan Automobile Club, 208; Morehead, 213; New Orleans, 48; Oneonta, 150; Royal Automobile Club, 104, 196; Southern California, 143; Washington, DC, 142

automobile fatalities, 32, 72, 73, 99 142, 204. See also traffic fatalities

automobile industry: in Britain, 50, 223n55; in France, 38, 97, 207; in Germany, 186, 207; in the United States, 46, 61, 76, 93, 113–14, 158, 175–78, 189, 212

automobile press, 38, 119, 223n55

automobile racing: French Light Car Race (1911), 132; Indianapolis 500, 132; New Orleans Automobile Club Racing Carnival (1909), 48, 225n26

automobile salons: New York, 38, 40; Paris, 97
automobile shows: American Motor Car Manufacturers' Association, 46; Automotive Dealers' Association Show, 49; Chicago Automobile Show, 149; New York National Automobile Show, 121; Olympia Motor Show, 50
automobile touring, 52, 66, 98, 115
automobility, 4, 198
automotive lifestyle, 38, 48, 76, 132
autophobia, 18
Autophone horn, 26
autotopian, 14
Axis powers, 154, 159, 163, 172

Baltimore, 110
Barcelona, 209
Bartlett, F. L., 27
Baudelaire, Charles, 5–7
Beatty, Octavius Holmes, 25
Belgium, 21, 45, 190
Bell Telephone Laboratories, 195, 200
bells, 5, 12, 13, 22, 23, 24, 25, 32, 33, 55, 187, 221n6; bicycle, 20, 25; carriage, 16, 19; church, 155, 173, 186, 187; electric, 17, 40, 79
Benjamin, Walter, vii, 186
Berlin, 130, 140, 185, 187, 191, 210, 239n30
Bijsterveld, Karin, 13, 195, 205, 221n4
Bingham, Theodore, 35
Bird, G.E., 48
Blanchard French horn, 27
Blériot, 97–99, 132–34, 156
"blow your horn" signs, 33, 143, 149
Boccioni, Umberto, 140. See also Futurists
Boissy-Saint-Léger, 98
Boston, 32, 33, 76, 125, 171
Bourcier, Emmanuel, 154
Bourdieu, Pierre, 127, 142
branding, 78, 91, 96, 185; brand ambassadors, 143, 146; branded sound, 66, 132; rebranding, 214; reinvigorating brand, 51, 122, 148, 181, 183, 213

Brazil, 124, 151
Britain, 8, 14, 21, 24, 32, 58, 134; law, 28, 101, 189; British market, 129; military, 155, 160, 162, 163, 168, 174; Ministry of Transport, 199, 212; Parliament, 103, 137, 199, 208; War Ministry, 62
British ads, 130, 178, 179
British Medical Association, 195–96
Buick, 159
bulb horn, 1, 22, 26, 28, 29, 30, 34, 36, 40, 43, 48, 81, 88–89, 98–99, 101, 104–5, 107–13, 116–17, 134, 141–42, 192, 196–97, 204, 241n70
buzzer horn, 40, 43, 79–80, 104, 134, 193

Calais (France), 116
California, 112, 143
Canada, 97, 116, 150
Cantor, Eddie ("Automobile Horn Song"), 199
Carey, James, 8, 9, 15
Carriages, 6, 11, 19, 40, 58
Châlons-sur-Marne (France), 116
Chaney, Verne, 160
Charles E. Miller, Ltd., 118
Charleston, 48
Chattanooga, 113
Chatfield, Judge Thomas, 119
Chevrolet, 159, 181, 214
Chiappé, Jean, 205–6
Chicago, 110, 165; City Council, 20, 28, 109, 211; city ordinance, 109, 114
Church, James Robb, 166
Cincinnati, 104, 112, 115
Clayton Act, 121
"clear the road" terminology, 104, 105, 130, 141, 165, 175, 182, 190, 212
Cleophas, Eefje, 13
cocooning, acoustic, 207, 212, 216
Cocteau, Jean, 191
Coghlan, Walter P., 149, 151, 175
compressed-air horns, 159, 198, 199, 213, 215, 238n6
Connecticut, 37, 40, 113
Conference on Street and Highway Safety, 189
Continental Calliope, 29